Bn
4.00

D1095696

JOURNEY
TO
WASHINGTON

Senator Daniel K. Inouye

with

Lawrence Elliott

PRENTICE-HALL, INC., Englewood Cliffs, N.J.

Journey to Washington
by Senator Daniel K. Inouye with Lawrence Elliott

© 1967 by Prentice-Hall, Inc.

Library of Congress Catalog Card Number: 67–18918

Printed in the United States of America

T 51122

Prentice-Hall International, Inc., London
Prentice-Hall of Australia, Pty. Ltd., Sydney
Prentice-Hall of Canada, Ltd., Toronto
Prentice-Hall of India Private Ltd., New Delhi
Prentice-Hall of Japan, Inc., Tokyo

This book is for my son
Daniel Ken Inouye, Jr.

A Foreword by
The President of the United States

❀ Daniel K. Inouye, my cherished and admired friend, is one of America's great egalitarians. His autobiography reflects his relentless struggle to achieve freedom of opportunity and equality for Americans of Japanese ancestry, and for all racial and religious minorities.

Born of Japanese parents in the Territory of Hawaii in 1924, he grew up in a climate of racial prejudice and discrimination. Throughout his youth he was determined to transcend social bias, and to achieve equal rights for his people.

The attack on Pearl Harbor was a source of humiliation and estrangement for the Japanese population in Hawaii, and it aroused widespread suspicions among other Americans. For a time, the *nisei* were not permitted to enlist and fight for their country. Yet Franklin Roosevelt expressed his confidence in his fellow countrymen when he said: "Americanism is a matter of the mind and heart; Americanism is not, and never was a matter of race or ancestry."

Thereafter the *nisei* formed a regimental combat team that emerged from the campaign in Italy as one of the war's most heavily decorated units. Dan Inouye was a valiant member of that team.

Dan's heroism in action resulted in the loss of his right arm. Despite this personal tragedy, his courage never failed him. For he had decided that "There wasn't a thing in the world I couldn't do with my left hand—if I wanted to do it badly enough."

Returning to Hawaii after the war, he felt the time was ripe for Japanese-Americans to achieve full participation in the political life of the Territory. He became successively a legislator and majority leader of the Hawaiian House of Representatives. When Hawaii attained statehood in 1959, Daniel K. Inouye was sent to Congress as the first representative of the new State of Hawaii. In 1962, he became the first American of Japanese ancestry to be elected to the Senate of the United States.

Dan Inouye has lived by the code of personal courage—on the battlefield, and in the political arena. He has faced the aggressor's bullets, and the bigot's contemptuous stare. He has gained the admiration and respect of his fellow men. Even more important, he has, by his example and witness, helped to make the hearts of his fellow men more tolerant, more free of the awful burden of racism.

I believe that this story will become part of the heritage of our nation, inspiring others to find within themselves the strength to say: "There isn't a thing in the world I couldn't do—if I want to do it badly enough."

Lyndon Baines Johnson

A Foreword by the
Vice-President of the United States

❀ The people of the State of Hawaii elected Dan Inouye to the Senate of the United States in November of 1962. But the third man ever elected to the U.S. Senate from our newest state already was familiar with the Nation's Capital and with Congress.

Dan first came to Washington in 1950, where he studied law for two years. He returned to his native Honolulu after receiving his law degree from George Washington University. But by 1959 he was back in Washington—the first American of Japanese ancestry to serve in the United States House of Representatives.

Dan Inouye was a war hero who served in Italy and France as a member of the United States Army during World War II. But as a Congressman and now as a Senator he never once has fallen back on the uniqueness of his heritage or his distinquished war record. Instead, he relies on his native ability and calls on the lessons of politics he learned so well in the campaigns of Hawaii. And he con-

stantly maintains an inborn belief in the essential worth
and dignity of his fellow man.

The soft-spoken Senator from Hawaii has done well in
the Congress. As a Senator, he won places on two major
committees (Armed Services and Public Works), was
chosen as Assistant Majority Whip and, in the election of
1966, held vital posts with Democratic campaign committees.

Dan Inouye and I fought side by side many times on the
issues that came before the Congress. He is a good and
effective fighter and a skilled parliamentarian. When I was
Assistant Majority Leader of the Senate it was reassuring
to know that he was on my side. And with Dan supporting
your position, you are afforded the luxury of being a little
more certain that your side is the right one.

Never did we fight harder together than for the historic
civil rights legislation of the middle 1960s. And never was
I more proud to have for my friend and colleague the distinguished gentleman from Hawaii. When he seconded my
nomination for the Vice Presidency in 1964, the honor was
mine.

This is an American story. Dan's boyhood in Honolulu
really was not so different from mine in South Dakota. He
had the ocean and I had the prairie. But we both had the
great gift of discovering that there is no limit to the aspirations of an American boy. His father worked in a jewelry
store and my father was a druggist. We both learned that in
this land of ours a man's beginnings are not nearly so important as his hopes for the future.

In the pages ahead you will read how a remarkable
woman named Kame Inouye made a single egg serve as
breakfast for a family of six, and how her oldest son Dan,
through personal will and sheer ability, eliminated the prejudices among his classmates. You will know how it felt on

a December morning to see your beloved island attacked, and to wonder if your own cousins were up there, dropping the bombs that changed the way of the world.

Dan Inouye has written as stirring and significant a story as I have read in a long time. It is his story. It is a story that reveals the spirit and heart of America. It is the story of a man who worked and studied and fought hard to make his dream come true. And because this dream was realized, we all have come to benefit.

Hubert H. Humphrey

A Foreword by the
Senate Majority Leader

❀ The roots of this nation reach out to all the continents of the globe. In the faces of America are reflected every mutation in the human race. Whatever national distinction exists anywhere, an offshoot is to be found somewhere in the United States. We are a people woven of many strands.

Some strains loom larger than others in our history. Some are more intense; some more muted. There are many nuances in the pattern of American life. From earliest times, much has come from Europe and Africa. These are the predominant sources of the present inhabitants of the United States. Over the decades and centuries, those who migrated from Europe and Africa came for obvious reasons or for no apparent reasons. Some came eagerly, some hesitantly and some under the lash of slavery, penal servitude, or indenture.

However they came, these streams of humanity poured their ideas and ideals, their confidences and fears, their strengths and weaknesses into the American heritage. They shed blood and they mixed blood, as they settled in the

East and South and Southwest of the nation and then spread inward and onward over a continent.

The sagas of European and African migration are well-known parts of the American heritage. We have long been aware of the contributions which issued from the Anglo-Saxon and Celtic islands of Western Europe. Much had been written of the surge of industrious peasants out of Germany, Scandinavia, Italy, Poland and other European centers—men and women who sought eagerly for something in a new land and often found it, if not for themselves, for their children or their children's children. The same is true of the migrations to and through Hispanic America into the Southwest. Of late, we have also learned something of the struggle of African descendents in America out of slavery, out of the limbo of the post-slavery century and into the promise of constitutional fulfillment in these times.

Less known is the Oriental aspect of the immigrant inheritance of America. It is one which has not loomed large in the totality of American life and its blend into the whole has been neither rapid nor easy. World War II was a catalyst in bringing this element more fully into national view and absorption. The advent of Statehood to Hawaii, where the Oriental strain predominates in the population, served to seal forever its merger with the main body of America's humanity.

The Oriental migration into Pacific America varied in character and rhythm from the streams of people which reached the United States from Europe and Africa. Those who arrived in the thousands from China and Japan in the nineteenth century came with great reticence, leaving behind as they did cultures which had given stability and satisfaction to countless generations of their ancestors. The original migrants from the Orient clung to the strong family-clan society which Confucian-Buddhist tenets and a sense of oneness with the land had produced in the Far East. When they left for America, they carried away with them a deep longing to return to the quiet smoke-hazed villages and the placid rice paddies.

The great bulk of the immigrants to America from Asia, in fact, did not choose to leave their homes. Rather, they were compelled to leave by the inadequacy of crowded lands and a rigid social system to meet the growing human demands which were imposed on them in the nineteenth century. Often these early immigrants constituted individual "sacrifices" who went forth into an alien world in a desperate, last-ditch effort to save the family-clan structure. They travelled to where there was a demand for the only resource which they had to sell, their physical strength. They poured out that strength in bitter labor (that is what the term "coolie" means) on behalf of the families left behind and to which they dreamed one day of returning.

The dream of going home came true for some of these early immigrants, although, in many instances only after their strength was gone and their years spent. For countless others, the dream came to an end along the tracks of the railroad networks which, with the participation of coolie labor, were then spreading through the empty vastness of Western America. Or sometimes the dreams were shattered in the raw misery of a frontier town or in the boisterous coastal cities or in the gold fields or somewhere on the great plantations which were burgeoning on the islands of Hawaii.

A substantial segment of the early Oriental immigrants, however, neither returned to the old nor met a bitter end in the new. Rather, some dared to evolve new dreams of a new life in a new world. Those who had come only to labor in Pacific America remained also to live. They sent for women to wive them. They founded families in the old traditions. Generation succeeded generation. The old ways slowly evolved into new ways. And, as already noted, with World War II and Hawaiian Statehood, the Oriental stream in America broke out of ancient self-imposed barriers, rose above imposed prejudices, and flowed fully into the life of the nation.

It is the story of the Oriental migration, and particularly of Japanese migration—from its painful beginning to its permanent rooting in the United States—which Senator Daniel Ken Inouye tells. He speaks in the inimitable accents of his beloved Hawaii and with the frankness of his World War II generation of Americans.

The story he tells is poignant in tracing the evolution of the Asian migrants from the early, bewildering and painful years. It is especially revealing of the "go-for-broke" courage which characterized the most decorated military unit in the American military forces of World War II. In the Italian campaign Lieutenant Dan Inouye and other Americans of Japanese ancestry sacrificed much of themselves. In so doing they gave expression to their respect for the heritage of their fathers and, at the same time, won for that heritage an incontestable place in the American heritage.

The life of Dan Inouye has carried him from the streets of Honolulu into war, into law and political leadership in Hawaii and, now, into the Senate of the United States as the first American Senator of Japanese ancestry. Dan Inouye's life is a personal triumph, a triumph of a man's courage and determination. But his triumph is, in the end, the triumph of America. The recognition which has come to Dan Inouye, like others before him, reveals the resilient capacity of this nation for replenishment, with energy and wisdom drawn from the many well-springs of the human race. The story of Daniel Ken Inouye, American, is, in truth, an enduring chapter in the story of America.

Mike Mansfield

CONTENTS

Introduction

❀ I think it is important that I say a few cautionary words to the reader before turning him loose on the highways and side trails of my life. For one thing, I cannot help feeling that anyone with the presumption to write his autobiography at the age of forty-two ought to have a very sound reason. Despite certain pressures I resisted the idea for a long time; I really did not think I had all that much to tell.

What changed my mind was the birth of my son. Maggie and I had waited a long time and when Dan, Jr., finally did arrive on Bastille Day in 1964, it seemed suddenly important that I remember for him every way station along the roads that had led to his appearance on earth. So that's number one. I finally agreed to write this book, not because I have made any earth-shaking contributions to man and his society—God willing, perhaps that is yet to come—but because it was an opportunity to set down for my son, and for anyone else who might be interested, the record of a single life at midstream.

Number two is that my life, as I see it, is not really

so very different from all the millions of others that have contributed to the American melting pot. My forbears came from the Orient and it is true that their facial characteristics set them apart from Americans whose roots are in the Western world. But their problems of assimilation were exactly the same: to find work, to maintain a pride in their heritage while adapting to the culture of a strange new land, and slowly, step by painful step, to work their way up the social and economic ladder toward independence and full acceptance by their fellow-countrymen.

I have not intentionally meant to hurt anyone in this book and if I have I am truly sorry. Except for Larry Elliott and myself, no one saw the full manuscript before it went to the publisher, not my wife and not my parents, and so if there are errors in it I must bear the full responsibility. Some things have been left out—names where a direct identification might cause pain or embarrassment; certain incidents and episodes, particularly in the more recent past, whose telling seemed better left to some future time. But what is here is the truth as I best remember it. May you, the reader, enjoy reading about it at least a fraction as much as I have enjoyed living it.

Daniel K. Inouye
Washington, D.C.

❊ JOURNEY TO WASHINGTON ❊

Chapter I

A Fire in Yokoyama Village

❀ No one could say how the fire started. One moment all Yokoyama slept and the only sounds were the wind and the whispered rush of the stream that fell from the mountain and ran hard by the thatched roofs of the village. And then a spurt of flame broke from the house of Wasaburo Inouye. There were shouts in the night: "Fire! Fire!"

Men tumbled from the dark houses and raced for the stream with their buckets. But the easterly wind gathered strength as it blew down the long valley where the village lay, and for all the water the scurrying, sweating men could fling at the flames, they leaped unimpeded from the Inouyes' house to the next house, and then to the one after. Only when the men doused the roof of the third house in line was the fire's deadly rush halted. And by then three homes lay in smoking ruin.

Early in the morning, the elders assembled in the village meeting house. Of course the destitute families would be cared for until their houses were rebuilt. But of even graver importance was the matter of assessing the costs for the disaster. For it was the code of the hill country of southern Japan that he who lived in the house where a fire began must pay for the restoration of any other house that burned and for all the lost possessions.

At last the talk and the tallying were done. It was Inouye who must pay, the elders decided, and fixed the amount at $400. Then they sent for him to deliver their judgment.

Wasaburo Inouye accepted it in bleak silence. There was no question that the fire had started in his house, from an unbanked stove perhaps, or a smoldering lamp. Nor had he any thought of protesting that such a sum seemed forever out of his reach, that his long hours of labor in the rice paddies and among the tea plants on the mountainside, and the labor of Asakichi, his eldest son, barely sustained the family. Everyone knew this to be true, for everyone in the village labored as hard and earned as little. But what was ordained in the unwritten laws of the hills was explicit and immutable, and so there was nothing for Inouye to say.

He left the meeting house and walked slowly along the single dirt street of the village. He was an intense, stocky man, a grandfather many times over, and now the years weighed heavily on his stooped shoulders. At the end of the street, he could see the curious still clustered around the blackened remains of the three houses. Women and children stared at him as he passed, for everyone now knew the verdict of the elders—"It is Inouye who must pay!" they whispered—and Wasaburo fixed his eyes on the dusty road as he walked and tried to think of what must be done.

He could, of course, flee. He could take his family and, in the dead of night, slip away from Yokoyama, and even if the villagers knew where he had hidden they would not follow.

They didn't have to, for at hand was a punishment far more agonizing. The elders would march ceremoniously to the meeting house and there, in the registry books that went back for generations, they would scratch out the name of Inouye wherever it appeared. It would be as though the entire family had never lived and no matter how far they fled their shame would follow them. Having given up their home, they would find no other anywhere in Japan. Worse, no respectable father would give his daughter in marriage to an Inouye son and soon the name, honored in the village for five centuries, would die out.

No, fleeing was unthinkable, as was remaining without satisfying this debt of honor. He was a Japanese and his home and his name and his family honor were more precious than life—more precious, even, than the first flesh of his flesh.

When he reached what was left of his home, Wasaburo beckoned his family to sit with him on the charred mud floor. They were solemn, even the little ones, regarding the head of the house attentively, as oblivious to the persistent onlookers as he was.

They must pay the other families $400, Wasaburo told them. It was a matter of honor. And since there was no way to earn such money in the village, Asakichi, the eldest son, must leave the village and earn it.

Asakichi's gaze remained fixed respectfully on his father's face. But Moyo, his wife, reached out toward their three small children and tried to encircle them with her arm. She knew her husband would do as his father bade, and she was frightened.

Wasaburo went on: tomorrow the son would go to Fukuoka City where he would find the recruiters for the

Hawaiian sugar plantations, and he would sign the contract. From his earnings he was to send back as much money as he could until the debt was paid. Then he might return.

Asakichi nodded. "Yes, father," he said, for just as Wasaburo had had no choice, neither, now, did his eldest son. To a Japanese, the word of the father was as immutable as the unwritten law.

But Asakichi Inouye's heart was heavy as stone. He trudged alone up the mountain, as he did every day, to pluck the tender young flushes from the tea shrubs, stuffing them into a sack that filled and grew heavy on his back. He had the dark, earnest look of his father, with tough, muscular arms and legs on his short body. He was twenty-eight years old.

Now and then he paused for a moment to gaze out over the green valley and the village and the clear stream that wound past the thatched roofs like a silver thread, the water wheels turning slowly, endlessly. As a boy he had splashed in that stream, as Hyotaro, his own son, now did, or sat quietly and watched the fish flash through the crystal water. To leave it, to leave everything he loved, was a sorrow such as he had never known and was not now certain that he could bear. How long before he looked out on this village again? How long before he could return to his wife and his family and his people? And what temptations and travail lay in wait for him over the huge Pacific, in the place they called Hawaii?

Only the month before the recruiters had come through Yokoyama. They had painted glowing word pictures for the people. Hawaii, they said, was a land of wealth and promise for anyone who would sign a five-year contract to work in the sugarcane fields. The great companies of the Islands were prepared to pay transportation costs and, to each worker, a wage of $10 a month, a sum unheard of among the farmers and laborers of the hills. But though the people of the village had talked much of the journey and the lavish wages—as they might of some awesome happening in another province, or another age—not one signed the contract and, disgusted, the recruiters moved on to the cities, where it was said they had better luck.

They didn't understand Yokoyama, nor could anyone from another land. This was the people's eternal home. Since they had enough to eat and their simple houses sheltered them from the rain and the wind, it was a good home. Here their ancestors lived and died, and in this ground they were buried. No Japanese could lightly surrender such a heritage, the tradition of so many centuries.

It had been said that an Inouye founded Yokoyama, 500 years before. Legend had it that he had been a samurai, a warrior who acquitted himself bravely in many spectacular battles during the civil wars. Then, in the most crucial battle of all, his warriors had been beaten. But instead of dying by his own hand as a defeated samurai was expected to do, he had heeded the importunings of his wife and fled with his family into the hills of Kyushu, southernmost of the main Japanese islands. And here, in this green valley, he had established the village that came to be known as Yokoyama.

Hidden by the mountains of Fukuoka prefecture, in the district of Yame, it had changed little through the generations. There were neither nobility nor samurai among the people, only poor farmers who tended the rice and the tea and the mushroom beds, and carried their harvest down from the hills on their backs. So remote from the cities and the great roads was the little village that rarely was a strange face seen and never, until the recruiters from Hawaii came, a Western one. And through all the years the name of Inouye had been honored, the disgrace of the samurai, if, in fact, the legend were true, long lost in the haze of the years.

And now, to preserve that honor, Asakichi Inouye must leave this valley and venture into a world that was alien and frightening, and he prayed that the gods give him courage to do what must be done and permit him to return safely, quickly. At dusk, he looked one last time across the valley, at the sparkling green tea leaves and, below, at the nodding stalks of ripening rice and the dark lines of the Buddhist temple against the darkening sky. Then he went back to the ruined house and told Wasaburo that he wanted to take his wife to Hawaii, and his only son, Hyotaro.

He would leave his daughters in his father's care, he said, but five years was a long time for a man to be alone.

The father pondered. He knew that with the woman and child to care for, Asakichi would be able to send that much less home. But his heart was heavy, too, and he could not deny this wish of his eldest son. "Very well," he said. "Take them. Let them be a reminder that you will come back to us."

That night, Asakichi and Moyo gathered together their few possessions and bade their two daughters a melancholy farewell. They were ready to start with the earliest light.

It was customary in a Japanese home that a celebration be held for a departing son, with all the villagers invited and much food and sake offered. It was fitting, too, that the family accompany the travelers at least part way on the 100-mile journey to Fukuoka City. But Wasaburo had decreed that from that moment until the debt was paid, the Inouyes would live in austerity: there would be no money spent for celebrations, nor would there be unnecessary travels to wear out shoes. And so the parting of Asakichi and his family was doubly sad.

His mother embraced him and his father's voice was thick as he said, "Let there be health in your body. Return to us well. And remember that you are a Japanese."

And Asakichi and his wife turned their backs to the rising sun and set forth on their incredibly long journey. Moyo carried four-year-old Hyotaro. In a parcel on his back, Asakichi carried everything else they owned: his father's suit, which had belonged to his father's father, Yataro, and a boiled shirt; Moyo's kimono, in which she had been married and in which she would be buried; a few things for the child; the Buddhist scrolls and the small family temple to the Shinto gods.

It was September 28, 1899, and their first steps down that dusty village road in southern Japan were the unimagined beginnings of a uniquely American odyssey.

In a single generation, the harvest from the Hawaiian sugar fields had multiplied 20 times. The cane grew straight in the volcanic soil and swelled under a beneficent sun, and day by day great ships sailed from Honolulu and Hilo, their holds full. And still the nations of the world called for more sugar, and still more. As early as the 1850s, the great planters had sent to the Orient for desperately-needed laborers. Their agents combed the cities and hamlets of China first, and shipped 30,000 field hands to the Islands by the century's end. But as the Chinese saved a few dollars and grew comfortable in their new surroundings, they abandoned the sweltering canefields and opened shops in the towns. Back to the Far East went the recruiters, to Japan this time, and later to the Philippines, and by 1900 three of every four people in Hawaii were Oriental.

The Japanese came with a special dream. Most were city people and of the 65,000 who crowded into the immigration stations between 1885 and 1899, virtually every one had vowed to return to his homeland. It was their plan to work hard, to accumulate a little money and, at the end of the five-year contract term, to sail back to the land of their ancestors. There they would buy a small farm, perhaps, and live out their years freed from the fear of hunger that forever haunted the teeming cities.

So it was with Asakichi Inouye and his wife Moyo, this dream of going back. And they clung to it urgently, blindly, in the turmoil of Fukuoka City, and through all the 15 days that it took the sailing ship *Peking Maru*, cramped and smelly with unwashed bodies at painfully close quarters, to cross the Pacific, through the bewildering days of quarantine when at last they reached Honolulu.

And then came the morning when they were herded into lines with hundreds of others and led into a great shed. White men wearing boots and immaculate breeches walked along the ragged rows of humanity, peering into the frightened faces, gauging the girth of a man's chest and the strength in his back with their sharp blue eyes, as a farmer would assess an ox he thought to buy.

"This one to Camp One, McBryde," they snapped as they passed along. "This one to Camp One. Camp One. Camp One. This one to Camp Two, McBryde. Camp Two . . ."

And in this manner was Asakichi Inouye's new home chosen for him, that small, splintery shack in Camp Number Two of the McBryde plantation, not far from the town of Wahiawa on the island of Kauai. And in this place, Asakichi and Moyo were destined to spend five times the five years of the contract.

Each morning by 6:30, the workers were in the canefields. Asakichi's muscles hardened to the strength of steel, for slashing the fat cane was far more arduous than tending the rice or picking tea leaves. He worked until the sun vanished behind the western mountains and darkness had closed over the cane and the ugly cluster of unpainted shacks, 12 hours a day, and as spring came and slipped into the long days of summer, 13, 14, 15 hours. And on the last day of each month, he waited on the pay line and was given whatever was left of his $10 after his indebtedness at the company store had been deducted. On that night, he and Moyo would separate from their small pile of silver and bills something for their needs in the month ahead—a pair of work pants, shoes for the boy—and the next day they would send whatever remained home to Yokoyama, vowing always to send more the following month. But a dollar or two was all that was ever left and before long Asakichi came to realize that it would take him a lifetime to pay off the family debt.

Unless he found some way to earn more money! And day by day his mind wrestled with the problem, until one night, as he lay in the darkness fighting sleep and grasping for some elusive idea, he said aloud, "A bathhouse."

"What?" Moyo asked sleepily.

"I will build a bathhouse! What Japanese would not pay to bathe himself in warm water, as we all did at home? I will find the wood and build a bathhouse, and I will charge a penny a bath."

And he did. He was skilled with his hands and soon he had constructed a square tub on stilts that held water without too many serious leaks. Each day he hurried home from the fields to heat the water in a stone pit outside the wood shack, and the men came, and the women, too, as they had come to the community bathhouses in Japan, grateful for the chance to clean their bodies after a long hot day chopping cane. Each one was handed a tin of soapy water before climbing into the tub, and each was given precisely five minutes in the luxurious warmth of the bath before the next one tapped his shoulder and clambered in. It was, above all, a small touch of home, and they paid their pennies gladly.

Most of the hands in Camp Number Two were bachelors. Already the tyranny of the company store—where everyone was forced to trade—had entrapped many beyond the terms of their first contract and they had had to sign a second, and a third. The company made it easy to buy on credit but often, at month's end, a man owed more than his wage would cover. Inexorably, the debts mounted until there were those who were bound, seemingly forever, to the company and the canefields. Some, who said that such indentured labor was little different from slavery, were hustled out of the camp and seen no more. Others complained that the wage was too low, to which the company overseers replied— in truth—that it was more than any of them had earned in Japan. But then nothing seemed to cost so much in Japan, nor were there so many things to be bought. And of course, in the end, there was the contract, against which all argument was futile.

And so the workers resigned themselves to this place. In time, they were joined by their "picture brides," girls from good Japanese homes chosen from the photographs sent to the homesick and desperately lonely men. And despite their fervent intentions, fewer than half the Japanese who had come to Hawaii, flushed with the dream of returning home in wealth and triumph, ever went back at all.

As for Asakichi, despite his extra labors and the steady lines at his bath, he was discouraged by the painfully slow accumulation of pennies. Then it was Moyo's turn to be smitten with an idea: she would bake *tofu* cakes to sell! In Japan, *tofu*, a bean curd cake made from soya beans, was a diet staple and, like the community baths, the men hungered for them as a reminder of home. And now the coins in the Inouyes' money jar began to mount!

But Asakichi and Moyo had to rise at 2 o'clock in the morning to build the fires and bake the cakes, for they peddled them through the camp before the people went to work. They carried the bland white cubes in cans of water that hung from long poles and, as they walked through the narrow streets, they called, "Tofu! Come buy Inouye's tofu!" Before long, young Hyotaro was pressed into service. Each evening, when the plantation train had come and gone, he walked between the narrow-gauge tracks and picked up the chunks of coal that had fallen to the ground, and these were used to fire the bakery stove.

Day by day Asakichi kept the burden of the family debt in the forefront of his mind, and begrudged never a moment of the incredible toil that he and his family had inflicted on themselves in its redemption. It was what had to be done. But life went on in its inexorable way and the time soon came to see to Hyotaro's schooling. Reluctantly, Asakichi sent him off to the priests at the Buddhist temple in Wahiawa village—how he would have preferred sending him to the priests in Yokoyama!

"It is a sadness," he said to Moyo. "It is one more tie with this place."

Moyo said nothing. She, too, longed for home, but she sensed, even with all their labor, that the debt would not be paid by the time the five-year contract ended, perhaps not even when a second five-year contract had ended. But she had no heart to further sadden her husband with such dark intuitions. They would come to him soon enough. In the meantime, there was nothing to do but work and worship the Shinto gods from whom, if it were so ordained, all good things would come.

Hyotaro was not quite ten when he finished his education with the priests. He could now write in Japanese and do small sums, which is all the learning his father, or his father's father, had ever had. But there were some in the camp who were sending their sons to the grammar school in Eleele where they were taught English. On the day Hyotaro asked if he, too, could go there, Asakichi had just decided to work in the canefields for another five years. He had come to see, as had Moyo earlier, that Hawaii might be his home for a long time to come, indeed, perhaps forever, for not a quarter of the debt had yet been paid. And he saw, too, that here in these islands, there might be a life for a Japanese that was not necessarily bound to the red soil where the cane grew. A Japanese who learned to speak English could become a clerk, or even open a small shop, as the Chinese had done. And if they were not to return to their homeland, Asakichi wanted this better life for his son. And so, sad, yet strangely hopeful, he registered the boy in the Eleele school, and he told Moyo that henceforth they would save out some money from the debt payments each month until there was enough to send for their two daughters.

Hyotaro's education was hardly uninterrupted. At fourteen, lean and wiry, he was considered old enough to wield a machete and day by day through the harvest seasons he worked by his father's side, and proudly. He stood in the pay line that first time and strained skyward in a vain effort to seem as tall as the men in front and behind, and he handed his little sheaf of bills to Asakichi with a dignity that barely suppressed the inner glee of the small boy. It was a moment he never forgot.

Working when there was work and snatching a few weeks of school whenever he could, Hyotaro was eight years finishing grammar school. But his hunger to learn was whetted and, with the debt now more than half-paid, he was emboldened to tell his father that he wanted to continue his education. And, in September of 1913, Hyotaro left Kauai for the first time, sailing the inter-island steamer to Hawaii, the Big Island, where he was enrolled in a boarding school to prepare for Mills High School in Honolulu. He was considerably older than his classmates and disdained their boyish games and pranks. It was just as well. Since there could be no money diverted from the debt to pay for his schooling, he was obliged to earn his keep. This, in halting but earnest English, he explained to the headmaster and was promptly appointed master of his dormitory at $20 a month. Added to his wages for summer work in the canefields, this sum, and the almost inborn prudence of his people, saw him through high school.

Mills was run by Congregationalist missionaries. Each Sunday, Hyotaro, heir of uncounted generations of Buddhists, was required to attend Protestant church services. Stoic and unyielding in the beginning, he slowly found himself touched by the liturgy and moved by the uncomplicated Christian faith. Sometime during his third year at Mills, he timidly presented himself at the River Street Methodist Church and applied for membership. No one can say what Asakichi and Moyo felt when he wrote them this news, but there was never a word of rebuke in their letters to him.

Hyotaro was twenty-five years old when he graduated from Mills, older by six years than anyone in his class. Momentous things were about to happen to him. He won a job as a file clerk with Theo. H. Davies, Ltd., wholesalers, shipping agents, sugar factors, and one of the Big Five, Hawaii's great family companies. And in the River Street church, he had seen a girl, a small, bright-eyed Japanese whose name was Kame and who, Hyotaro knew in his heart of hearts, would become his wife or all the days of his future would be blighted.

The days of Kame Imanaga's past had been blighted. Her parents had come from the village of Mitamura in Hiroshima prefecture and, like all the others, they came to Hawaii steadfast in the belief that they would return sufficiently enriched to live a life of modest comfort in their native land. They settled in Puukoli village, near Lahaina, on the island of Maui, and there, in 1902, Kame was born. Her name meant turtle, the Japanese symbol of longevity, and there was a melancholy reason for the choice: of five children earlier born to the Imanagas, only a son survived the first hours.

The mother remained weak and sickly after the birth of Kame and two years later, delivering yet another stillborn child, she began to hemorrhage and died within the hour.

This ironic turn of events was the undoing of the father. Goro Imanaga had been much buffeted by the fates and had fallen into the habit of seeking comfort in the warm sake which numbed his pain and diffused his troubles. Now, with his wife, the last mainstay of his battered and wasted existence, stolen away, he surrendered himself completely to the sake bottle. Kame, who loved her father, remembers him returning from day-long labor in the fields too spent to do more than smile sadly at her before sinking into a corner with his bottle. Kindly neighbors did what they could to care for the little girl and her brother, Shuzo, feeding and bathing them and providing what small warmth and affection came into their lives. When Kame was ten, the father, as though arranging his affairs for the inevitable end, sent the boy Shuzo back to Japan to live with relatives in Hiroshima. When, soon after, he died, Kame found a home, first with a Methodist minister and, when the extra burden proved too much for his meager salary, with one family, then another, most of whom were not Japanese but Hawaiian. She was never to forget the abiding kindness of the people who cared for her in those troubled years and held ever after a special regard for the Hawaiian people.

When she was fourteen she was sent from Maui to the Susannah Wesley Home, a church-run orphanage in Honolulu. Here she lived only one week, going to school and pretending to herself that happiness does not necessarily mean a home, a real home of your own. Then one day, Reverend Daniel Klinefelter, an official visitor inspecting the facilities of the Home, was caught by the longing in Kame's dark eyes. He turned back and asked, "What would you like best of all, my child?"

"A home," Kame promptly answered.

"Then you shall have one," the good Reverend said, and that very day made the arrangements necessary to take Kame into his home.

There, for the first time, the girl basked in the security of knowing that *this* bed was *her* bed, and that if she were late for dinner someone would worry, and if she cried someone cared. She was like a big sister to the two Klinefelter daughters and the warmth of those years as part of a loving, large-hearted family slowly erased the blight of her childhood and readied her to face her life as a sound, whole human.

From her first days with the Klinefelters, Kame began attending the River Street Methodist Church. It was, if you will, segregated, as were most Hawaiian churches, along language lines. At River Street the service was conducted in Japanese so mainly Japanese were members. Kame came to know them all and a strange face quickly sprang into her consciousness. So it was when that young man came—Inouye, someone said his name was—and stared at her, Sunday after Sunday. One evening there was a church social and Kame surely thought—and, to tell the truth, hoped—that he would speak to her. But, no, he stood in a far corner of the church basement and continued to stare.

At twenty, Kame had learned much from life about resourcefulness. If she could not entice the newcomer over with her great concentration and the most encouraging of expressions, *she* would go to *him*. Carrying a cup of punch, she crossed the floor and offered it to the dark and intense-looking young man who, for just a moment, seemed on the verge of fleeing.

"Would you like something to drink?" she said, extending the cup.

"No," he replied, taking it and downing the punch in a single gulp.

They stood staring at each other, stiff, wary, miserable. Once they started to speak at the same time, then lapsed

back into their unhappy silence. Long minutes passed before
Hyotaro touched her arm—to indicate that he was, finally,
about to speak, and that she should please not start at the
same time—and he said:

"I mean, yes, I did want something to drink, and I thank
you. My name is Hyotaro Inouye and I would be honored if
you would allow me to call on you."

A year later, in September 1923, they were married by the
Reverend Komuro. Reverend Klinefelter gave the bride in
marriage, and the groom's parents, who had come from
Kauai for the wedding and had never before seen the inside
of a Christian church, sat in stony silence through hymns
and prayers. They were, of course, aghast that their son was
marrying outside the Buddhist faith—and marrying an or-
phan, at that!—but he was their eldest son and in all other
ways had been faithful, and so they clenched their teeth,
held their peace and hoped for the best.

The young couple went to live on Queen Emma Street, a
teeming Japanese ghetto with two-family houses pressed one
on the other and a streetful of children screeching a piercing and inimitable jangle of Japanese and English.

And there, in the early evening of September 7, 1924, I
was born.

Chapter II

Up from Queen Emma Street

❈ Years later the sociologists and planners would point to Queen Emma Street with horror, and describe it as a poverty pocket and a pesthole, and eventually it became the site of Honolulu's first slum clearance project. The ramshackle lines of houses were knocked over by bulldozers and the remains carted away. Grass was planted in the places where I grew up, and trees, and today it is a public park, a green oasis in the city.

I suppose that is progress. Certainly it is an aesthetic improvement over those crowded and chaotic duplexes of my earliest memory. But the thing is that I was much too young to realize how underprivileged I was and foolishly I enjoyed every moment of my childhood. As for my parents, they were so caught up in the adventure of raising a family, and worked so hard to preserve and protect it, that apparently they had no time to worry about being poor. There was always enough to eat in our house—although sometimes barely—but even more important there was a fanatic con-

viction that opportunity awaited those who had the heart
and the strength to pursue it.

Almost directly across the street from our house stood the
Pacific Club, shrine and symbol and watering place for all
the *haole* (white) wealth and power in the Islands. There
are places like it all over the world, the very private retreats
of men of proper station. But it is a neat little irony that this
particular bastion of Hawaii's planters and great merchants
and their ladies, which rigidly barred all Orientals, should
have been set down in the very heart of a Japanese slum. Of
course the irony eluded me completely during all that time I
lived on Queen Emma Street, and if I ever thought about
the Pacific Club at all, it was probably with passing regret
that no native kids lived there; the immaculate lawns
seemed a perfect place for a ballgame.

I was enchanted with the swift-moving and colorful world
into which I'd been born and the world, I must say, seemed
pretty pleased with me, too. As the eldest son in a Japanese
household, I was, to begin with, accorded a very special
esteem. And since I was the most recent descendant of five
generations of eldest sons, my father and grandfather
swelled with paternal pride at my every yowl.

My mother had her own reason for showering me with
affection for, as the nonmedical saying goes, I had been born
dead—no heartbeat, no breath, just a bluish lump of flesh
held head-down by a nervous midwife, responding neither to
coaxing nor to several smartly-delivered whacks across the
backside.

"Bring ice water!" the midwife cried out to my father, who
blithely waited in the kitchen to be congratulated.

Poor man. Everyone had been so persuasive about the
ease of modern childbirth that, finally, he had turned com-

pletely relaxed about the whole thing, so that at the midwife's shrill cry of emergency he came bounding up out of
his chair as though stroked with a hot iron. Without a
wasted motion, he sprang to the icebox, flung it open and
scooped the whole huge block of ice into a pail, vegetables
scattering, milk spilling and eggs crashing in the process.
Into the pail he splashed water, and splashed more on the
floor as he dashed for the bedroom—where the midwife
rewarded him with a look of withering disdain.

"Did you think I meant to give him swimming lessons?"
she snapped as she dipped her fingers into the cold water.
Then, brushing them across my forehead and the back of my
neck, she crooned a little incantation. A moment later I
wailed with first awareness of this world, and my mother fell
back on her pillow with a prayer of thanks, and my father
grinned with great pride and relief.

I was not, to put it mildly, a prepossessingly handsome
infant. My head was too large for my body and, as my
mother has had occasion to remind me, my face resembled
nothing so much as a great dark prune. Passed into family
legend is the story of the Klinefelters' first visit to our house
after I was born. The good Reverend seemed struck dumb at
the sight of me, and Mrs. Klinefelter, struggling for some
tactful way out of the disquieting confrontation, could manage only a feeble, "Well—well, he certainly has nice ears."

The matter of selecting a name for this newest heir to the
Inouye name and fortunes precipitated one of those inevitable encounters between East and West, old and new. In
traditional fashion, my father wanted to name me Taro, the
second part of his own first name. My mother, with her
confirmed Methodist upbringing, opted for Daniel, a
prophet she revered for his steadfast courage. That this was

also the Reverend Klinefelter's first name buttressed her enthusiasm for it.

But one did not lightly fly in the face of one's heritage, especially when one's in-laws—who, in an earlier day, would have chosen their grandson's name and no nonsense—stood silently but purposefully waiting for the decision. On the evening when the judgment was to be made, I am told, my mother idly flipped open the pages of the Bible—and lo! the pages parted at the Book of Daniel. "Look! Look!" she whispered in awe, and my father looked and was equally moved by what seemed an incontrovertible sign, and Daniel it was.

Naturally I have never had any reason to doubt the story. It is only that knowing my mother's great dependence on the Bible, I would accept a reasonable wager that, eyes closed, she could open it to the Book of Daniel nine times out of ten.

My middle name was to be Ken, a concession to the old tongue and the old ways. Ken in Japanese means to build and in my earliest years I thought that my father, in choosing that name, intended for me to be a builder or, as I understood it at the time, a carpenter. Not until long afterward did I realize the true significance of my middle name, given with the devout hope that, as the eldest son, I would continue to build the Inouye family. In any event I was later baptized Daniel Ken Inouye by the Reverend Harry Komuro, son of the good man who had married my parents.

If loveliness of face was not my strong point, I managed apparently to compensate my parents for their enormous devotion by a certain precocious wit. My mother, admittedly a prejudiced witness, says that I was fluent by the time I was two, singing songs and conversing with adults in chirpy but completely intelligible Japanese. English was another matter. I limped along in that tongue, picking up a word here and another there—most of them on the street and hence not very serviceable for polite conversation—until I entered kindergarten, at which time my mother and father abruptly dropped Japanese and began to speak English and only English at home.

Of course this was a hardship and a sacrifice and a great personal wrench for them, but they stuck painstakingly with it, perhaps the most striking demonstration of how far the Inouye family had traveled since my grandfather set out on that long road from Yokoyama village just 25 years before. There would remain ties of tradition and sentiment with the old country, but there would never be any confusion about my parents' allegiance: they were Americans, the proud distillation of the union between the girl from Maui who had been raised a Methodist, and the boy from Kauai whose forebears had been Buddhists.

This is not to say that either one could or would summarily slam the door on their Japanese heritage. "I take from the old ways what I think is good and useful," my mother used to say. "I take from the new ways what is good and useful. Anyone would be foolish not to."

And so there were no jangling conflicts between East and West in our house, but a kind of stimulating blend of the two that characterized the entire Japanese community in Hawaii. When we ate chicken or beef, we used knives and forks. When we ate sukiyaki or tempura, we used chopsticks. Although I went to a Japanese school every afternoon, it was never permitted to interfere with my American education. Perhaps the most marked evidence of our Japanese background was a deep sense of respect and discipline. I wasn't ever spanked because it would never occur to me to disobey my parents. And when my sister and brothers were born, I was clearly given to understand my responsibilities as the eldest son, being held personally accountable for all of their childish transgressions and misdemeanors. I was furthermore required to set an excellent example for them in all things, as this was the best assurance that the family would flourish and its honor remain untarnished.

There were, inevitably, some minor confusions. I noted the reverence in which the old folks held the Emperor and once asked my mother if a boy like me could ever aspire to marry his daughter. She did not consider the question at all foolish, but weighed it in all seriousness and at some length before answering me. "Remember always," she finally said, "that there is no one who is too good for you." I felt myself grow taller. "But remember, too," she went on, "that there is a difference between pride and arrogance, for *you* are no better than anyone else, either." I came quickly back to earth and have never forgotten that little talk. In all the years to come it would help me feel comfortable in the company of presidents and longshoremen, among people whose skin was white, brown, black or yellow.

I remember a great celebration in my house. There were songs and much sake, and though I was not yet five years old I sat on my grandfather's lap and took a sip of the potent warmth in his cup. When my mother protested, Grandfather said, "A Japanese should learn to drink his native potion as a boy so that he will hold it with honor as a man." And my father shushed his wife: "It is a special occasion."

It was special, indeed! The debt had been paid, and the honor of the Inouye name had been secured. After nearly 30 years of persistent and painful effort, Asakichi had redeemed the family obligation. Had he chosen to do so, he could now have returned to Yokoyama village and been received with esteem and the great respect of all the villagers—and this surely had been the shining goal toward which he had labored all the long years.

But many things can happen in three decades, and sometimes even the most rigidly-held notions of yesterday must give way to the realities of today. Asakichi's mother and father—my great-grandparents—had passed on to their reward. His sons and daughters had made a permanent home in Hawaii, they were Americans, and he himself had now passed more years in this new place than he had in the land of his fathers. And so the decision was made: he would stay in the Islands, which had been good to him and to his children, and when the time came, he would be buried there, too.

But it was far from only a simple and straightforward matter of so deciding. There was, for one thing, the inflexible tradition that a Japanese who is so unfortunate as to die far from his homeland must have made—or have made for him—necessary provisions for his remains to be cremated and shipped back to the homeland so that he might be interred close to his ancestors. For a true son of Nippon to be buried anywhere else would be a sacrilege. But Asakichi's commitment was made and it was total: he gave instructions that, when his time came, he was to be put to rest in the cemetery in Honolulu.

Next he gave up his place, reserved for the eldest son, as head of the Inouye family. In a poignant letter to his brother Yahei in Japan, Asakichi tried to explain the reasons for his momentous decision: "My children are here, and my grandson, and it is here that I have passed most of the days of my life. I do not believe that my wife and I, in our last years, could find contentment in Yokoyama, which has become for us a strange place." In consequence whereof, he formally relinquished his rights to all the Inouye goods and property in Japan, traditionally reserved for the eldest son, and renounced the venerated position as head of the family.

The brother was understandably horrified, it was as though Asakichi had died. Indeed, when my grandparents returned to Japan for a visit some years later, the great joy with which they were greeted was tinged with amazement— just as though they had returned from the dead.

Asakichi's decision was to have a profound effect on my own life. In 1927, when my father had managed to save enough to build a modest little house on Coyne Street, my grandparents, having grown bent and weary in their years of bondage to the family debt, finally left the plantation and came to live with us, bringing with them, of course, my two uncles and two aunts. This formidable addition to our household my father accepted without question—a Japanese tradition that the Inouyes were *not* giving up was the inherent responsibility of the eldest son to care for his aging parents. The problems, however, were awesome. With the birth of my sister, May Masako, there were ten of us in those small quarters. At night, we overflowed the three bedrooms and one was apt to stumble over a sleeping body anywhere. By day, any two people moving at the same time created an immediate traffic jam.

Even more serious was a real collision of East and West. Naturally my grandfather became the new head of the family, and naturally he expected my mother to accept the place reserved for daughters-in-law in all Japanese house-

holds which, not to mince words, was that of a servant. She
was to cook and clean and cater to the needs of everyone in
the family in strict accordance with their station, her father-
in-law first and her children last. She was to speak when
spoken to—and reply with all deference—and was to otherwise make herself as inconspicuous as possible.

But my mother was no ordinary Japanese girl. She had
been raised in a Western home and was imbued with a firm
belief in the worth and dignity of every individual. For my
mother, you might say, democracy began at home. After a
period of returning from work to find his young wife increas-
ingly silent and tight-lipped my father decided that something would have to be done. True to his obligation, he
would provide for his parents and brothers and sisters as
long as they remained in the house on Coyne Street. But
true, too, to his own family, he moved us to half of a small
duplex—one bedroom—on Thompson Street (now called
Hausten Street) in the Moiliili district, managing, somehow,
to maintain two households on his pay of $100 a month. Not
until 1940, when my uncles and aunts were grown and gone
and my grandparents passed on to their reward, did we
return to the house on Coyne Street, and it is in that house
that my parents have lived to this day.

For her part, the experience left my mother with a view-
point that was far advanced for her generation: when I
married, it was obvious that one of the three bedrooms could
have been made available to Maggie and me. Mother acknowledged this, then said to me, "Perhaps it would be
easier financially for you to stay with us for a while, but I
have a feeling your wife would be happier in even the tiniest
rented room." Her "feeling" was absolutely right, as I was to
find it to be in almost every instance through my growing-up
years.

Moiliili was a teeming and turbulent section of Oahu, occupied mostly by Japanese with only the most tenuous handhold up from poverty. McCully, where we moved three years later, was its economic and social twin. And both these districts were to play a significant part in my life, first as a child, and then 20 years later when I plunged into politics: in Moiliili and McCully I regularly carried all but a bare handful of precincts.

We were poor, but since all of our friends and neighbors were equally poor, I never felt deprived or sorry for myself. As far as I knew, every mother sliced a single hard-boiled egg into equal parts—six in our case—for the family breakfast, and every father gave his sons their monthly haircuts— who had 20 cents to spare for the barber? Not until I was in high school did I see the inside of a barbershop.

Although once I almost had a wig made of my own cuttings. I had long admired my grandfather's glistening dome, shorn and shaven in the Japanese tradition, and one day I told my father that I wanted all my hair cut off, too. Both men, instantly ascribing to me an instinctive racial loyalty—whereas, in truth, I was only childishly taken with the fierce look that Grandfather's bald pate gave him—delightedly proceeded to give me a true ceremonial haircut, beaming with pride at every snip and razor scrape. Just as they finished, my mother, who had been out shopping, walked in the door.

I suppose the three of us must have started with the same expectant expression on our faces, as if to say, "Well, how do you like your son now?" I am certain that we all reacted the same way to her reaction, her thunderstruck look driving us closer together, making us try to seem as small and inconspicuous as possible. She said, "What have you done to him? What have you done to him?"

Then the silence was shattering. As she glared at us, I huddled close to my father and grandfather, completely baffled by my mother's anger. And they huddled close to each other, suddenly understanding it perfectly. Not only did my shaven head make me look like some owl-eyed dwarf, but the very idea of the ceremonial haircut ran directly contrary to her commitment, to the commitment of all of us, to Western ways and ideals.

"Oh, what have you done to him?" she moaned once more, and dropping her parcels she fell to her knees and began scooping up clumps and snippets of my hair. And suddenly we were all helping her, not quite sure why, three generations of proud Inouye eldest sons, scrambling around on all fours searching for every stray locket to mollify a little wisp of a woman with very firm ideas. And having gathered it all, Mother spent days trying to figure out some way to make a temporary hairpiece with it to cover my naked scalp, giving up only when I began sprouting a bristling new crop of hair. It itched fiercely, which seemed to give my mother some small measure of gloating satisfaction. I never heard her mention the episode to my father, but of course words weren't really necessary; everyone in the house understood with crystal clarity that I had had my first and last ceremonial haircut.

As for my poor grandfather, his way of making amends was to present me with a replica of a samurai sword. Naturally I thought it the most marvelous toy in all the world and proudly flaunted it wherever I went.

"Isn't it beautiful!" I cried triumphantly to my mother.

"Hmph," she said.

When I was twelve, I was formally admitted to a sort of family council. This was definitely not in the Japanese tradition to which the very idea of decision-sharing in the home was alien; the head of a proper Japanese house decided everything. But this was my parents' way of broadening my sense of responsibility. The three of us would gather around the kitchen table and ponder the problems of the moment. Mother had managed to save $2 out of her monthly allotment: should we use it to buy John a pair of shoes, or was a blanket for May's bed a more pressing need? Mostly I contributed little, content to play my heady role on the family board of directors in silence. But my mother occasionally came up with a truly fantastic suggestion and one of them, I remember, startled me into speech.

"I think," she announced at one of our sessions, "that we should have a piano."

My father could only gasp with astonishment. But I, thinking, I suppose, that this must be some kind of test of my common sense—I mean, we didn't even *know* anyone who owned a piano!—blurted out: "But none of us can play the piano!"

By which time my father had found voice and echoed, "And who among us can pay for one!"

To all of which my mother responded with tranquil silence, waiting until the sound and the fury had died down. Then she calmly faced up to each of our objections, and some we hadn't even thought of, as well, and met each one with her half-exotic, half rigidly practical logic. None of us could play because we had never had the opportunity, she said sweetly. When we got the piano, we would play. As for paying for it, she had found a suitable one for $50 that could be paid for on an installment basis. Finally, she pointed out that a piano would give the family pleasures and cultural advantages such as were available to us in no other way. Once he had gotten over his shock, my father could see that she was right—as she usually was—and gave his assent, which I seconded with still some bewilderment. And so the momentous decision was made. A few days later, the piano arrived, a massive, far-from-new upright that had to be wrestled, this way and that, into our tiny quarters, and whose great bulk thereafter dominated the entire house. It was three years before it was fully paid for, but there is no way of calculating how much joy it brought into our home. Just as Mother had predicted, each of the kids learned to play, me least expertly of all, and it was a rare waking hour when someone was not thumping away happily on that battered instrument.

Of course the piano stands out in my mind just because it was such an incongruity in our circumstances. I mean, we were poor! My mother cooked on a tiny kerosine stove and among all six of us we had not enough clothes to fill a closet—which worked out very nicely since none of the places where we lived had a closet. Nor was there ever anything resembling leftover food at the Inouye table. With some uncanny mental gauge, Mother prepared precisely enough so that each of us got up from the table feeling a little hungry.

But we were surely not undernourished and rarely sick, and Mother never missed an opportunity to capitalize on any unexpected opportunity to stock the larder. A neighbor who raised fighting cocks responded to my enormous admiration by giving me a chick of my very own. It quickly became my pet, trailing after me and even fluttering up to my shoulder on command. My mother didn't object to the few grains of rice and corn I appropriated for its food, which ought to have given me fair warning, and for a while I was as happy with my pet as if I'd been given a best-of-show collie. It grew plump and sassy, and Mother bided her time.

One night we had chicken for supper and there was much smacking of lips and sighing of contentment, and for once everyone ate his fill. Next morning, having checked the house and yard to no avail, I came inside to ask if anyone had seen my chicken. "We all saw it," said my mother without turning from the sinkful of dishes she was washing. "We ate it at supper last night. And we all thank you for taking such good care of it until it was ready to eat." I suppose I was absolutely devastated for at least half a day—I honestly don't remember that part of it. But I will never forget my mother's words, gentle, toweringly practical, absolutely conclusive: "We all thank you for taking such good care of it until it was ready to eat." She really meant it.

My sorrows were few and momentary and my most vivid memories are of the fun we had. We enjoyed each other. We even turned Mother's fixation about vitamins into a family lark. A voracious reader, she had somewhere become smitten with the importance of the nutritional values in certain foods. Eggs, milk and fresh fruit were prime vitamin sources, said the good book, and since the first two were expensive, Mother plied us with the third, which in Hawaii is available for the picking. Off we'd go on a mountain picnic and, almost automatically, we kids would scatter out into the bush, to return with armloads of guavas, mangoes, mountain apples and wild plums. This was our picnic feast, and there was always enough to cart home for the rest of the week. Whatever else we had to eat—and sometimes it wasn't much—the fruit, a quart of milk and that egg divided six ways were as unvarying as the Hawaiian sunshine.

In a nearby woods we built an elaborate treehouse and imagined ourselves to be so many Tarzans, pitting ourselves against villains of the jungle, human and animal. And even this childish fantasy was turned to practical use. My father showed us how to trap the tricky little mongoose, introduced to Hawaii by the sugar planters in hopes it would control the rat infestation introduced by the trading vessels of the eighteenth and nineteenth centuries. But having done this, the mongoose turned its attentions to the Islands' plump poultry and became quite a pest. Oh, I can still savor that sense of triumph with which I bore each one home, nor could the mightiest hunter ever have felt more handsomely rewarded than I did when Mother flashed me that smile of pride.

The mongooses remind me of the time Frank Buck, the world-famous bring-'em-back-alive hunter, came to Hawaii with his celebrated snake collection. Of course our island paradise has always been free of reptiles—except for a rare sort of earth snake, perhaps eight inches long—and quite naturally the powers-that-be, wanting to keep it that way, had passed a law forbidding the introduction of any live snakes. Enter Frank Buck whose famed wild animal act, widely advertised in the Honolulu newspapers, featured a collection of boa constrictors, pythons and other specimens of reptilian ferocity. And plain on the statute books was the law subjecting him to arrest if he deposited so much as a garter snake on the dock. Buck faced a Hobson's choice: he could either return to the States—canceling his show and refunding every penny of the substantial advance sale—or he could somehow get rid of his snakes. In the end, the show went on, with a splendid display of snake *skins*.

I didn't wear shoes regularly until I was in high school, —none of us *nisei* kids did—and it was as much a matter of comfort as money. After all, this was Hawaii, a truly blessed place for a boy to grow up in.

We were a trial to our teachers, I'm sure. Many of them were *haoles* from the Mainland, properly reared and educated young ladies, and they must have been disconcerted, to say the least, to be suddenly confronted with a ragtag crew of barefooted, sport-shirted kids whose English was liberally larded with Japanese, Chinese, Hawaiian and some exotic combinations of each. But they were a wonderfully dedicated group and they did their best to make educated Americans out of us young savages. And even more important, they accepted us on our own terms—they didn't despair over us, or patronize us, or slough us off as inferiors and hopeless delinquents. They treated us as exactly what we were, a bunch of kids from poor homes with hard-working parents, with a sort of built-in eagerness to become part of the mainstream of American life, and there is no way in which I can adequately express my thanks to them.

I loved school. Each day brought its own separate reward and learning became a constantly intriguing challenge. Of course when you're a boy there is always a danger of being tagged a bookworm and, in natural consequence, a sissy-pants. And so I was careful not to be caught studying or doing more homework than was absolutely necessary, and I warily cultivated a manner of dress and classroom manner that, even by our group's casual standard, was pretty flamboyant.

By this time we had returned to Coyne Street, in an area officially known as Bingham Tract but more readily recognizable by its popular name: Chinese Hollywood. Here Chinese families clustered together, and here came aspiring Americans from China with every new ship bound east from the Orient. The Inouyes were one of only two Japanese families in Bingham and, perhaps inevitably, we were soon virtually adopted by our sweet-natured neighbors. To this day I am known by our old neighbors as Ah-Danny-Jai, affectionate Chinese for little Danny.

As for me, I acquired a highly-cultivated taste for Chinese delicacies, not the least of which was dried water beetles. When these were roasted, the tails could be pulled from the body and made a delicious snack, like peanuts. One day, hungry as usual, I took a whole bagful of these morsels to school with me and whiled away the afternoon cracking them and stuffing the tasty tails into my mouth. So long as there was activity in the classroom I was safe, the teacher couldn't hear me and I took care that she didn't see me. But toward the end of the day, with all of us hushed in assigned study, the sharp crack of a beetle back sounded through the silent room like a rifle shot. Miss Dolton, who was blond and beautiful, looked up and I looked down. Miss Dolton looked down and—CRACK!—went another beetle.

"Dan!"

"Gmmm?" I mumbled, my mouth stuffed with tails.

"Are you *eating* something?"

I nodded, trying to express an apology with my eyes alone.

"Well!" said the proper young lady indignantly. "You know the rule about eating in class. Now you may bring whatever it is you have there up to me and I will take my share and pass it around to the class."

Now, as you can see, this was truly punishment to fit the crime—forcing any of us kids to give up food was like shredding a tobacco addict's last cigarette. Crushed and contrite, and still unable to speak a word in my defense, I carried my precious bag up front and deposited it on Miss Dolton's desk. Whereupon she righteously reached in, produced a beetle and, on the verge of popping it into her mouth, caught sight of what she was holding and delivered herself of a shriek that, they say, was heard on the far side of Diamond Head. Into the wastebasket went my bag—punishment enough!—and back to my seat I marched, directed by Miss Dolton's quivering finger. Years later, when I went back to see her, we had many laughs over my school days. But when I brought up the matter of the Chinese water beetles, the same look of dread crossed her face, and she said, "Oh, Dan, how could you!"

The trouble I got into at Japanese language school was somewhat more serious and crystallized for me, once and for all, the matter of who I was and where in this cultural melting pot I was headed. Most of my contemporaries quit at the end of the tenth year, by which time they had a fair grounding in Japanese history and tradition. In deference to my grandparents, I suppose, I was enrolled for the eleventh grade and sat through excruciatingly long afternoons listening to lectures on the sacredness of the royal family and being admonished to preserve the centuries-old customs of my people. Then, all in one cataclysmic afternoon, I unburdened myself of my smoldering resentment and, in consequence, was flung bodily from the classroom, never to return.

The year was 1939 and already times had turned tense in the Far East. The Japanese government was in the iron grip of fanatic warlords and the Imperial Army was waging aggressive war in China and menacing all of Southeast Asia. Day after day, the priest who taught us ethics and Japanese history hammered away at the divine prerogatives of the Emperor, and at the grand destiny that called on the Japanese people to extend their sway over the yellow race, and on the madness that was inducing the American government to oppose them. He would tilt his menacing crew-cut skull at us and solemnly proclaim, "You must remember that only a trick of fate has brought you so far from your homeland, but there must be no question of your loyalty. When Japan calls, you must know that it is Japanese blood that flows in your veins."

I had heard his jingoistic little speeches so many times that I suppose they no longer really registered on me. He was an old man, to be respected for his station, but when he began spouting nonsense I could easily tune him out. But one day he shifted his scorn to the Bible and I reacted by instinct—and violently. He had been discussing the inadequacy of Christianity compared to Shintoism, the state religion of Japan, and already my hackles were up. Then he favored us with an elaborate grin and, mockery dripping from his every word, he said, "I give you the Bible itself as the best evidence of this Christian foolishness. Their God made the world in seven days, it says. Ha! Then he made a man and from a rib of that man—a rib, mark you!—he made a woman. Ha! Anyone with only part of a brain can see that this is the wildest nonsense!"

I never realized that I was on my feet and shouting until I saw the grin on his face twist, first into astonishment, and then into fury. Then my words echoed in my head:

"That's not right! That's not fair! I am a Christian, a lot of us here are, and you mustn't talk that way! I respect your faith. You must respect mine."

"How dare you!" he roared.

"I do. I do dare! You have no right to make fun of my beliefs."

"You are a Japanese! You will believe what I . . ."

"I am an American!"

He flinched, exactly as though I had struck him. With a single compulsive jerk, he threw the book he had been holding through the open window, and we watched the pages flutter in the wind for a moment. Then he started toward me, and the class watched in silent terror, and his face was black as a thunderhead and his mouth worked violently as he cried, "You are a Japanese!" Now his fingers clutched at my open collar and he was shaking me back and forth. "Say it!" he screamed into my face. "You are a Japanese!"

And barely able to bring my voice up out of my tortured throat, I muttered, "I–am–an–American."

With that, he lifted me from my feet and half-dragged, half-carried me to the door, and he threw me with full force into the schoolyard. "You are a faithless dog!" he screamed, and slammed the door closed.

Dazed and trembling, I stumbled to my feet. My trousers were torn and one knee was scraped and bleeding. Crazily, my first thought was how to hide this from my mother. But I had only taken a few steps toward home when I realized that I didn't want to hide it. I had had all I could take of that Japanese teacher and if it took this catastrophe—and the punishment I was sure to get for it—to free me, well, so be it.

But, of course, I had underestimated my mother again. She took one look at my tattered pants and the mutinous expression I wore, and she demanded the whole story. And I told it to her, and all the time I spoke she was washing and bandaging my skinned knee, so that I could not see her face and could not gauge how she was reacting to this great crisis in my life. But when I was all finished, she got to her feet and said, "Come, we are going back there."

This was something more than I had bargained for. Maybe I had used up my day's supply of bravery, but the fact is that I had no desire to face the priest's wrath again. "Mama," I began hesitantly . . .

She shushed me. "You have nothing to fear or to be ashamed of," she said crisply. "But there is a matter of honor to be settled."

Nor did she waste any time on the teacher. Instead, she went directly to the office of the principal, a gentle and distinguished Japanese. And Mother stood before his desk, a tiny figure whose massive indignation strengthened her words, and she told him exactly what had happened. "I do not send him here to become a Shintoist or a samurai. I want him to learn the language and traditions of his ancestors, but we are Americans and shall always remain so."

Amazingly, he nodded his agreement. He would speak to the priest, he assured my mother. There would be no more such authoritarian teaching, and I could return to my class without fear of retribution.

"That is up to Ken," my mother said looking straight at me and using, as she almost always did, my Japanese name. "He is old enough now to decide this for himself."

And I said, "I don't want to go back. I've learned enough about the old ways." My mother thanked the principal for hearing her out, and we left, and for the first time, I suppose, I knew what it was to *feel* like an American.

Up through the ninth grade in intermediate school, I did well enough scholastically but, like nearly all of my friends, I had no goals that stretched beyond graduation and getting a job somewhere, and even that seemed a long, long way off. Meanwhile I was fully occupied with a whole array of

hobbies and the occasional yardboy jobs I could pick up to pay for them. Thanks to my mother's incredible foresight in the matter of the piano, I had grown up with a love of music that ranged from swing—Benny Goodman was one of my first heroes—to the classics. I only studied the piano for a year because my fingers seemed to be perpetually bruised from playing baseball, but I switched to the saxophone and sang in the church choir, and once even represented my school in a city-wide singing contest. I didn't win, which is probably just as well, but because my voice didn't drop down into the lower registers until I went into the service, some of my friends dubbed me Japanese Bobby Breen.

I collected tropical fish and homing pigeons, and more than once I walked the 25 dusty miles to the Army signal center at Schofield Barracks where, if I did a good job cleaning the coops, the soldiers would give me a couple of pigeon eggs in payment. These I would tenderly carry home, and unless you have been a fifteen-year-old boy who has loved pigeons, no words of mine can fairly express the thrill of seeing those shells crack open to reveal a ragged, skinny —but living!—pigeon chick.

In the traditional city-boy fashion, I progressed from yo-yos to billiards and secretly envied the older fellows who swaggered, unimpeded by law or conscience, into the pool parlors that seemed to be on every corner in downtown Honolulu. It was illegal for anyone under eighteen to set foot inside any of those dimly-lit and constantly alluring places so my crowd did its billiard-playing at the local YMCA, pretending, I think, that those antiseptic halls were really some downtown den of hustlers and pool sharks, and every time we picked up a cue stick we were Willie Hoppe, about to rack up an unbeatable run.

One Saturday afternoon, goaded by who knows what sudden need to assert our too-slowly approaching manhood, a few of us actually smuggled ourselves into an authentically dingy pool hall. We pulled ourselves as tall as we could, assumed the proper expressions of disdain, and trembling inwardly, sauntered past the door checker. And, honestly, we had not been inside long enough for our eyes to grow accustomed to the dimness when there was a sudden flurry at the door, a piercing whistle—and police all over the place. And we were all under arrest!

Luckily, I was too bewildered to be scared; I mean, we hadn't *done* anything. Everyone in the place who looked even remotely underage was hustled down to the station house where a tough-looking desk sergeant read us the riot act. Then, without formally charging us, he said, "Now go on home and next time you come up to a pool hall run, don't walk, past it."

I took his advice, to the letter. And although I thought nothing of it at the time, I have since often wondered how my life would have been changed if that sergeant had taken it into his head to record our names on the police blotter. For small events can cast large shadows, especially in politics, and I think it's safe to say that if he had I would not now be a member of the United States Senate.

The one unalloyed joy of being an adolescent in Hawaii was the beach. One could swim and surf and spearfish the year 'round, and if one was lucky, even get paid for it. During the tourist season, I would run down to Waikiki as soon as school was over to serve my apprenticeship with the older beach boys. Mostly they were Hawaiians, and without organization or a written regulation, they operated an impenetrable closed shop that would have won the admiration of the largest international trade union. In order of seniority, they would station themselves along the choice spots by the seawall outside the Royal Hawaiian Hotel, waiting, in turn, for the guests who were interested in surfing to hire them for the afternoon.

There was nothing to the job. You paddled the tourist's board out to where the great waves were beginning to crest, showed him how to get on and shoved him off on the long ride to shore just as the wave broke. If he was thrown, a not uncommon occurrence, you were obliged to rescue the board, but that only gave you a chance for a good swim.

In my sixteen-year-old eyes, such a life offered everything anyone could ever ask for—the ocean and the everlasting sun—and to think that anyone would pay you for this was proof enough that there really was a Santa Claus. Of course the real trick was to ingratiate yourself into that tight little beach boy monopoly, and toward this end I exercised all the wiles and flattery at my command. I admired this one's swimming style, remarked on how beautifully that one had ridden his surfboard in on a particularly tricky breaker. And always I was there, patient, agreeable, and secretly swelling with hope.

And one afternoon the leader of the group summoned me to his side and pointed out to the beach: "See that guy dragging his board? He's a beginner and he'll only pay you ten cents an hour. But if you want him he's yours."

I flew. *If I wanted him!* Why, to me that paunchy, milky-skinned tourist looked like Clark Gable and I was to be his trusted right hand man in an assault on the raging Pacific! And so I was officially inducted into apprenticeship in the order of Waikiki beach boys. Of course the pecking order was firmly maintained: I was assigned only those less affluent tourists who walked to the beach from the relatively inexpensive hotels on the far side of Kalakaua Avenue and, at ten cents an hour—the journeymen beach boys got twenty-five—the most I could hope to make, even on a Saturday or Sunday, was perhaps seventy-five cents. But to me it was found money and even my clumsiest, most obstreperous patron seemed to me to have a touch of that Clark Gable devil-may-care.

The money I earned not only provided for further investments in tropical fish and pigeons but substantially bettered my nutritional situation. Although my mother gave me five cents each day for lunch in the school cafeteria, more often than not I used to walk across to the auditorium and join the poorer kids in the penny soup line, thus saving four cents for my hobbies. And now I could afford both!

Soon I had acquired a fine collection of American stamps which I still treasure. Then I bought the parts for a crystal radio set, and put it together and listened to it in the darkness each night before I fell asleep, marveling at the miracle that could bring music and voices into my bedroom from the faraway mainland.

It was around this time that I became something of an expert on the illegal sport of cockfighting. Our neighbor, the same one who had unknowingly donated that ill-fated cock to the Inouye dinner table, joined the National Guard and asked me if I would look after his flock while he was at camp. I was happy to do it, although it was an exacting and complicated business. The birds had to be fed precisely on time, and their legs had to be oiled regularly, and their combs cut. But this experience served me well when I became a Honolulu County public prosecutor. By then, fortunately, my old neighbor was no longer involved in this illicit trade, for I couldn't help feeling I had an unfair advantage when it became my responsibility to act against the gamblers and trainers of fighting cocks.

It was in my sophomore year in high school that I first came under the warm and rewarding spell of Mrs. Ruth King, a teacher whose influence in my young life ranked just behind that of my mother and father. She certainly didn't look inspiring, a short, plump lady in her middle forties with graying hair and eyes that seemed to look vaguely out from behind a pair of rimless glasses and to see practically nothing. But the truth was that she saw practically everything, surely nothing of any real importance that happened in her classroom escaped her notice.

Hers was the top tenth grade class at McKinley High. I don't know how I got into it and, from the very first day, I wanted out. In place of all my old live-and-let-live buddies from Moiliili and McCully, I found myself rubbing shoulders with a breed of kids who kept trying to pretend that their skin was white and their eyes were blue. And there in the midst of this pretense, surrounded by all those starched white shirts and shined shoes, was rough-and-tumble Dan Inouye, to whom a necktie was a garrote on the spirit, and shoes an encumbrance to be suffered through at funerals and in church.

In those days, McKinley High School was jokingly referred to as Tokyo High. Thanks to an ingenious system of segregation, nearly all of us there were of Japanese ancestry, and from the least affluent *nisei* families, at that. It worked through a device known as the English Standard School and neatly sidestepped the law that, theoretically, opened all the public schools to everyone regardless of race, color or creed. To be admitted to an English Standard School—which by

invariable coincidence had better facilities and better facul-
ties—one had to pass an examination. The written part was
fair enough since everyone had an equal chance. But the
oral test served as an automatic weeding-out factor, for rare
indeed was the student of Asian parentage who could properly pronounce the "th" sound, the "r" and the "l." The
obvious result was that the English Standard Schools became almost the exclusive province of Caucasian youngsters,
and that handful of Japanese and Chinese whose parents
could afford to give them private tutoring. Not until 1955
was the last of this subtle segregation eliminated from
Hawaii's public school system.

I was too young and unknowing then to be troubled by
the concept of "Tokyo High." Only my stiff-necked classmates bothered me and sometimes it seemed that the only
person who ever talked to me in that grade was Mrs. King.
"Your grammar leaves something to be desired, Dan," she
would say to me privately. "Why don't you stay after school
today and we'll work on it?" And I would, happily, because
to be in her presence was suddenly to glimpse something
beyond the narrow horizons of the life I'd known, to sense
that being a clerk, or even a beach boy, was not the ultimate
and only hope for a kid like me. She took me seriously,
which is something that no one, not even I myself, had ever
done.

All at once literature was exciting and history was real.
Washington and Jefferson and Lincoln suddenly stepped out
of some mythical haze and became men of flesh and blood,
men with great problems and the great courage to face
them. I felt the bitter cold and despair of that winter at
Valley Forge. I felt a sharp sense of personal loss at the
death of Lincoln, the lost opportunity to bind up the nation's
wounds. Whereas Japanese history had always sounded like

some great impersonal pageant, the story of America had the ring of an adventure in human progress, troubles and set-backs and the inexorable march down to the present.

But most important of all, I came to believe that the giants who made American history were *my* forefathers. Always before, I had been a little embarrassed singing about the "land where my fathers died," and I always spoke of *the* fathers of *the* country. It was Mrs. King who, in some wonderfully subtle way convinced me of the essential rela-tionship between America's founding fathers and all of America's people.

In mid-year, Mrs. King recommended me for membership in McKinley's two junior honor societies, the Torch Society and the McKinley Citizenship Club. My mother and father glowed with pride and although I tried to pretend that it didn't matter to me one way or the other, the truth is that I was really excited by the prospect. On the appointed after-noon, beaming with good fellowship, I strode up before the Student Council for my interview. They sat behind a long table, four seniors trying to look as stern as bankers. They didn't ask me to sit down.

"Why do you think you belong in an honor society?" one of them asked.

I shrugged. "It was Mrs. King's idea. I . . ."

"Why don't you wear shoes?" another suddenly shot at me, a Japanese kid I'd known for at least five years.

"Because I only have one pair," I said to him. "They have to last." It was a silly question, he knew I only had one pair. He probably even knew that they'd been bought two years ago, and bought two sizes too large so I wouldn't grow out of them, and that until only recently I'd had to stuff the toes with paper to keep the darned things on.

But the silly questions were only beginning. "Why don't

you wear a white shirt?" they asked. "Why don't you wear a tie?"

I didn't know what to say. I looked from one to the other, a gathering fear inside me, like dirty fingers squeezing my stomach. What was this all about? I thought they were going to interview me about my interests and ideas, about my schoolwork maybe. Why did they care what I wore?

"Are you going to answer the question?"

"I don't know," I said. "My shirt is for church . . ."

"Don't you care how you look in school?"

Not wanting to, I looked down at my sports shirt and my denim pants and bare feet. "My clothes are clean," I mumbled. "I don't know what's wrong."

"What about your friends?" one of them barked, and rattled off a list of kids from my neighborhood. "Are *they* your friends?"

"Yes," I said, and all at once I knew that they were going to turn me down. "What's the matter with them?"

"Delinquents!"

"Because they don't wear shoes?" I said, and it was not a question. "Because they're poor? They're no more delinquents than I am. Or you are." All the disappointment, all the fear had suddenly boiled up in anger, and when they tried to interrupt me I shouted them down: "Hey, listen, I thought this was an honor society—honor, scholarship. But if all you're looking for is guys who wear white shirts and shoes, you don't want me and I for sure don't want you. I wouldn't trade one of my friends for . . . for both your honor societies and all four of you, so just forget the whole thing!"

For a long, long time afterward I would stiffen with an inner fury every time I remembered those moments of humiliation, and I remembered them often. Nor was that the end of it. Somehow I had to explain to my parents that I had not been accepted into the honor societies without telling them the real reasons, for they would then have blamed themselves. So I stammered and stuttered through some lame explanation that fooled them not a bit, and their eyes grew sad and there was no more for any of us to say. As for Mrs. King, who seemed to know everything there was to know about my unhappy encounter with the Council without my saying a word, she was so deeply hurt by their behavior that not once in my next year at McKinley High did she recommend another candidate for the Torch Society or the McKinley Citizenship Club.

But the most important effect of the entire episode was to convince me of the essential truth of that old saw about it being an ill wind that blows no good. It left me enraged and a little confused, but most of all it left me with a fiery resolve to "show those guys!" Never before had I felt so challenged, nor so determined to make something of myself. As a matter of fact, I don't think it's unfair to say that those four snobbish seniors are at least partly responsible for whatever successes I subsequently enjoyed. Their faces stuck in my mind, and do to this day, and for years afterward I charged at every obstacle in my path as though those four had personally put it there and it was absolutely essential for me to overcome it to prove that shoes and neckties were no measure of a man.

I should explain that there was no racial prejudice connected with my rejection, unless it was a kind of reverse bigotry. It was not my Japanese ancestry that the panel attacked, but my refusal to make any attempt to hide it in slavish imitation of *haole* dress and manner. And in this regard the Japanese members were my severest critics. They were very much in tune with a sizable segment of the Japanese community in Hawaii which, in their fawning anxiety to please their white neighbors, behaved as though they were white, too. They bought automobiles beyond their means, were sensitive to any change in *haole* fashions and mimicked them, and bitterly resented those of us who refused to conform to their twisted notions of what made an American. We were letting down all Japanese-Americans, they cried, and never missed an opportunity to crack down on us, more severely than our *haole* neighbors ever did.

My newfound ambition was soon channeled in a single direction, and a most unlikely one at that for the son of a poor *nisei* family: I had decided to become a doctor! I suppose the seeds of that dream had been sown years before when my grandmother was stricken with cancer. I remember the sad reliance of all the family on good Dr. Sato, not to save Grandmother's life, for we were all too painfully aware that the dread disease would take its inexorable course, but to ease her suffering and help her over that incredibly hard journey to final release. He came nearly every day over those long weeks, and always found time for a word of comfort to the rest of us after he had seen to Grandmother's needs.

What nobler goal could a young man aspire to, I daydreamed, than to minister to the sick and to provide strength when people most desperately needed it? Soon I was haunting the Library of Hawaii, reading everything about medicine and the men who practiced it that I could find. Without getting their hopes up, my parents encouraged me—to have a doctor in the family was the absolute peak of achievement to which a Japanese household could aspire—and my single Christmas gift for each of the next two years was a chemistry set.

My ambition was reinforced by a personal disaster. Some years before, playfully wrestling with my good friend Shigeto Kanemoto I fell hard on my left arm and suffered a compound fracture. Mother rushed me to the only doctor she could think of, a fine eye, ear, nose and throat man then treating my brother for an ear infection. He set the arm as best he could, but unhappily he had had little practice in orthopedics and his best was not good enough. The break was a tricky one and when it finally mended, my arm hung limp and crooked and I could barely move it.

My mother and father were distraught. Of course they were not unmindful of my personal loss—bad enough!—but there was also an odd sense of family shame involved: how would it look to the world for the Inouye's eldest son to turn out to be a cripple! It was too bitter a prospect to even contemplate and they were absolutely determined that if there was any single thing on God's earth that they could do to prevent that happening, they would do it.

So began a bleak two-year period during which my mother took me from one doctor to another, seeking to have my misset fracture properly mended. Everywhere she asked who was the best orthopedic surgeon in Hawaii, and everywhere they told her someone different. Finally, one sunny morning Mother ordered me into my shoes and sole white shirt and took me to the Children's Hospital and asked for a doctor named Craig. He took only one look at my arm and said I would need an operation if I was to have any chance at all to regain its full use. Mother asked no questions, not how much the operation would cost, nor whether it was dangerous. She spoke only one sentence: "When can you do it?"

I remember little about my hospital stay or the actual surgery. Only Dr. Craig sticks in my mind, a white-headed, seamy-faced, ever-smiling man who always had a small joke for me—"You a baseball player? You better start learning to throw lefty because when we get finished your left arm will be stronger than your right." And it almost was. Soon after the operation I could bend it and not long after that it was as tough as it had ever been.

When I went back for my final checkup, Dr. Craig had still not said a word about his fee, but Mother was now ready to get down to cases. "We will not be able to pay you at once," she said, "but we will bring you a small amount each month until the whole amount is paid. I hope you will allow this and not worry for we are grateful to you and even if it takes a lifetime . . ."

"You owe me nothing," Dr. Craig said.

"Nothing?" Mother whispered.

"You will have to pay the hospital's costs, I believe that comes to $30, but the operation is my gift to Dan." He grinned at me. "You going to be a left-handed pitcher?"

"No," I said, unsmiling and never more serious in my life. "I'm going to be a doctor—like you."

For a long time afterward, I made regular trips to his office, carrying produce from our little garden; eggs, now and then a freshly-killed chicken, and not wanting to bother him, just left my basket in his waiting room. And often I saw on his table little baskets just like mine, and soon I understood that the Inouyes were not the only recipients of Dr. Craig's generosity.

Somewhere, far back in my mind, I was conscious of the growing tension between the United States and Japan. It was a worrisome thing, like a forecast of showers for a day on which you'd planned a picnic. But deep inside you had this feeling that the forecasters were wrong, that the sun would shine. That's the way I felt about the trouble in the Far East. It was disturbing because the newspapers were full of it and people talked about it, and because a conflict between my country and the country of my ancestors was too terrifying to even think about. But I never believed such a thing would come to pass, nor did hardly anyone else in the Japanese-Hawaiian community. And as that last peacetime summer edged into autumn, all of us took heart from the news that two envoys had been sent to Washington from Japan to iron out the difficulties.

By this time, the Japanese in Hawaii made up some 40 percent of the population and were the largest single ethnic group in the Islands. In the homes of the old folks, it was not uncommon to see a picture of the Emperor, or even a Shinto shrine. But except for a hard-shelled handful, there was no question about where their ultimate loyalty lay. We were Americans.

In response to official urging, I enrolled for a Red Cross first aid course. I think my real reason for taking it was not any expectation that I would ever need to put my new knowledge to use in an emergency, but that it contributed to my personal ambition for the future. I was pretty good at it and once I had my certificate began teaching classes of my own.

Otherwise my life was pretty typically teen-age. I played tenor sax and clarinet in the school dance band—oh, how I loved that solo opening of Glenn Miller's *In the Mood*—was active at the YMCA (I still am, as a member of the board of directors of the Nuuanu YMCA) and had even had my first date. All this was all right with my parents—although I suspect that they felt that playing in a band was something like being the piano player in a burlesque house—so long as I was faithful to the strict family code of behavior. For one thing, no matter what the occasion, no matter where I was, I had to be back in our living room by 10 P.M. and there were no exceptions.

So it was that one Saturday night at a dance at school, I had to cut out of the band at 9:30. At that I had to run the last few blocks to make it on time and came panting into the house.

"Why do you run?" Mother said. "You'll wear yourself out."

"I had to be home by ten. I was late."

"You should start earlier," she said with that unanswerable logic.

We chatted for a while, then my father stretched and said, "Let's go to bed. Tomorrow will be a long day."

He could not know how terribly right he was. At that very moment, 1,000 miles away in the North Pacific, Japanese carriers were steaming toward Oahu, the hundreds of airplanes on their decks primed for a pre-dawn takeoff. It was December 6, 1941, and by 7:30 next morning the way of the world would change and never be the same again.

Chapter III

One Sunday in December

✿ The family was up by 6:30 that morning, as we usually were on Sunday, to dress and have a leisurely breakfast before setting out for 9 o'clock services at church. Of course anyone who has some memory of that shattering day can tell you precisely what he was doing at the moment when he suddenly realized that an era was ending, that the long and comfortable days of peace were gone, and that America and all her people had been abruptly confronted with their most deadly challenge since the founding of the Republic.

As soon as I finished brushing my teeth and pulled on my trousers, I automatically clicked on the little radio that stood on the shelf above my bed. I remember that I was buttoning my shirt and looking out the window—it would be a magnificent day; already the sun had burned off the morning haze and glowed bright in a blue sky—when the hum of the warming set gave way to a frenzied voice. "This is no test!" the voice cried out. "Pearl Harbor is being bombed by the Japanese! I repeat: this is not a test or a maneuver! Japanese war planes are attacking Oahu!"

"Papa!" I called, then froze into immobility, my fingers clutching that button. I could feel blood hammering against my temple, and behind it the unspoken protest, like a prayer— *It's not true! It is a test, or a mistake! It can't be true!*— but somewhere in the core of my being I knew that all my world was crumbling as I stood motionless in that little bedroom and listened to the disembodied voice of doom.

Now my father was standing in the doorway listening, caught by that special horror instantly sensed by Americans of Japanese descent as the nightmare began to unfold. There was a kind of agony on his face and my brothers and sister, who had pushed up behind him, stopped where they were and watched him as the announcer shouted on:

". . . not a test. This is the real thing! Pearl Harbor has been hit and now we have a report that Hickam Field and Schofield Barracks have been bombed, too. We can see the Japanese planes . . ."

"Come outside!" my father said to me, and I plunged through the door after him. As my brothers John and Bob started out, too, he turned and told them: "Stay with your mother!"

We stood in the warm sunshine on the south side of the house and stared out toward Pearl Harbor. Black puffs of anti-aircraft smoke littered the pale sky, trailing away in a soft breeze, and we knew beyond any wild hope that this was no test, for practice rounds of anti-aircraft, which we had seen a hundred times, were fleecy white. And now the dirty gray smoke of a great fire billowed up over Pearl and obscured the mountains and the horizon, and if we listened attentively we could hear the soft *crrrump* of the bombs amid the hysterical chatter of the ack-ack.

And then we saw the planes. They came zooming up out of that sea of gray smoke, flying north toward where we stood and climbing into the bluest part of the sky, and they came in twos and threes, in neat formations, and if it hadn't been for that red ball on their wings, the rising sun of the Japanese Empire, you could easily believe that they were Americans, flying over in precise military salute.

I fell back against the building as they droned near, but my father stood rigid in the center of the sidewalk and stared up into that malignant sky, and out of the depths of his shock and torment came a tortured cry: "You fools!"

We went back into the house and the telephone was ringing. It was the secretary of the Red Cross aid station where I taught. "How soon can you be here, Dan?" he said tensely.

"I'm on my way," I told him. I felt a momentary surge of elation—he wanted me! I could do something!—and I grabbed a sweater and started for the door.

"Where are you going?" my mother cried. She was pointing vaguely out the window, toward the sky, and said, "They'll kill you."

"Let him go," my father said firmly. "He must go."

I went to embrace her. "He hasn't had breakfast," she whispered. "At least have some breakfast."

"I can't, Mama. I have to go." I took a couple of pieces of bread from the table and hugged her.

"When will you be back?" she said.

"Soon. As soon as I can."

But it would be five days, a lifetime, before I came back. The kid who set out on his bicycle for the aid station at Lunalilo School that morning of December 7 was lost forever in the debris of the war's first day, lost among the dead and the dying, and when I finally did come home I was a seventeen-year-old man.

The planes were gone as I pumped furiously toward the

aid station, more than a mile away. The acrid smell of the smoke had drifted up from Pearl and people, wide-eyed with terror, fumbling for some explanation, something to do, had spilled into the streets. What would become of them, I agonized, these thousands, suddenly rendered so vulnerable and helpless by this monstrous betrayal at the hands of their ancestral land? In those first chaotic moments, I was absolutely incapable of understanding that I was one of them, that I, too, had been betrayed, and all of my family.

An old Japanese grabbed the handlebars of my bike as I tried to maneuver around a cluster of people in the street. "Who did it?" he yelled at me. "Was it the Germans? It must have been the Germans!"

I shook my head, unable to speak, and tore free of him. My eyes blurred with tears, tears of pity for that old man, because he could not accept the bitter truth, tears for all these frightened people in teeming, poverty-ridden McCully and Moiliili. They had worked so hard. They had wanted so desperately to be accepted, to be good Americans. And now, in a few cataclysmic minutes, it was all undone, for in the marrow of my bones I knew that there was only deep trouble ahead. And then, pedalling along, it came to me at last that I would face that trouble, too, for my eyes were shaped just like those of that poor old man in the street, and my people were only a generation removed from the land that had spawned those bombers, the land that sent them to rain destruction on America, death on Americans. And choking with emotion, I looked up into the sky and called out, "You dirty Japs!"

Why had they done it? Why couldn't they let us live in peace? My mind reeled with tormented, confused, unanswerable questions. Once, with the sharp pain of a fresh wound being freshly plucked, it came to me that any one of the men in that armada of planes flaunting the rising sun could be my cousin, and to this day I do not know but what it might have been so, for I have never wanted to find out. I remembered my teacher in Japanese language school preaching, "When Japan calls, you must know that it is Japanese blood that flows in your veins." And in another spasm of fury I muttered, "Fool! Blind and bigoted fool, see what the likes of you have brought us!"

And so I rode on, filled with grief and shame and anger, not knowing how they would receive me at the aid station, uncertain even if they would let me stay in school. All my dreams seemed to be spiraling out of reach, like the great, greasy billows of smoke from the oil fires at Pearl Harbor, and by the time I reached my destination, I carried the full and bitter burden shared by every one of the 158,000 Japanese-Americans in Hawaii: not only had our country been wantonly attacked, but our loyalty was certain to be called into question, for it took no great effort of imagination to see the hatred of many Americans for the enemy turned on us, who looked so much like him. And no matter how hard we worked to defeat him, there would always be those who would look at us and think—and some would say it aloud—"Dirty Jap."

It was past 8:30—the war was little more than half an hour old—when I reported in at the aid station, two class-rooms in the Lunalilo Elementary School. I had gained the first six years of my education in this building and before the day was out it would be half-destroyed by our own anti-aircraft shells which had failed to explode in the air. Even now confusion was in command, shouting people pushing by each other as they rushed for litters and medical supplies.

Somewhere a radio voice droned on, now and then peaking
with shrill excitement, and it was in one such outburst that I
learned how the *Arizona* had exploded in the harbor. Many
other vessels were severely hit.

And then, at 9 A.M., the Japanese came back. The second
wave of bombers swooped around from the west and the
anti-aircraft guns began thundering again. Mostly the planes
hammered at military installations—Pearl, Hickam, Wheeler
Field—and it was our own ack-ack that did the deadly
damage in the civilian sectors. Shells, apparently fired without timed fuses, and finding no target in the sky, exploded on
impact with the ground. Many came crashing into a three-
by-five-block area of crowded McCully, the first only moments after the Japanese planes reappeared. It hit just three
blocks from the aid station and the explosion rattled the
windows. I grabbed a litter and rounded up a couple of
fellows I knew.

"Where're we going?" one yelled at me.

"Where the trouble is! Follow me!"

In a small house on the corner of Hauoli and Algaroba
Streets we found our first casualties. The shell had sliced
through the house. It had blown the front out and the tokens
of a lifetime—dishes, clothing, a child's bed—were strewn
pathetically into the street.

I was propelled by sheerest instinct. Some small corner of
my mind worried about how I'd react to what lay in that
carnage—there would be no textbook cuts and bruises, and
the blood would be real blood—and then I plunged in,
stumbling over the debris, kicking up clouds of dust and
calling, frantically calling, to anyone who might be alive in
there. There was no answer. The survivors had already fled
and the one who remained would never speak again. I found

her half-buried in the rubble, one of America's first civilian dead of the Second World War. One woman, all but decapitated by a piece of shrapnel, died within moments. Another, who had fallen dead at the congested corner of King and McCully, still clutched the stumps where her legs had been. And all at once it was as though I had stepped out of my skin; I moved like an automaton, hardly conscious of what I was doing and totally oblivious of myself. I felt nothing. I did what I had been taught to do and it was only later, when those first awful hours had become part of our history, that I sickened and shuddered as the ghastly images of war flashed again and again in my mind's eye, as they do to this day.

By the time we had removed the dead to a temporary morgue set up in Lunalilo School, more shells had fallen. It was now, by one of those bitter ironies, that our aid station was hit by our own shells, and we lost precious minutes evacuating what was left of our supplies. Nearby, a building caught fire and as the survivors came stumbling out, we patched their wounds as best we could and commandeered whatever transportation that passed to get them to the hospital. For those still trapped inside there was nothing in the world anyone could do. The flames drove us back to the far side of the street, and by the time the firemen brought them under control, there was nothing left alive in that burned-out hulk. Then, carrying corrugated boxes, it became our melancholy duty to pick our way through the smouldering beams and hot ashes and collect the charred, barely-recognizable remains of those who had perished. We tried to get one body in each box, but limbs came away as we touched them and it was hard to tell an arm from a leg, and so we couldn't always be sure of who, or what, was in any given box.

There are moments I can never forget. An empty-eyed old lady wandered screaming through the wreckage of a house on King street. A boy of twelve or so, perhaps her grandson, tried to lead her from danger, for she could scarcely keep her footing in the ruins. But the old woman would not be budged. "Where is my home?" she would cry out hysterically in Japanese, or "Where are my things?"

I climbed up to where she tottered on a mountain of wreckage and took hold of her shoulders. "Go with the boy," I said to her.

But it was as though I wasn't there. She looked right through me and wailed, "What have they done to my home?" And without thinking about it, for if I had thought about it I could never have done it, I slapped her twice across the face, sharply. Later, I would be awed by my audacity—my whole life had been a lesson in reverence for my elders—but at that instant I remembered only what I had been taught to do in cases of uncontrollable hysteria. And it worked.

"Go with the boy," I said again, and the light of reason returned to her eyes, and she went.

A man burst into the improvised morgue, snatching at the arms of strangers and begging to know if they had seen his wife and baby. Finally someone recognized him and, gently as such a thing can be said, told him that they were dead. "Where are they?" he cried out, his face torn with anguish. "Let me see them!"

And so he was led to one of the corrugated boxes and he saw them. The woman lay nude, staring back at him sightlessly. One arm ended in a bloody wrist and the hand had been tossed haphazardly into the lower corner of the box. The other arm, rigid in death, clutched the body of a child without legs.

"Yes," the man said softly after a time, "that is my family." And they led him away.

We worked on into the night, and were working still when the new day broke. There was so much to be done—broken bodies to be mended, temporary shelter to be found for bombed-out families, precautions against disease, food for the hungry and comfort for the bereaved—that even our brief respites for a sandwich or a cup of coffee were tinged with feelings of guilt. We worked on into the following night and through the day after that, snatching some broken moments of sleep wherever we happened to be when we could move no further, and soon there was no dividing line between day and night at all. Now and then my mother or father would appear with a change of clothes, or some food, and they would look at me, worried: "Are you all right? Will you come home soon?"

"Yes," I'd tell them. "I'm fine. I'll be home as soon as I can."

I had been listed as a part-time volunteer. But right after the bombing, the aid station was absorbed into the civil defense command and most of us were put on a full-time basis. I was designated a medical aide, given the night shift, 6 P.M. to 6 A.M., so I could go to school in the daytime, and put on salary of $125 a month.

It was a wildly incongruous life. In the morning I was a senior at McKinley High, just as before, trying to be concerned with congruent triangles and passive verbs and the French Revolution. In the afternoon, I fell exhausted into my bed and slept like a dead man until 5:30, when my mother would shake me awake and, as I dashed for the door, hand me a sandwich to munch on while I bicycled to the aid station. And all through the night I tried to cope with the real problems of innocent people caught up in a tragedy of terrifying proportions. And always, day and night, I expected at any moment to hear the wailing air raid sirens signaling the return of those Japanese planes.

I was amazed at myself. Overnight I had been thrust into a position of leadership: in charge of a litter squad, training new volunteers at the aid station and directing the high school first aid program. Like everyone else in the military or civil defense command, I wore a steel helmet, carried a gas mask and a special identity card that permitted me on the streets after curfew. Me, Dan Inouye! Only a few weeks before, my biggest worries had been marks and dates and whether I'd get that neat saxophone riff in *Little Brown Jug* just right. And now I was earning $125 a month, more money than I'd ever seen in my life. It meant less than nothing to me. All I could really focus on was that I was at war.

On the afternoon of December 7, a Pathé News camera crew had been around the neighborhood shooting pictures of everything in sight. And a month afterward, on my first day off since the beginning of the war, I went to a movie— and there I was, running over the ruined streets with my litter team, grim-jawed, calm, purposeful. Again I was astounded. That was me? Dan Inouye? But then war does astounding things.

Remembering those traumatic days, the great turning point of my life, I can see how my need to become totally involved in the war effort sprang from that invidious sense of guilt, the invisible cross lashed to the back of every *nisei* at the instant when the first plane bearing that rising sun appeared in the sky over Pearl Harbor. In actual fact, of course, we had nothing to feel guilty about, and all rational men understood this. And still I knew of no American of Japanese descent who didn't carry this special burden, and who didn't work doubly hard because of it.

The provocations were sometimes severe. We began to hear disturbing stories of what was happening to the Japanese on the mainland. Along the West Coast, thousands of families were summarily uprooted, taken from their homes, often on 12 hours notice, and moved to "relocation" camps on the incredible grounds that this whole class of Americans, rich and poor, alien and citizen, men, women and children, was a security risk. Herded onto trucks and trains, they were taken inland, to places like the Santa Anita racetrack where they lived in stables within barbed wire compounds, and in hastily-erected barracks that afforded no privacy, nothing resembling a normal family life. And for what? Because they had had the bad luck to be born in Japan, or of Japanese parents.

I think that most Americans now agree that this was a dreary chapter in our history. But I believe it to be equally important that they understand that greed, as much as war hysteria, made possible this momentary triumph of the vigilante mentality. In every city and town where Japanese-Americans settled, there were those who envied their neat little farms, those who coveted their homes and gardens and jobs. And when their hour came, these human vultures struck with cunning and cruelty, offering $200 for land that was worth $2,000, $5 for a nearly-new refrigerator. And stunned by this upheaval in their lives, unable to make a better arrangement in the few hours given them to settle their affairs, the *nisei* were forced to surrender the fruits of a lifetime's labor, for a pittance.

Had it not been for a few courageous and outspoken men,

the same bitter situation might have prevailed in Hawaii. There was, as a matter of fact, some talk about evacuating all of the Japanese population from the Islands, whipped up by politicians desperate enough to capitalize on this human tragedy, and by a few unscrupulous businessmen rapacious enough to seek personal profit in it. But these ghouls were in a minority. Most Hawaiians stood by their Japanese neighbors and some of them spoke out for them in no uncertain terms. John A. Burns, our present governor, was then a police captain in Honolulu and in the earliest days of the war, when the anti-Japanese feeling was at its most feverish, he showed his backbone by announcing to the press, "I have complete confidence in Hawaii's Japanese-Americans."

His confidence was not misplaced. Despite widely-published concern that the *nisei* were a sort of built-in fifth column in Hawaii, not a single act of sabotage or subversion was ever charged to an American of Japanese ancestry from the day the war began until the day it ended. The *nisei* bought more war bonds than any other group in the Islands. And when the Army finally permitted them to volunteer for the service, more than 10,000 men showed up at their draft boards, approximately 80 percent of all qualified males of military age.

And still we could not escape humiliation, discrimination, even internment. Immediately after Pearl Harbor, martial law was declared in the Islands and some 1,500 Japanese, mostly aliens, were rounded up and confined in special compounds. Thanks to friends, Caucasian as well as Asiatic, who vouched for their loyalty, all but 277 of these were released by the war's end. But there were bitter scars.

And even those of us whose personal liberty was never threatened felt the sting of suspicion. We felt it in the streets

where white men would sneer at us as they passed. We felt it
in school when we heard our friends called Jap-lovers. We
felt it in our homes when military police and F.B.I. men
came looking for shortwave sets, letters in code and only the
good Lord knows what else. Everywhere there were signs
that admonished us to "Be American! Speak American!"

It was especially hard on the old folks, most of whom
could manage only the barest smattering of pidgin English.
But they tried. Samurai swords were turned in and pictures
of the Emperor vanished from the walls of Japanese homes.
Old ladies who had never worn anything but slippers and
kimonos ventured downtown to buy shoes and dresses for
the first time in their lives. And though Selective Service had
declared the *nisei* unfit for military service, they could not
keep them from volunteering for every other kind of war
work open to them.

It was all part of a desperate attempt to convince America
that the Japanese attack had not been intended for only 60
percent of Hawaii's people. We had *all* been attacked, and
the dead on December 7 were not only the brave soldiers
and sailors at Pearl Harbor and Hickam Field, but the
unarmed civilians in McCully, too. Unhappily, I don't think
we ever wholly succeeded. There were always those to
whom the only good Jap was a dead Jap, and never mind
whether he happened to be an American citizen.

Not long after the war began, the military government
ordered all radios with shortwave bands to be reported. As it
happened, my father had just bought such a set, and it was a
real beauty, picking up Tokyo and the Philippines just
perfectly. Of course we were all enormously proud of it, we
had so few possessions and had waited a long time to
accumulate enough money to pay for so expensive a luxury,

and we promptly complied with the order to report it. One day about a week later, three men came to the door, one of them flashing a card under my nose that said something about naval intelligence. "Does Hyotaro Inouye live here?" he said.

"Yes," I answered, and my father, hearing, came to the door.

"Where is your radio?"

"It is in here," Father said. "Please come in."

"No, no. Bring it outside."

I helped my father carry it out. He seemed puzzled but not concerned as we set the radio down on a little table that stood against the side of the house. Without another word, the man who had spoken to us upstairs dug a screwdriver in behind the backing and ripped it off. The other two watched impassively. I looked at my father. His eyes had narrowed, but he said nothing. And then I understood why they had had us bring the radio outside. The man with the screwdriver was using it to snap the wiring inside the set. Then he reached in and expertly removed one tube after another, smashing each one on the ground without ever changing his expression.

I was heartsick at this needless cruelty—he could have deadened the short wave band by disconnecting a single wire—and this time when I looked at my father I felt fingers of fear at my stomach; his face had turned black as a thundercloud and I knew he would not suffer this indignity in silence.

"Here," he said into the bleak silence between the crashing tubes, "let me help you." Whereupon he reached down to the pile of wood we used to heat the stove and hefted his ax.

Instantly all three of them reached for the bulges under their jackets and, in awe and terror, I whispered, "Don't, Papa." For like them, I was sure he meant to fight.

But not my father. He smiled sadly and said, "Put your guns away, gentlemen. I told you I only want to help." And he moved in front of them and with three great swinging blows, smashed the nearly new radio set into splinters of wood and glass. "There," he said, breathing hard with his effort, "that should do it. Now you'll never have to worry about it, eh? My son will clean up the mess."

He put the ax down and walked back up the steps into the house. The men just watched him. What did they feel? I wondered; they were human beings, and surely they had to feel something—and I watched him, too, and my throat grew tight and my eyes blurred in sadness for my poor father.

"He gave blood twice," I said to them, not knowing why I was speaking. "He works so hard and he's never been in any trouble and he'd do anything . . . anything. . . ." I lost hold of what I was trying to tell them and anyhow my throat grew too tight for me to talk. So I just stopped and we looked at each other for a moment and then they got into a car and drove away. And I began to clean up the mess.

From the very beginning, the younger Japanese in the Islands suffered under a special onus, a deep sense of personal disgrace. They were far removed from the ways of the old country. All their lives they had thought of themselves as Americans. And now, in this time of crisis and peril for America, they were cast from its trust and seemingly lumped with the enemy by official policy. Not only had the War Department turned them down for active service, but those already in the army were transferred to labor battalions. *Nisei* in National Guard units were summarily discharged, and those in the ROTC and Territorial Guard were stripped of their weapons.

But despite every derogation and disparagement, Japanese-Americans fought for a place in the war effort, no matter how small or menial. Older men, including my father, organized their own labor squads and volunteered for garbage details and ditch-digging. University students strung barbed wire and guarded beaches and important intersections, armed only with fury and a massive determination to make some useful contribution. And always, day after discouraging day, they struggled to persuade the government to reverse its anti-*nisei* ruling, writing letters, collecting signatures for petitions and imploring Caucasians of good will to attest to their loyalty.

For me, the nightmare quality of life went on. By night I worked at the aid station, and by day I went to school, where suddenly everything turned inconsequential and my classmates seemed to be children engaged in some insignificant charade, while just outside McKinley High the world we all knew was coming to a violent end. In a way, many of them *were* children, and proved it at mid-year during the senior class elections.

I was still in the top class and, as before, my fellow students were impeccably starched and groomed. Furthermore, there were among their number virtually every class officer, club president and school newspaper reporter. And there in their midst was I, Dan Inouye, considered by them, I am positive, the class rebel and the kid least likely to succeed. Which was all right with me—I was interested in learning what I could and going on to college to study medicine, having owned up to myself that I'd probably never be allowed into the army. The white-shirt boys had their lives and all I asked was that they let me have mine. But they wouldn't.

On the day we held homeroom elections, I was astonished to hear one of them nominate me for permanent chairman. Instantly another moved that nominations be closed and the next thing I knew I was standing up front with a gavel in my hand, not sure whether to laugh or cry. Let me be honest: for one stirring moment, I believed what my heart wanted to believe, that they really *wanted* me, that they had looked beyond my poor clothes and recognized some quality of leadership, and I was greatly moved. But as I said, this little act of self-deception lasted only a moment. I had only to look out over that class, at the girls barely able to suppress their laughter, at my nominator and his cohorts smirking back at me in anticipation of the imminent parliamentary disaster, and I knew that the whole thing had been planned as a monstrous joke. A class full of leaders and skilled debators had chosen Dan Inouye, that juvenile delinquent from some Japanese slum, to be their chairman, and now they had only to sit back and wait for him to make a fool of himself. Wasn't that just too funny for words?

Of course I wanted to quit on the spot. Actually, I wanted to throw first the gavel and then myself at them and at least mess up a few immaculate white shirts and ties tied just so before they overwhelmed me. I don't know why I didn't. Some part of me, I suppose, resisted the joke and wanted the honor, and some part of me so desperately wanted to show them that I could do it that I was willing to risk the most abject humiliation in the effort.

Somehow I stumbled through that first organizational

meeting and, at someone's sneering suggestion, called another for the following week to discuss a Valentine's Day party. The others had gone and I was collecting my books, still dazed by a kind of angry shame, when I realized my teacher Mr. Kirkpatrick, an exchange teacher from Evanston, Illinois, was standing behind me. "I'm sorry, Dan," he was saying. "I guess this is one time the democratic process was used for rotten purposes."

I shrugged, uncertain what to say. I suspected he thought I was a goofball, too.

"I'm glad you stuck it out, though. With a little experience under your belt, I think you'll make a fine chairman. Here, maybe this will help."

And he handed me a copy of *Robert's Rules of Order*, the first time I had ever heard of such a book. By the time of the meeting the following week, I could quote whole sections of it verbatim. That's how important it was to me.

I opened the meeting by announcing that in light of the national emergency, I thought we ought to forget about the Valentine's Day party and concentrate our efforts on something more constructive, perhaps a senior class Red Cross drive. I could see that some of the kids were considering this quite seriously. But the wise guys were not about to let me get off so easily.

"Will you put that in the form of a motion?" one of them said.

But I spotted the trap. "No, I will not," I answered evenly. "And I certainly am surprised that someone as active in school affairs as you are doesn't know that according to *Robert's Rules* the chairman is not permitted to introduce a motion. But I will entertain one from anyone who agrees that a Red Cross drive is a worthy project for us."

My heart sang with every jaw that dropped in amazement. But they were far from finished with me. Someone did make the Red Cross notion and then the big guns opened up. We had always had a Valentine's Day party, said one. Why should we suddenly drop it now? echoed another. And so on. All of which was perfectly all right with me. I had some big guns to bring up, too. Now I felt confident up there, sure of myself, and I was more than ready to match wits with the white-shirts.

"Why should we drop the party now?" I repeated, and answered the question: "Because there's a war on—or hadn't you heard?"

The one who had nominated me stood up, angry now because he could sense that he was losing and this was certainly an outcome he could never have anticipated. "We know there's a war, Dan. *We* were the ones who were attacked." He came down especially hard on the *we,* then said, "I move that we set February 13 as the date for the Valentine's party."

I smiled. I really had him now. "I'm sorry, my friend," I said, relishing my tone of father talking to a rambunctious child. "You are out of order. There is already a motion on the floor. Really, your grasp of parliamentary rules is pathetic. Now, if there is no further discussion, I suggest we vote on the motion to launch a senior class Red Cross drive."

The motion passed handily and I could have jumped with glee. I had beaten them at their own game!

In the spring of the year, Mr. Kirkpatrick invited all who were interested to submit entries for *Scholastic* magazine's essay contest and though I had never even written anything for the school paper, I decided I would have a try at it. I had something to say. I wanted to tell how it felt to be a *nisei* on

Oahu on the morning of December 7, how it was to be
picking up the torn and burned bodies of men and women
born of Japanese parents and killed in a brutal assault by
Japanese airmen. I put all of my shock and anger, all of my
agonized questions, into that essay, and I suppose that some
of those intensely-held feelings were conveyed to the reader.
It surely was no Day-at-the-Beach composition. Anyway, my
little story took the Territorial Board's first prize and when it
was sent on to the national contest, it won an honorable
mention and was printed in a summer issue of *Scholastic*.

When the time came for our annual assembly, at which
the year's prizes were to be handed out to the winning
students, there I stood just offstage, waiting my turn, wearing, as always, my denim pants and a sport shirt. As a matter
of fact, I had intended to come barefooted, but at the last
minute decided I would make at least that one concession to
the proprieties. Nevertheless no one would have had a speck
of trouble spotting Dan Inouye in that assemblage of
pressed jackets and rigidly-tied neckties, and when I was
called out to receive my award a great roar of approval went
up from my McCully and Moiliili buddies, and I grinned out
at them, the local boy who made good. But I couldn't escape
a small look of pain on the face of Dr. Miles Cary, the
principal of McKinley High, who was making the presen-
tations.

He found me in the hall right after the ceremonies. "Do
you have a minute, Dan?"

"Yes, sir."

"You own a suit, don't you?"

"Yes, sir."

"Why didn't you wear it?"

I shrugged. "This is what I wear every day."

"But this isn't every day, Dan." He put his arm on my shoulder and walked me off, away from the noisy crowds of students gathering outside the auditorium, and he talked quietly as we went. "I've heard a lot about you from your teachers, most of it good. And I can certainly understand how you'd feel angry, maybe even a little vindictive, toward some of the kids who've put you through the wringer here. But don't carry it too far, Dan. In a few years, by the time this war is over, your people will have as much opportunity as any white man in these islands, in the army, in business, in politics. It's bound to happen, it's already been too long happening. And all I want to tell you is that I'd like it if you were ready for those opportunities because you're a fine boy. Don't spoil things for yourself by being a hardhead. Do you understand?"

"Yes, sir," I said softly. "And thank you."

But the truth is that I was only beginning to understand, for he had said so much that was important and meaningful to me that it would take a long time to absorb it all. But I would never forget that little talk, nor would I forget Dr. Cary.

But since this is a true account of my life, I have to confess that I was incapable of blossoming into a perfect gentleman overnight. Now that I had won one of the Territory's highest prizes, the National Honor Society of Mc-Kinley High School invited me to become a member. I played hard-to-get for a while. It wasn't easy to just forget that sense of shame they'd saddled me with when I'd tried to get in before, but then, I recalled the recent words of Dr. Cary. A few days later I was initiated into the membership of this honor society.

The following week I received a brief note from Mrs.

King. It said: "Dear Dan: We finally made it. Congratulations."

I passed my college entrance exams and in September 1942, just turned eighteen, I enrolled for a premedical course at the University of Hawaii. For those of us in that wartime class, study as we might, a substantial portion of our thoughts and hopes were directed outside, fixed on that world in conflict, concentrating our fiercest aspirations on the chance that somehow they would allow us into the army. I was still doing my job at the aid station, but with the emergency in Hawaii past and the grim reports of Japanese victories at Bataan and Corregidor, working at the aid station didn't seem like much of a vital contribution any more.

The War Department had given us some small hope that their harsh preconceptions about Japanese-Americans might be changing. A few months earlier, *nisei* Guardsmen and early draftees had been organized into the 100th Infantry Battalion, a combat unit not assigned to any regular outfit. Then, little more than a year after the attack on Pearl Harbor, we got the news that did most to unshackle us from stigma and help us really believe that we would be allowed to fight for our country: the War Department announced that it would accept 4,000 *nisei* volunteers to form a full-fledged combat team for front-line service without restriction, without constraints. The outfit was to be activated on February 1 and would consist of the 442nd Infantry Regiment, the 522nd Field Artillery Battalion and 232nd Combat Engineer Company.

President Franklin D. Roosevelt, who personally passed on the plan, had this to say about it: "The proposal of the War Department to organize a combat team of loyal American citizens of Japanese descent has my full approval. No loyal citizen of the United States should be denied the democratic right to exercise the responsibilities of his citizenship, regardless of his ancestry. Americanism is a matter of the mind and heart; Americanism is not, and never was, a matter of race or ancestry."

It is hard to express our emotions at this expression of faith by the President. It was as though someone had let us out of some dark place and into the sunlight again. And what chaos in the University auditorium that January morning when Colonel Clarke, head of the ROTC, called us together and announced that the draft boards were now ready to receive our applications for enlistment! It was as though he'd revealed that gold had just been discovered at the foot of Diamond Head. He later told me that he had a little pep talk all prepared for us, how we now had a chance to do our duty as patriotic Americans, but it was about as necessary as telling those navy gunners on December 7 to open fire. As soon as he said that we were now eligible to volunteer, that room exploded into a fury of yells and motion. We went bursting out of there and ran—ran!—the three miles to the draft board, stringing back over the streets and sidewalks, jostling for position, like a bunch of marathoners gone berserk. And the scene was repeated all over Oahu and the other islands. Nearly 1,000 *niseis* volunteered that first day alone, and maybe because I was in better shape than most of them and ran harder, I was among the first 75.

Everything changed that day and, because there are no fairy tale endings in real life, not all the changes were for the best. Dozens of boys I knew from the premed courses crowded into the draft board, some of them with only the rest of that last semester to go before graduation. And the long years of war took their toll on every one of us. Some hadn't the heart to go back to school when peace finally came, and some, with families to support, hadn't the money. Many never came home at all and among those who did there were those so severely wounded that a career in medicine was out of the question. And so it was that of all those students who had entered the University with such high hopes, and with the hopes and prayers of their parents, not a single one ever became a doctor.

The army's original plan called for a *nisei* outfit of 1,500 from the Islands and 2,500 from the mainland. But the crush of volunteers in Hawaii persuaded them to reverse the proportions. We were given three weeks to wind up our affairs—which most of us would have been happy to do in three days—and there were sentimental and sometimes tearful farewell parties from Koko Head to Kahuku. I suppose mine was fairly typical: the parade of aunts and uncles and cousins, the last whispered words—"Be a good boy; be careful; make us proud!"—and the crumpled $5 or $10 bill pressed into my hand.

And then my bag was packed and my ukelele slung over my shoulder and with my mother and father standing nearby, sad and already a little withdrawn, I elbowed my way into that great swarm of about-to-be GIs on the grounds of the old Washington Intermediate School, just outside the draft board. Girls were draping leis around our necks and the long line of trucks stood waiting to carry us off and in each little family group you could see the mood alternating between piercing sharp anticipation and a kind of melancholy as the men abruptly realized what their mothers and fathers and sweethearts already knew: that this was good-bye and what lay ahead was no boy scout outing.

They started to call out the names and a tight little hush took hold of us. We edged closer to hear—"Aimoto, Aka-hoshi, Arakaki"—and each man who was called took time for a last kiss, then ran for a truck. As soon as one was loaded, it rumbled off in a hail of farewells and a wild flutter of handkerchiefs.

"Fukuchi, Gora, Hamano." The names droned on and the line of trucks grew shorter and I was suddenly conscious that my mother was trying very hard not to cry. "Higa, Ikegami, Ito, Kaneko."

They had gone past my name!

". . . Nagata, Odo."

They were reading the list in alphabetical order and they had skipped mine!

My father knew this almost as soon as I did and he looked at me uncomfortably, but I was unable to meet his gaze. What had happened? It was true that I hadn't been formally accepted—none of us had—but I had passed my physical and we were given to understand that that was the final hurdle.

". . . Sagata, Sakuma."

There had to be some mistake! That was the only explanation my mind was capable of accepting, and I said to my father, "There must be a mistake. I have to go ask them." And I pushed off through the crowd, still carrying my bag, and the ukelele bounced on my shoulder and my ears rang with all those names they were calling—and mine wasn't one of them. Wouldn't they ever finish? Was there nobody to listen to me?

At last I found a captain, a *haole*, who must have read the panic in my eyes. "They didn't call me," I burst out. "They went right past my name."

"I'm sorry, son," he said gently. "If they didn't call you, you're not accepted."

"But why? What did I do? I . . . I passed the physical. They told me . . ."

"I don't know why. I only know about those men on the trucks."

I turned away, trying to hide the tears that stormed to my eyes, trying not to look as the last of the trucks filled up, or to hear as some sergeant bellowed out, "That's it! All aboard!"

God bless them, my parents asked me no questions. I just shook my head quickly and they understood. But as we walked slowly away, a fellow I knew on that last truck called out, "Tough luck, Dan! Sorry!" And I never felt so ashamed in my life.

When we got home, I just dropped my bag on the floor and went to sit by myself at the back window. It was my mother who opened it and began carefully to put my things away again, no one speaking. I kept thinking: *it's a mistake; it has to be a mistake!* In the morning I would go to the draft board and find out. I'd tell them they'd goofed up somewhere. There would be another shipment going out in a couple of weeks and I'd be among them!

"What is this, Daniel?"

My mother used my Christian name only when there was trouble ahead. Otherwise she called me Ken. Now she was standing in front of me and holding out her hand and in her hand was a pair of dice. I swallowed and stuttered, struggling to shift my thoughts from one disaster to this newest catastrophe. "That?" I finally managed with a hopeless attempt at confidence. "That's—uh—that's a pair of dice, Mom."

"Yes, I can see that," she said icily, her strict Methodist hackles stiff. "What I want to know is what a pair of dice is doing in your suitcase."

And terribly conscious of defeat pressing in on me from every side, I told her the only lie that I ever have. "A friend asked me to get them. He didn't have time. I was supposed to give them to him today, but—uh—in the excitement . . ."

"I see," she said—and did, perfectly. She put the dice into my hand and said no more about them, but she knew beyond a shadow of a doubt that if her Dan's sheltered Methodist upbringing had successfully diverted him from cigarettes and whiskey and wild women, he had, indeed, acquired one small vice.

The fact is that it was the husband of one of my mother's own oldest and dearest friends who, in what he truly conceived to be my own best interests, had introduced me to the manly art of crap-shooting, and when my mother reads this book, she will be learning it for the first time. I hope she is not too shocked and will forgive that gruff old warm-hearted sailor.

He was a *haole* and when he married Mother's best girl friend, both became like members of the Inouye family. When they'd heard that I was about to go into the army, naturally they came to visit and the husband, a five-hitch navy man, drew me to one side and announced that he was going to instruct me about a few aspects of the military life that no one, least of all my parents, were apt to tell me. "I know you're a good kid," he said in that clipped navy way he had of talking. "I'm not worried about you getting in trouble. But gambling—now there's a lot of gambling in the service; it's hard to stay away from—and you ought to know enough not to get rooked. Right?"

I nodded dumbly, overwhelmed by his logic and awed to be so casually invited into the robust world of the fighting man. Whereupon he hauled a pair of dice out of his pocket —the same ones Mother was to confront me with in my most desolate hour—and rattled off the basic precepts of the game, a bewildering series of odds and the final stern admonition: "Never bet against a hot shooter, even if he's your worst enemy."

Frankly I didn't glean too much in that brief session. For one thing, I was scared to death one of my parents would discover our nefarious doings and I couldn't concentrate too well, and for another the argot of the crap-shooter was as alien to me as Hindustani. I mean, you take the average Methodist choir boy and I think you'll find the chances are not too good that he'll understand what you're talking about if you pepper your conversation with "boxcars" and "snake eyes" and "little Joes." What I did get from my sailor friend was the bug: if he thought it was important for me to know about craps, I was going to know about craps. And so in the next week or so, I spent several hours in the library with a copy of Hoyle, and before long I had learned the language, memorized the odds and, most important, come to understand what my mentor was trying to say when he cautioned me against betting emotionally. For the game of craps is essentially an invocation of the laws of probability. The hotheaded player will ignore them or, worse, fight them— and will lose. But the player with respect for the mathematical inevitability of averages, if he plays long enough, must win. And so, armed with this new knowledge and my gift from our old family friend, I felt manly, and confident that I could pick up a dollar or two when the dice came out and blankets were spread on the barracks floor.

Of the twin calamities that descended on me soon after, my rejection and getting caught red-handed, the former was infinitely more depressing. Aware of my misery as only a parent can be, my mother never again mentioned the dice and, whatever her private relief that her son was not about to be sent off to battle, she commiserated with me and always pretended disappointment when I returned from the draft board without an iota of fresh hope.

I haunted the draft board. Starting the very day following the departure of that first contingent, I was there morning and afternoon, day and night. And I learned absolutely nothing. "No," they would tell me, "we have no new information. We don't know why you were turned down." The most outlandish notions flashed through my head: did they think I was a security risk? was there some dark family secret that my father had never told me? was the F.B.I., even now, closing in on us?

Of course I had to return all the gifts to my relatives. That was a cheerful day! Riding the trolley car all over town, handing over the money with some mumbled apology about "not leaving just yet" while trying to avoid looking into anyone's eyes. Naturally I was absolutely useless as far as school was concerned, nor was I much better at the aid station. My poor brain had room for only one galling thought: they didn't want me; all my buddies had made it, but I was still a sad sack civilian. Dr. Hamre, my zoology professor, tried to cheer me up: "God means for you to do other things, Dan. You're going to make a fine doctor."

"Sure, sure," I answered, and died a little more.

Finally I came to grips with myself. Either I was going into the army or I wasn't! And if I wasn't, I had to quit moping and get down to some serious work. All of which meant that I needed an absolutely straight answer from the draft board, I just had to have it! And so I marched in one Tuesday afternoon, blood in my eye, and laid the whole thing out for them. "I'm not leaving here," I said, "until I find out why I was rejected and whether I have any chance at all of getting in."

There were whispered conferences, much shuffling of papers and a 20-minute search through the files. I'm not knocking them, really—I know how badgered and over-worked all those people were in those first critical months of the war—but try to imagine my feelings as I waited there while the bureaucratic process groped its way to a decision on my fate. At last I was summoned to an inner office where a distinguished gentleman sat peering into a file that was plainly marked, "Inouye, Daniel Ken."

"Yes," he said as I stood there icy-fingered and barely breathing, "well we've located your records and there seems to be no mystery about the decision. You're putting in 72 hours a week at the aid station, which we consider an essential defense contribution, and you're enrolled in a pre-med course at the University, and Lord knows we'll be needing doctors. Does that clear it up for you, Inouye?" He looked up at me and smiled, certain, no doubt, that he'd settled that little problem for all time.

"Yes, it's clear, sir," I answered quietly, amazed at the brash thing I was about to do. "Except that I'd appreciate it if you gave me about an hour. Then if you call the aid station and the University, they will tell you in both places that I've given my notice to quit by the end of the week."

"Now see here, Inouye . . ."

"Yes, sir," I interrupted, and lost some of my calm. "I'll be honest: I don't know if it's right or wrong, whether I'd be doing more good here or in the service. I just know that if there is any way in which I can humanly get into the army, I'm going to do it."

And I left. In 45 minutes, I'd told my aid station leader and the Dean of Students that Friday would be my last day. Then I said a silent prayer and settled down to wait for the call. It came on Thursday. They sent for me during a zoology class and I went to the office and picked up the telephone with a shaking hand.

"Daniel Ken Inouye?"

"Yes," I whispered.

Some woman from my draft board announced her name. Then she said, "You're to report to the Nuuanu YMCA at 8 A.M. Saturday morning for transportation to Schofield Barracks. Your induction orders are being cut now."

"Yes," I whispered again, then sounded off loud and clear: "Yes, *ma'am!*"

I suppose I went back to class and got my things. I don't remember that part. From then on things just registered in snatches. I was standing in the zoology lab handing out my dissecting instruments to my classmates. They were no $2 bookstore set, either, but true surgical instruments which had cost me nearly a month's pay. Then I was saying goodby to Dr. Hamre, shaking his hand, feeling my grin, saying something like, "I finally made it."

He didn't return my grin. He said, "I was hoping you'd stay, Dan."

"I can't. But I'll be back. I will! And I'll pick up right where I left off."

Then my mother was looking up from her work in the kitchen and saying, "What are you doing home so early?"

"I'm in the army, Mom! I have to report Saturday morning." Then I grabbed her around the waist and squeezed her as hard as I could. "I'm in the army, Mom!"

"God keep you," she murmured, making no attempt to get free, and reaching up to my cheek with hers. "I'm happy if you are, my son. I ask you only to be a good boy. Bring honor to our name."

"I will, Mom. I will! I'll come home a corporal!"

"Just come home safely."

She seemed to be looking deep into the future. "You will go off now," she said carefully. "You will be a man. I want to tell you something, of my feelings." We sat opposite each other at the little kitchen table, and she kept her eyes on me as she spoke:

"You will be good. You will do the right things. Still, I know that the old ways, the ways of your father and me, will not be so important to you. When you marry . . ."

"But Mama . . ."

"Please listen! When you marry, it would make me most happy if you married from among our own people, a nice Japanese girl. Still, I know, I understand, that this may not come to pass, that it is not so important to the younger people. Well, then, I will tell you again of how kind and good the Hawaiian people were to me when I was young and needful, and I will say to you that if you do not find it in your heart to marry a girl from a good Japanese family, then I will not be unhappy if your choice is a Hawaiian girl. I have wanted to say this to you for a long time, and now that you are going into the world I must wait no longer. Do you understand?"

"Yes, Mama, I understand." And I went around the table and hugged her very hard.

Then there was a flurry of packing, the goodbyes, all hasty now, and my father and I were riding the bus to Nuuanu. Saturday was a regular working day for him, but he had said, "I think they will understand if I do not come in this morning," and picked up my suitcase. He was very somber. I tried to think of something to say, some way to tell him that he was important to me, and dear. But nothing came out.

"I will not talk to you of women and drinking," he said unexpectedly, "for you are nearly full-grown and have always been good."

"I always tried, Papa."

"But far from home, in strange places and among strange people, men's weaknesses sometimes get the best of them. Only remember not to get into waters too deep for you to walk out of." He was quiet for a time, then said, "You know what *on* means in Japanese?"

"Yes." *On* is at the very heart of Japanese culture. *On* requires that when one man is aided by another he incurs a debt that is never canceled, one that must be repaid at every opportunity without stint or reservation.

"The Inouyes have great *on* for America," my father said. "It has been good to us. And now—I would never have chosen it to be this way—it is you who must try to return the goodness of this country. You are my first son and you are very precious to your mother and to me, but you must do what must be done. If it is necessary, you must be ready to . . . to . . ."

Unable to give voice to the dread words, his voice trailed off. "I know, Papa. I understand."

"Do not bring dishonor on our name," he whispered urgently.

And those same infinitely meaningful words must have

been spoken thousands of times all over the Islands in those
climactic last weeks when the men of the 442nd were coming together.

And now I was clambering up into the back of a GI truck,
struggling to hold my balance as it rumbled off and I stood
waving to the diminishing image of my father. "Goodbye!" I
called long after he was out of earshot, a forlorn but resolute
figure, standing there alone as if he never meant to leave.
"Goodbye, Papa."

We were to sail four days later, the 2,686 Hawaiian
Japanese of the 442nd Regimental Combat Team. I had
been No. 2,685.

Chapter IV

"The First Battle Will Be Bloody"

❀ Everything goes by numbers in the army. By the time
my number came up, the quartermaster seemed to be out of
everything that was even remotely the right size. I had been
issued winter-weight O.D. shirts and khaki pants, a glaring
mismatch whose extremities were two inches too long and
had to be folded back before I could regain the use of my
hands and feet. My mother had managed to sew these up,
but my overseas cap, a trim 6⅝ths, perched precariously
on my size 7⅜ths head. Somebody took a picture of me in
this garish outfit, one arm flung confidently around my
mother. I am told that she treasured it—but burst into tears
every time she looked at it.

The inexorable demands of war had shortened the supply
of amenities all over the world. Some more needlework had
me looking almost soldierly, but I sweltered in that heavy
O.D. shirt—although I'd be blessing its warmth as soon as
we hit the chill Stateside spring. Our first quarters were four-
man tents that no one thought it necessary to wire for
electricity, and we took our chow in messhalls scattered all

over the post, eating the leftovers of more senior outfits. But we were in the army and if there were any complaints, they were softly spoken.

Besides which, now officially deemed old enough to get killed, we had a whole new set of experiences to try, each one symbolic of our sudden manhood. And so beer bottles were opened, cigarettes cavalierly passed around, fresh decks of cards awkwardly riffled and dice rattled self-consciously in sweaty fists. I tried them all, with varying results. I turned down a Lucky Strike for a Chesterfield, choked just the same, guzzled a beer—and won $600 shooting craps.

The game was in our messhall. I walked over with some of the guys, bet my few dollars cautiously enough to build up a $50 stake, then got the dice. "Shoot ten," I said with what I hoped was the proper note of unconcern and really only worried—as I'm sure now that all beginning crap-shooters must worry—that I would at least lose gracefully.

"Shooting ten," the house man said, and two crumpled fives were tossed down on the blanket.

I rolled a natural seven and just stared at it, astounded, until my buddy Jenhatsu Chinen whispered in my ear: "You won, Dan!"

"Let it ride," I croaked, and rolled another seven, and another.

"Shooting seventy-five," said the house man in that never-changing monotone.

That brought me out of my stupor. "It's eighty," I informed him. "I made three passes."

It was as though I wasn't even there. "Shooting seventy-five," he said again.

"Hey, wait a minute!" I yelled—no dinky corporal was going to milk me!—"I started with ten and rolled . . ."

". . . three passes, I know all about it. And after you've been in this man's army a whole week you'll know that the house cuts five dollars on every second pass."

"Cuts five on every second pass," I echoed numbly. They were all staring at me, even my buddies, and I'd have given him the whole $80 if I could have vanished into thin air. "Yeah, sure," I finally managed. "Sorry. Shooting seventy-five."

Luckily, my ignorance about the functions, and rewards, of the house man didn't affect my game. In a little less than three hours, betting strictly by calculation, I had won $600. In the same period, the house man had cut over $100 from the pot, but with absolutely no risk! And although I was properly impressed with my haul—it was five times as much money as I'd ever held in my hand before—I couldn't help thinking about that house man: $100 was a pretty good return for a pair of dice, a blanket and the ability to count by fives.

I won another $200 the next night, but then the party was over. Our shipping orders were cut and early on the fourth day, we climbed aboard a train at Wahiawa and clattered into downtown Honolulu, bound for Pier 11 and the onetime Matson luxury liner, *Lurline*. The only trouble was we had to get off the train a mile from the ship and make it the rest of the way on foot.

We were a motley crew, our straight black hair clipped, GI-fashion, to an ugly bristle; ukeleles and guitars poking up, down and sideways, and our mismatched uniforms sagging under the weight of our bulging duffle bags. And although our departure was supposed to be secret, the streets were jammed with parents, relatives and friends, so that the MPs, marching on the outsides of our double column, had to physically hold the well-wishers off.

It was, in truth, a sad leavetaking. We Japanese, you know, average only about five feet five in height, and we had had no training in marching with a weighty burden on our backs. And so, far from parading boldly off to war to the inspiring strains of martial music (the streets were dead silent) we staggered along, sweating, stumbling, some of the smaller men dropping their bags altogether. Often when this happened, a heartbroken father or brother would rush out into the street in a vain attempt to help, and be muscled back by the MPs: "Back! Get back there, you!"

"But that's my boy. Please, sir, let me help him. I carry something . . ."

"I said *get back!* Now *git,* before I . . ."

And so we shuffled on toward the great looming ship, painted a dingy wartime gray, and we tried not to search the faces of the people who lined the streets, or to hear when they shouted: "Goodbye, Jackie! Hey, Takashi, so long. Aloha!" Deep in my heart I knew that my own folks were out there in that crowd, but I kept my eyes straight in front of me, conscious only of a kind of shame in the very moments when I'd expected to feel exultant. And I thought about the mothers and fathers who were seeing their sons for the very last time this day, and how all they'd have left in all the years to come was this memory of him, struggling along the street under an outsize burden, and looking more like a prisoner than a soldier. And I thought that if only it had been possible for the army to provide a couple of trucks to transport our baggage that last mile, and maybe a small band, it all needn't have been so sad for the old folks.

Because of the *Lurline's* great speed, we traveled without convoy and crossed the Pacific in four days. For nearly all of us, this was the first time away from home, but except for the first view of San Francisco's Golden Gate, we had scant opportunity to enjoy the splendors of the mainland. We were hustled aboard a train as soon as we docked and began wending our way through the back alleys of America toward Hattiesburg, Mississippi. When we stopped—only at night —for a few minutes of calisthenics, people would gather to stare at us, and though some of them brought us coffee and doughnuts, you could tell that others, hanging back in awe, were convinced that we were Japanese POWs.

It was mid-April when we got to Camp Shelby, and it was as though we had stepped out on another planet. We had come from a land of color and warmth and great mountains falling to the sea, and Mississippi was cold and flat and desolate wherever you looked. They marched us to our barracks—"One big draft surrounded by boards," someone called them—and divided us into companies and platoons and without any fooling around, we began those thirteen long, hard months of training that would make us soldiers.

I had been assigned to E Company in the 2nd Battalion, 3rd squad, 1st platoon—and I couldn't have been happier. For one thing, my pals Jen Chinen and Ralph Fujii were in the same outfit, and for another, it was a rifle company, which meant that when the time came we'd be right up there in the thick of things. But as things turned out, I had to lie, bluff, beg and then fight like a tiger to stay there. When S1 began combing the records in Regimental Head-quarters, they found out, first of all, that I'd been in the ROTC band at college.

"Inouye!" the first sergeant bellowed at me one morning at reveille formation. "Report to the band!"

"No, sir!" I bellowed back. And before he could assign me

to a week of latrine duty, and *then* to the band, I squeaked, "I mean, do I have to?" The very thought horrified me. Imagine spending the war blowing a saxophone! What in heaven's name would I tell my grandchildren?

The top kick was a *nisei* and I think he understood. "You don't want to?" he yelled across the parade ground while 200 men shivered in the dawn cold and undoubtedly wished me in the guardhouse.

"No, sir! I want to stay in this outfit."

"I'll see what I can do." And that was the last I heard of that.

But a week later they discovered I'd worked at the aid station in Honolulu and a T4 from the medics came to pay me a visit. "We need experienced men, Inouye," he said, then leaned toward me as though he were conspiring to get me promoted to lieutenant-colonel. "Just say the word and I can get you transferred to the regimental medical detachment—like *that*." He snapped his fingers for effect.

"Hey, do me a favor, will you, Sarge?" I whispered back. "Don't."

But the narrowest escape of all came when some very determined Intelligence guys came down from Camp Savage, Minnesota, to recruit Japanese-speaking GIs for the Pacific. They were looking for interrogators and interpreters for the G2 sections of a dozen different divisions and, naturally, they sent for me. I remember sitting in a little cubicle in battalion headquarters while this stony-faced master sergeant barked questions at me in Japanese. And I kept thinking that there must be millions of GIs in line companies who would have preferred the Quartermaster Corps or the medics or G2, and me, all I wanted to do was carry a rifle, and they wouldn't let me.

"What about it, soldier?" my tormenter of the moment was barking. "Did you understand me or not?"

"Umm, sorry, Sergeant, I . . . uh . . . didn't get it."

"No eh? Your record says you studied Japanese for eleven years."

"Yeah, well I was never very good at it. Didn't pay attention, you know."

He glared at me and for a wild moment I thought I'd pulled it off. Then he hunched in close and said, "Don't play games with me, Inouye. We don't need your permission to make this transfer. All I have to do is sign my name on this paper and you'll be on your way to Camp Savage in the morning."

At that I panicked—I mean, I believed him!—and I did the only thing left to do: I threw myself on his mercy. "Hey, Sarge, I didn't mean to try conning you. It's just that—well, I don't want to leave this outfit. And anyhow, I'd be a lousy Intelligence man. I just want to be a plain dogface. There's lots of other guys who'd . . ."

"Okay, okay!" He was standing up, walking to the door, and taking that accursed paper with him. "Only don't try to put anything over on anybody from the 2 section again."

"No, sir!" I breathed fervently. I was delighted to let him have the last word, so long as he let me hang on to my M1. "Never again!"

You wouldn't think that a single eight-by-ten card could get anyone in as much trouble as my record got me. But there was still one more near-disaster I had to survive before things simmered down. Apparently someone had reported to the first sergeant that my file showed that I had been a lieutenant in the ROTC. Of course, they'd neglected to notice that I had been a lieutenant in the band and so, that first week, testing a few candidates for assignments as assistant squad leaders, the sergeant had me take my squad out for some close order drill. Now to say that I knew *nothing* about close order drill would be an exaggeration—I had once spent ten minutes watching the boys at school going through their paces. And now, visions of myself as an acting corporal dancing in my brain, I decided that I'd already aggravated the top kick enough: if he wanted me to take the squad out for some close order drill, well, by gosh, I would!

I stood before them on the edge of the parade ground just outside our barracks. I took a deep breath and hollered, "Atten—*shun!*"

They snapped to, which was pretty good considering that they'd been in the army all of two weeks and knew even less about close order drill than I did. I sneaked a look at the sergeant. "Get going," he snapped.

"Right—*face!*"

Eleven out of twelve of them turned the right way and the twelfth finally got squared around.

"Forward—*march!*"

And off they went. For a moment or so I trotted happily after them, the first sergeant following, and I felt as though they were in the palm of my hand. And as they marched inexorably on toward the farther reaches of the parade ground, I groped through my mind for some command that would stop them, or turn them around—or anything—but all I could think of was, "Mail call!" and I knew that wasn't right. I turned to look frantically at the sergeant, but he just strolled impassively along, staring straight ahead. By now the squad had moved well into the F Company area and in another 100 paces, maybe less, would be lost, maybe forever, in some other non-com's calisthenics class. What was the command? *What should I do?*

And at last the first sergeant spoke: "You better say something, Inouye. Even if it's only goodbye."

And in the absolute nick of time the words popped into my head. "Squad—*halt!*" I yelled, damp with perspiration, and wheeled to report to the sergeant, as I'd seen him report to the Company Commander. "Sir," I said, "3rd Squad all present and accounted for."

"Yes," he said, "but barely."

Our C.O. was a *haole* who had gone to Roosevelt High in Honolulu, Captain Ralph B. Ensminger, and from the very beginning there wasn't a man in E Company who wouldn't have followed him into General Rommel's command post. He looked like a soldier, six feet of lean hardness and a straight-in-the-eye firmness when he talked to you. But more important, we felt that he was one of us. To be honest, there were some Caucasian officers in the early days of the 442nd who sounded off about the injustice of having to lead a bunch of Japs into battle. That would change—we had to *show* them—but Captain Ensminger knew it all along. He knew that though our skin was browner than his, we were no less citizens of these same United States. And he also knew that because not everyone thought so, we had some special problems and anxieties.

In the third week of our training, when the period of our restriction to the company area was almost over, he assembled us between the barracks of the 1st and 2nd Platoons and ordered us to stand at ease. Then, squinting into the harsh sun, he began to speak:

"Most GIs signed up to fight the enemy. That's all. No-body has called on them to do anything else, just to get the job finished so we can all get back to what we were doing before the war started. You men have an additional battle to fight. You have to overcome the prejudice and discrimination that will be thrown at you, that *has* been thrown at you, because your forefathers came from a country that is now our enemy."

You could hear the breathing of the man next to you. No one moved. No one made a sound.

"To anyone who has grown up in Hawaii as I have, to anyone who has gone to school with you people and worked with you and played ball with you, it's an insult to hear your loyalty called into question. It's personally painful to me to know about the indignities you've suffered: the relocation camps, the questions, the slurs. But war does strange things to otherwise sensible people and I suppose there are those who haven't yet gotten over the shock of December 7. It's not enough for them to blame it on the Japanese warlords. They need someone closer to home to blame, and they picked you."

Now there was a slight stirring in the ranks. He was getting uncomfortably close to hurts that every one of us had experienced.

"What can you do about it?" he said. "First, you can be the best damn soldiers this country has ever known. You can fight your first battle with everything you've got. And second, you can conduct yourselves with the honor for which your people have been known. You must begin in Hattiesburg, Mississippi. Men, I have been instructed to tell you that during your time in this state, you will be treated by its people as white men."

"Well what d'you know!" I heard someone mutter. "Now I'm a *haole!*"

"Don't do us any favors," mumbled another.

"You may not like it," the Captain went on. "I don't like it. But that's the way they do things here and that's the way it's going to be. When you go into Hattiesburg, you will see that public facilities—restaurants, movies, waiting rooms, toilets —are divided into white and colored sections. Much as this will rub you the wrong way, I am asking that you abide by it as long as we are in the state of Mississippi." He stopped and now his gaze took in the whole company, and then he said those words that would stay with me—with all of us, I guess—all through the war: "Men, the first battle will be bloody. But those who survive it will have a chance to make a world where every man is a free man, and the equal of his neighbor. Let's not blow that chance. Let's win the first battle first!"

And that's how it was. We'd have done anything Captain Ensminger asked us to do, and though we often felt foolish, and maybe a little hypocritical, standing in the crowded front section of the bus though there were plenty of empty seats in the back, we did it, and performed all the other asinine rituals of a segregated society, too. But we smoldered inside because, believe it or not, when you've suffered at the hands of prejudiced men, it's almost as painful to be on the other side of the fence.

And so there were problems. Once, an outfit that had fought the Japanese at Attu came through Shelby and, whether they were honestly confused or just feeling their oats, they threw that hated word "Jap" at us, and accumulated quite a collection of black eyes and fat lips by the time they shipped out. Another time, one of our boys got thrown out of a 69th Division PX and a couple of hundred of us marched on the place with blood in our eyes. The MPs had to call up a couple of tanks to turn us back.

Ever conscious of Captain Ensminger's appeal, we had little trouble in town, although the South's peculiar concept of democracy took a little getting used to. The first time I saw a colored GI turned away from the YMCA swimming pool, I felt sick to my stomach. I had always been active in the Y—and am, today, a director of the Nuuanu YMCA— and I simply could not grasp how an organization that so emphasized its Christian beliefs could exclude a man because he was Negro. I remember dressing in a kind of daze, and going back to camp to write a bitter letter of protest to my friends at the Nuuanu Y. They never answered me.

But of course it wasn't all bad. A Hattiesburg businessman named Earl Finch practically adopted the men of the 442nd, inviting groups of us to his ranch, arranging dances for us and generally making us feel warm and wanted. And months later, when the wounded of the 442nd began coming back to the States, he traveled hundreds of miles to visit them and spent thousands of dollars of his own money helping them get settled and rehabilitated. To this day, *nisei* all over America owe Mr. Finch a profound debt of gratitude.

Meanwhile, day in, day out, our all-important mission was getting ready to fight. In the field we put out as though every training exercise was the real thing. Assigned a 25-mile hike with full packs, we were out and back in little over seven hours, a new camp record. What was really remarkable, though, is that every man in the outfit made that march—cooks, supply sergeants, headquarters personnel— and every man finished it, although a few had to be carried down the home stretch, literally. In maneuvers against the

69th Division, the 442nd was assigned the role of Aggressor Force, which meant that we were only supposed to provide the opposition while the 69th, three times our strength, polished up its tactical skills. I guess we didn't follow the script or something, because by the time the exercise ended, the umpires were forced to rule that we had "wiped out" two of the "Friendly Force's" three regiments.

I don't know how it got started, but pretty soon our pidgin-English expression, "Go for broke!" became the Combat Team motto. What did it mean? To give everything we did everything we had; to jab every bayonet dummy as though it were a living, breathing Nazi; to scramble over an obstacle course as though our lives depended on it; to march quick-time until we were ready to drop, and then to break into a trot. The words were to become part of the language, but in those spring and summer days of 1943, if a newcomer to Shelby asked what "Go for broke" meant, chances are he'd be told it was that crazy *nisei* outfit that fought every tactical problem as though it was the Battle of Bataan.

I had progressed from rifleman, to ammunition bearer for the Browning automatic rifle, to lead scout. After that first fiasco at close-order drill, I did pretty well in my tests for assistant squad leader, and when the written grades came back, I was promoted to corporal. "The time-table is a little off," I wrote the folks. "I was going to come home a corporal and they went and made me one today. Guess I'll have to shoot for sergeant now." My mother and father were naturally proud, but also a little concerned. I had a very great responsibility, they wrote back, and all the family was counting on me to fulfill it.

There were a couple of guys in the squad who doubted that an 18-year-old college kid who shaved every third day would make an effective leader. I honestly don't know when they became persuaded otherwise, but it probably coincided with the time I became house man for the E Company crap game, one of the liveliest in the whole battalion. It goes without saying that there were crap games going on all over Camp Shelby, and the stakes generally ranged from a nickel and a dime to rolls of maybe $10 right after payday. But on the entire post, there were only three or four games where a man could count on getting a $100 bet faded. One of those games was in the E Company dayroom, and I ran that game.

To put it simply and succinctly, I cleaned up. Of course there is no way the house man can lose, taking for himself, as he does, a small sum out of every second roll. But when the stakes are high and the game goes on until nearly dawn three and four nights a week, the piles of bills in his fists and his pockets grow to staggering proportions. I was averaging $1,500 a month and, had I hoarded it, could have come home with substantial wealth, certainly as wealth was calculated in the Inouye family. But the truth was that my conscience troubled me—it was all so pathetically easy—and I worked very hard not to save any of it. Each month, I sent $30 or $35 home, not more for fear that my parents would begin to suspect that there was more to my generosity than met the eye. And full of pride, Mother would write back to tell me how all the other boys were asking their parents to send them some extra money, and only her Dan—"such a good son!"—managed to save enough to send home.

As you can imagine, this sort of thing left me with a slightly sour taste in my mouth and I took to searching out the guys Mom said had been writing for money and slipping them $25 or $50. Then I hit on the practice of keeping a three-inch roll of dollar bills on the top tray of my footlocker, which was never locked. The understanding was that any man who needed it could help himself to any part of that roll, no questions asked, repaying the loan on payday. And in all the months that that money was available and common knowledge throughout the outfit, I don't think there was ever more than $10 that was unaccounted for.

When I got leave, I always took six or seven of the boys to Chicago or New Orleans, and all expenses were on me. This was sometimes a little aggravating—as when they went into a bar for a few drinks and I had to wait outside because I was too young to be served—but it was all worth it. I never had the feeling that that money was really mine in the first place, and I did my darndest to put it back in circulation among the boys.

The training got rougher. No longer could we be sure that there'd be a hot shower and a soft bed waiting after a day in the field. As squads and platoons learned to work together, we spent days and nights far from the comforts of the post, getting used to K rations and rain on, and often in, pup tents. Then, suddenly, it was over. And we could sense it: we were ready. And on a May afternoon in 1944, we shipped out for Newport News and a couple of days later became part of a huge convoy bound for the places where the shooting was.

It took us 29 days to make the crossing. That was the period when German submarine packs infested the Atlantic, and we swerved north and south in our efforts to elude them. One day the wind would blow in your face with bitter cold, and three days later you would be sweltering under a broiling sun. And so we knew that we were backtracking and zigzagging, but exactly where we went in those 29 days, no man could say.

Submarine alarms punctuated the long hours of deadly

sameness. Reveille was at 5 A.M., and the steamy holds
would come to slow life as we dressed and waited our turn
at the head to brush our teeth with brackish water. A slight
smell of seasickness hung over the whole ship, and seemed
especially acute in the messes, where the men were jammed
elbow to elbow in a great echoing cavern that denied the
existence of a sea or a sky or the faintest trace of fresh air.
We ate the same dreary foods—I remember an endless river
of chipped beef and beans, great bottomless jars of apple
jelly—and we had the same spiritless sessions of calisthenics,
followed by an orientation class, followed by an inspection,
followed by the next meal; and so on through the endless
days. I found myself thinking of my grandparents a great
deal during that trip, realizing, for the first time I suppose,
what an irrevocable passage their voyage from Japan must
have been. For there seems no turning back on the sea, only
that far horizon, forever out of reach, and the teeming hold
of the ship where there is neither privacy nor solace, just the
pulse of the great engines and the sense and smell of frightened humanity in the very next bunk. I loved my grandparents very much on that long trip overseas; I felt I understood the forces that shaped their lives, the courage.

In every free moment and all through the night there were
crap games and poker and blackjack in the unoccupied
corners and crannies of the ship. Only the barest handful of
men came up on deck for church services on Sunday, and
when the Chaplain, pained but resolute, took the service
down to the hold the following Sunday, the gamblers, a little
awed, listened to the Invocation, then burrowed deeper into
their corners and went on dealing.

"We might as well go back up on deck next week," I said
to the Chaplain. "At least the air's fresher."

He smiled ruefully: "Yes, I suppose so. They'll find us when they need us."

And, of course, they did. As the weeks passed and it was plain that we were drawing close to our destination, more and more men—they seemed to come blinking into the sunlight as though they'd been all their lives belowdecks—turned up for the services. Then one day, a dark cliff stood up out of the haze dead ahead and no one needed to be told that we were passing through the Strait of Gibraltar and into the Mediterranean, for the great rock on the port side looked precisely like the Prudential Insurance symbol. That afternoon the officers broke open the sealed boxes on the quarterdeck and passed among us the little phrase book that began, "You will soon be landing in Italy."

Now a great stillness settled on the ship. Men came to the rail to gaze at the purple shore of North Africa. We could see an occasional house and a cultivated field, and it seemed incredible that only weeks before GIs—like us!—and soldiers of the British Eighth Army had clashed with Rommel's Afrika Corps on that peaceful shore.

In the night, we lay quiet in our bunks, each of us as alone as a man can be. There were no songs and no crap-shooting, only the thump of the engines and the silent prayers of men about to sever their last ties with home, about to be deposited on some alien battleground for a meeting with some unknown fate. Some of them prayed to be spared, some to be brave. I prayed only that God would help me to do my job. I had been promoted to buck sergeant just before we boarded ship and I was suddenly filled with an awesome sense of responsibility—for the men in my squad, for the folks back home whose honor now was so inextricably dependent on mine. How would it be when I heard the guns? How would I react? And I asked only one thing: *Please, God, let me do what must be done.*

We landed at Naples on a beautifully blue Mediterranean morning. In the far distance, the hills looked like some land out of a fairy tale, green and gently rounded and beckoning. But the scars of war lay everywhere before our eyes. The harbor was a ruin of sunken ships and demolished buildings. Just beyond, the gutted city seemed to quiver in expectation of another air raid. The roads, which had just been cleared, swarmed with lines of trucks and marching troops, and scurrying alongside, begging food and cigarettes and, I suppose, anything at all, was the pathetic refuse of the shattered city—men with haunted eyes and children in tatters of clothing.

They took us through the ruined streets to a bivouac area beyond the edge of town. When we had eaten and been settled into tents, most of the men were given passes and, anxious to unwind after the long, cramped voyage, vanished in the direction of Naples. Captain Ensminger had been transferred to command of the headquarters company and our new C.O., Captain Tom Crowley, had assigned me to help organize the company area. I was mighty busy setting up the kitchen and supply tent. It must have been mid-afternoon when I noticed a group of 12 or 15 Italians, men and women, hanging back among the trees at the edge of the area, watching the men in my detail with those dark and haunted eyes. Sometimes they would jabber among themselves and one would start forward. But always he seemed to lose his nerve, and he would fall back with the group, and they groaned and jabbered some more. At last, looking back over his shoulder for encouragement, he edged out into the open and called to me, and it was like a plea: *"Signor!"*

I walked toward him and we met in the open ground, under the hot sun, between his people and mine. "What can I do for you?" I asked.

"We work, eh?" He gestured back at the group behind him. "We clean—kitchen, clothes, eh? Whatever you want." His English was pretty good, but he was very frightened.

"*Quanta lira?* How much?" I knew this was common practice and I didn't think Captain Crowley would mind if some of the guys hired these people to do their dirty details. Lord knows they looked as though they could do with a couple of bucks.

"No, no *lira*," the Italian said. He smiled sadly. "Is nothing to buy. You give us garbage." He pointed to the row of cans outside the mess tent. "We work for garbage."

I thought they were farmers. I thought they'd take the garbage and use it for fertilizer or something. "Sure," I said. "Go ahead—help yourself."

He bellowed something at the group in Italian. They didn't make a sound. They just ran to those cans and plunged their hands in and crammed the slop they pulled out into their mouths, potato peelings and congealing stew and coffee grounds. The men in my detail had stopped what they were doing and watched in fascinated dread. I remembered the guys grinding their cigarette butts into their messkits before scraping them clean in the cans, and other men spitting into the cans, and I had to take a deep breath to keep from being sick. Now they were scooping the stuff into sacks and odd bits of cloth, still in absolute silence and, for all their desperate intensity, in perfect orderliness.

"Stop!" I heard myself yelling. I ran up to them and shoved them back. "You can't do that! You can't eat . . ."

"You said we could," their hollow-eyed spokesman said. "You promised. We work."

"No! No, listen," I told him, clutching him by the arm and pushing him away from the garbage rack, "I'll get you food. Clean food. Put that . . . garbage . . . back. Tell your people to put it back and tonight, six o'clock, come back at six o'clock and there'll be food for you!"

They backed off reluctantly, hanging onto their dripping, smelly packages, and as soon as they had disappeared among the trees, I ran to find Captain Crowley. I guess I managed to get the story out, the same look of horror crossed his face that I felt on my own, and he sent for the mess sergeant. And the order went out: starting at the next meal, no man would take anything he didn't mean to eat; and every portion that was not taken—a scoop of mashed potatoes, an apple, a piece of bread, anything—would be set aside in clean containers and given to the Italians.

And so I began to find out what war was all about. And what I saw that first day was only a bare beginning. The Battalion Surgeon said that if those people were to come into the regimental area, they would have to be deloused. The very next morning, a team of medics lined them up— there were 50 or more now, for the word had spread and other groups had found sympathetic ears in other company areas—and sprayed them with DDT. One medic walked down that sad and unresisting row of men and women, and he lifted up the women's dresses and opened their blouses, and the men's pants, and the other walked right behind him, ready to pump DDT into crotches and armpits and between breasts, and no one spoke, no one moved, and in 15 minutes the ghastly ritual was over. Now they could work in the regimental area. Now they could eat and carry away food for their starving families.

On the third day I got my pass and a chance to go into the

city. I walked the streets in a daze, actually unable to comprehend the enormity of what was happening before my eyes. Women and girls—some of them younger than my kid sister—sprang out at me from the heaps of shattered brick and masonry, and they begged, "Come on, Joe. We have fun. Five *lira*." Children of six and seven, but with the eyes of ancients, grabbed my sleeve and pleaded for money or candy. Men scrabbled for their possessions in the ruins of what had once been a home, and with every plane that flew over they cringed and searched the sky, terror-stricken. And soon I turned away and went back to the bivouac area.

But I came back. There was some awful lure in that desolated city, as there must have been for American soldiers in all of the wrecked cities of the world. I felt that I had to see it again and again, so that I would remember, so that I would always know the true face of war. The destruction of buildings and the great treasures of civilization—this was grievous, but what man has built he can rebuild. The death of millions of soldiers was an incalculable loss, but willingly or otherwise these men had been trained to fight and prepared to die. But the grinding down of the human soul and spirit, the utter degradation of innocent men and women, husbands pimping for their wives, children bargaining for their sisters, this was something I could not bear and can never forget.

Once I went with a girl, I suppose she was 14, to the hovel of a house where she lived with her mother and father and five or six other children, all younger than she. "Five *lira*," she had said, and though nothing in this world could have made me touch her, I went because I needed to know all of the horror of this time and place. The mother and father treated me as though I were of royal blood, bowing and scraping and shooing the little kids out of my way. Beyond a shabby curtain there was a shabbier bed—the only one in the place—and this, they plainly indicated, was for me and the oldest girl.

I shook my head, heartsick and sorry I had come.

The mother spewed a stream of Italian at me. I gathered she was saying that if I hadn't meant to go through with it, why was I wasting her daughter's valuable time? And the father tried bargaining with me: "Three *lira, signor?* Is worth!"

"How can you do that?" I said to him. "To sell your own daughter . . ."

He smiled sadly and turned his hands up in a gesture of surrender. "I have other little ones, too. They are all hungry. *Niente da mangiare.* What can a man do?"

The mother began yelling again. She was an old crone with a seamed and tortured face. By the time I made up my mind, she wailed, it would be too late for her daughter to find anyone else. I said no again and then emptied my pockets on the bed—a chocolate bar, some chewing gum and 30 or 40 *lira*, everything I had, and I walked quickly out. But all their faces clung to my brain for a long, long time.

Early in June, we boarded a fleet of creaky LSTs and sailed north to Anzio, debarking on a night the Germans chose to bomb a mammoth supply dump. We watched in nervous awe as each fiery explosion lit the sky and red tracer bullets zoomed upward and puffs of flak reached out for the *Luftwaffe* raiders. Before dawn, we were loaded into a truck convoy and driven to a bivouac area at Civitaveccia where for two weeks we worked out the kinks of the ocean voyage and honed our fighting skills.

Now everything happened swiftly. On June 10, the 442nd Combat Team was attached to the 34th Infantry Division. On June 24, we moved into an advanced bivouac and the next day marched 13 miles to a last assembly area. On June 26, just before dawn, we were sent into the line and had made contact with the enemy by 8:30.

It seemed so easy. We formed a line of skirmishers and advanced, squeezing off a shot whenever we saw movement across the barren land. I watched my men. I was proud of them, of the way they took advantage of every bit of cover, of the way they moved steadily ahead, as though this were no more than another tactical exercise at Camp Shelby. It was all automatic. There was no sense of danger. I felt no fear.

Our objective was the high ground around the town of Belvedere, with the 2nd Battalion driving forward on the right flank. We had gone 1,500 yards, maybe half way, when the regular crackling of German rifle fire began to be punctuated by the unmistakable *crrrump* of their 88s. The order came down to dig in. We burrowed as close to that warm earth as we could get, suddenly aware that death was flying overhead and crashing down on every side of us.

In a little while, squad leaders were called back for new orders. I crawled up a draw to a little grove of trees and got the word that the 100th Battalion was moving up in an attempt to encircle the town. We were to give them a chance to get in position and then drive straight forward. I went back to my squad and passed the word. Then we waited, listening to those 88 shells whistle over, feeling them shake the earth around us. And while we waited, one of those shells drove into battalion headquarters and killed the first man in the outfit. It was Captain Ensminger.

The first battle would be bloody, he had said, and at last we all knew what he meant.

Chapter V

Go for Broke!

❁ Everything exploded in a farrago of movement and light, men firing as they ran, German mortar shells seeking us out and machine gun bullets spewing up the ground we had to cross. Gone—and gone forever—were the handsomely -ordered formations of basic training, gone the precise tactical maneuvering that worked so neatly in the manuals.

It is almost always at this point, in the fury of that first battle, that an outfit finds out what it is made of. Some never get over the shock of realizing that the enemy is not bound by the book, or the fear that comes from standing next to a man who is suddenly torn to pieces by shrapnel. Casualties and attrition can change the personnel by 80 percent, but can never change the mark of caution stamped on such an outfit, and you better not count on it for much more than a holding operation.

The 442nd was shaken by its first bloodletting, too. There was a time of confusion, maybe even panic, when the shattering reality of death broke on us. Units that had lost their leaders floundered momentarily and there were deadly dangerous moments when not only the battle but the integrity of the entire Combat Team hung in the balance. Then we began to improvise. If the classic flanking movement we learned at Shelby wouldn't work, we'd bull straight ahead. If a company commander or platoon leader fell, the second in command took his place, and when *he* got hit, someone else moved up to take over. In one chaotic 24-hour period, I went from assistant squad leader to platoon guide, but we kept moving.

Our objective was Hill 140. It crouched across the line of our advance on the far side of the Cecina River, dominating the surrounding countryside with its heights, anchoring the enemy's main line of resistance and providing a haven for the German 88s. Dug in just behind the crest of the ridge, their fire directed by forward observers with an unimpeded view of our movements, the big guns rained shells on us all day and through the night.

It was a murderous baptism of fire. G Company, on our left flank, lost every officer but the company commander. In my platoon, I was the only squad leader unhit, and before the day was out I was made acting platoon guide. In late afternoon, burrowed down behind a narrow fold of ground and sweating out a particularly withering hail of fire, I heard the piercing whine of a shell that was headed in maybe 50 yards behind me—it's astounding how quickly you learn to track an 88 by its sound. I dug in even lower, twisting around so I could see the explosion, and in a great puff of smoke and earth and debris, I saw Jenhatsu Chinen killed. The shell all but tore his head from his body, smashing his shoulder so that his arm dangled crazily and laying his brains bare. I ran to him, totally oblivious of the continuing shelling, but of course he was beyond help. I lay beside him for a while in the ragged depression torn out of the ground by the shell that killed him, and I kept thinking of how we had horsed around together in college, of how proud his mother had been that her boy was studying to become a doctor. And now that fine mind and gentle soul were mashed into the dust and dirt of some rocky Italian field, and if I ever lived long enough to see Jen's mother again, what would I say to her? And then the shelling eased up a little and we got the word to push on, and I said so long to my friend Jenhatsu Chinen and moved back up to the head of my platoon.

In the early evening of July 6, with all three rifle companies on the line, we drove the Germans off Hill 140 and were relieved by the 100th Battalion. Our first battle was over. It had lasted four days and four nights, but to this moment the whole wildly furious thing sticks in my mind as a lifelong nightmare.

There were other days, other battles, each one leading inevitably to the next, through all the deadly weeks and months to come. Soon every man who lived bore his personal grief, and there were commanders for whom every single casualty was a personal grief. One of these was our own C.O., Thomas E. Crowley. Except for this one fatal flaw, there wasn't a finer leader in the regiment, nor one the men cared more about. He demanded a casualty report immediately after each battle or skirmish, and so two and three times a day the platoon sergeants would troop to the command post with our grim rosters. "How many this time, Inouye?" he would say, and you could read that stubborn hope in his eyes.

"One dead, three wounded, sir."

"Who's . . . dead?"

"Pfc. Fujikawa, sir."

"Oh, no! Not him." It was a protest, an outcry against some nameless and unjust fate, and he would turn away to hide the wrenching emotion that took hold of him. Then his voice turned low: "Who are your wounded? Are they bad?"

And you would tell him, and he would ask if they were cared for, and then you would leave him alone with his torturous introspections—until the next platoon sergeant reported. It was only a question of time before Captain Crowley's fatal compassion incapacitated him for command, just as surely as if he'd stopped a *Wehrmacht* bullet. He was transferred to regimental headquarters where he served valiantly until the end of the war, but convinced, I'm sure, that he had failed the men of E Company. This, then, is to tell him, this *haole* from the mainland, that the men of E Company loved him as he loved them, and every one of them would have laid down his life in Crowley's service.

We ran through several C.O.s after that, as did every company in the outfit, for the mortality rate among junior officers was very heavy. Then we got the man who would lead us to the end, Captain Thomas W. Akins, a onetime schoolteacher turned tough as steel by the pressures of war. He was a red-headed, ramrod-straight Texan, and every bone and muscle in his body was military. We felt a special confidence following Captain Akins, he always knew exactly what he was doing and he seemed to lead a charmed life. Though he was forever right smack in the forefront of the fighting, he was one of the few officers in the regiment who was never hit.

I fought through all but two of the 442nd's battles, but the war remains fixed in my mind, not as an orderly progression of setbacks and victories, but rather as a kaleidoscopic jumble of hours and minutes and seconds, some of which make me proud, and some of which I have been twenty years trying to forget. One such time was my first patrol.

North of Hill 140, fighting our way from ridgeline to ridgeline, we went into regimental reserve while the 3rd Battalion slugged its way forward through mines and a killing hail of rifle fire. In the early morning, I was ordered to report to the C.P. and there with Captain Crowley was the 2nd Battalion C.O. "Inouye," he said, "I've got a ticklish patrol for you. Do you have six good men to take?"

"Yes, sir." I was already ticking off their names in my mind.

The 3rd Battalion had been severely chewed up and we would have to relieve them immediately, he explained. I was to reconnoiter the route. He didn't have to go into too much detail about how dangerous this mission was: the interchange of hundreds of men on a front line position was a tempting invitation for the enemy to counter-attack—if they found out. For that reason, such reliefs were almost always carried out under cover of darkness. Now, because the 3rd Battalion was in such seriously weakened condition, the 2nd would have to replace them in broad daylight. And I was charged with finding the best way up for men who would have to be fresh for combat, as well as the best way back for those who would be bearing dozens of dead and wounded.

I didn't have too long to think about my responsibility, which is just as well, for time was of the absolute essence. In fifteen minutes, I had chosen my people and briefed them. Grenades stuffed in our pockets and dangling from our belts, we moved out. I tried to concentrate every particle of my attention on the terrain, which helped me avoid thinking about why the C.O. had chosen to entrust the fate of 1,000 fighting men to a nineteen-year-old buck sergeant.

In the beginning it was easy. We followed the protected trail over which the 3rd Battalion had moved up the day before. Then, with the firing up ahead growing louder in our ears, we came on a grisly sight. The first casualties of the battle had been moved back to a clearing just off the trail, and there they lay in the relentless sun, 20 or 30 of them, waiting for a lull in the fighting so they could be buried. They were already bloating with decay, the black flies swarming at their faces and in their wounds. The stench clutched at the pits of our stomachs.

"My God, there's Miura!" I heard one of my men whisper in horrified awe.

"Come on, Dan," gasped another, "let's get by them!"

"No!" I said sharply. "Follow me!" And I turned back and double-timed in the direction from which we'd come. When I reached a narrow valley that I hoped to God paralleled the trail and wasn't too thickly mined, I turned in, sweating profusely from the exertion and the battering emotional shock.

"This'll be longer, Dan," one of the men said, "even if it gets us there."

"Maybe so," I answered, "but I don't think the Colonel would want to take fresh troops past that open graveyard. Just keep your eyes peeled for freshly-turned earth. That's where the mines'll be."

Circling the mine fields and marking them, searching out every bit of cover in that rocky valley, it took us two hours to cover the 2,000 yards to the line. But I was reasonably sure the enemy hadn't spotted us, and as soon as we'd made contact with rear elements of the 3rd Battalion and told them to prepare to evacuate their positions, we turned and scooted back, running all the way.

The 2nd was all set to roll and we were on the move before noon, E Company in the lead and the Colonel and I at the very point of the column. When I turned off the trail and up the valley, he stopped me: "Why don't we go straight on?"

And I told him about the dead men. "I didn't think you'd want the men going into battle with that on their minds, sir."

He looked straight at me for a long moment. Then he said, "If you can reconnoiter as well as you can think, Inouye, we may pull this cockeyed maneuver off. Let's go."

And we did pull it off. With hardly a word exchanged, the 2nd Battalion filtered through the positions of the 3rd, and that poor, shot-up outfit pulled out to the rear. By 3 P.M., we were ready to drive on and the enemy had missed a prime opportunity to catch the 442nd at its weakest moment. When we were all in position, the Colonel gave me a gruff, "Good work, son," but I had an even clearer sign of his appreciation: whenever an especially tough patrol came up in the next weeks, he always sent for me.

Crazy things happened. Men go a little out of their minds in war—that's how heroes are made—and when you've lived with death and the idea of death for as long as we did, human life grows cheaper and cheaper. Once one of our boys got into a fire fight with a German not 100 feet away. Each of them took cover behind the only two trees still standing on an artillery-decimated field, and each seemed to take turns squeezing off a shot at the other. And it was like the showdown battle between the good guy and the bad guy in a cowboy movie. All of us behind our man quit firing and shouted encouragement at him—"Come on, buddy, put it between his eyes!" and we could hear the Germans cheering their man on. And at last our boy caught the German as he peeked around the tree and shot him flush in the face, and as he toppled into the open, every one of us squeezed off a round. We saw the corpse an hour or so later when we moved up: it must have had thirty bulletholes in it.

I remember the time I didn't get to Rome. We were in a rest area and half the non-coms, chosen by lot, were to have passes. I got mine, all right, but a man in the 3rd platoon, a guy I knew from back home, stopped me just as I was coming out of the orderly room. "I pooped out, Dan," he said sadly. "I didn't get one."

"Ah, too bad," I said. "But you guys'll get first crack next time we come through."

He shook his head. "Maybe the other guys will, but not me. I just have this feeling, you know?"

I knew, and it sent a shiver down my back. I made a feeble attempt at kidding him out of it—"Come on, you'll probably be talking Italian before we get home"—but I don't think he even heard me.

"I wouldn't ask this of you, Dan," he said in dead seriousness, "but I figure this is it for me, my one chance. I'm a Catholic, you know, and if I could get to the Vatican, maybe be blessed by the Pope, I'd be ready for anything that's coming down the pike my way. Dan, would you switch pass days with me?"

I felt my skin in the clean O.D.s, the first clean clothes I'd had on in weeks, and the fresh tingle of after-shave lotion on my face, and I fingered the fat roll of lira in my pocket, and I said, "Sure, pal. Let's go tell the first sarge."

And the thing is that he was right on every count. He *did* get to the Vatican, and he *was* blessed by the Pope, and he came back ready for anything. And four days later, in a little skirmish that didn't amount to much more than a scattering of machine-gun fire and a couple of mortar rounds, he caught a piece of shrapnel in the middle of the breastbone. They say the hole was so small that the medics had to open his blouse to find it, but it was in just the right place and he must have been dead before he hit the ground.

Men have to laugh. Even knowing that every agonizing second may be their last on this earth, a man has to vent the terrible pressures inside, and of course laughing is better than crying. So we laughed, sometimes heartlessly, sometimes hysterically and sometimes in the final instant of life. Under artillery barrages that often lasted for hours, we had devised a technique for not fouling our foxholes when the demands of nature could no longer be denied. Since it was suicidal to seek relief above ground when the 88s were booming, we pressed our steel helmet coverings into service, evacuating as necessary and then tossing the waste out. But the foxholes were only a few yards apart, and a man popping up between shell bursts to get rid of his own stool can hardly be expected to take careful aim. And so, amid the roar of death, you would sometimes hear outraged shrieks and violent cursing and dire threats:

"Hey, Terry, you bastard, cut the goddam shit!"

"Oh, I wish I had my diarrhea back—I'd drown you in it!"

"Terry, I swear, if the 88s don't get you, I will!"

And the laughter echoed among the explosions.

There were a few men who would turn blue with self-torment because the very idea of relieving themselves in their own helmets and within the confines of their own foxholes was more than their sensibilities could endure. One of them gave us all a terrific laugh during the battle north of

Orciano. The enemy barrage had lasted all morning and well into the afternoon when, all at once, there was a lull. Like a jack-in-the-box, a 4th platoon man leaped out of his hole, his pants already down around his knees, and ran stumbling to a piece of high ground just behind the defense perimeter. You can imagine the chortling wisecracks that flew his way as he squatted there in full view of half the company. Nor did it stop when the barrage began again and shrapnel spattered the ground at his feet and just beyond his bare bottom. Frantically he sprang erect, tugging at his pants, and the men yowled:

"Don't let them scare you, pal. Finish what you were doing!"

"Don't forget to wipe yourself!"

And then the shrapnel found him and a piece caught him in the throat, and he clutched at it as he spun around and fell into his own excrement. And the laughter was choked off by a sort of gasp, and for a while there was no sound on the battlefield at all.

I never got used to it. Deep down, I think no one did. We pretended to be calloused and insensitive because we understood the fatal consequence of caring too much. You were no good to your men; you were through as a soldier if you cared too much. But hidden in the core of every man's being, there must have been a wound, a laceration of the spirit, and the abrasives of war rubbed against it every day and you thought that even if you lived, and the years passed, it would never stop bleeding.

One morning I was leading a forward patrol along a gentle slope toward an ancient farmhouse that sat deserted and glaring in the sun. Only it wasn't deserted. We were barely thirty yards away when a machine gun spat fire from a darkened window and my lead scout was all but cut in half. The rest of us hit the ground and I hollered for the bazooka while bullets from that dark window kept seeking us out in steady, disciplined bursts of six. With a whoosh and a glowing roar, our rocket tore into the weathered frames of the house and it sagged crazily, and the machine gun was still. We ran forward in the sun, throwing grenades as we closed on that malevolent window, crashing inside before the dust of the explosion had fairly settled.

Two of the Germans were dead, torn to shapeless hulks by the bazooka. The third, an ammo bearer, I guess, had been thrown back across the room, and he lay sprawled against the wall, nearly senseless, one leg shredded and twisted completely around. *"Kamerad,"* he whispered, smiling sadly. *"Kamerad."*

I think I felt sorry for him. I don't know. I was thinking about my scout, lying dead out there in the sun. Anyhow, it didn't matter. He reached into his tunic and I thought he was going for a gun—it was war; you only had one chance to make the right decision—and I pumped the last three shots in my rifle clip into his chest. He jerked each time, and the last time, as he toppled over, his hand sprang spasmodically out from his tunic, and he held up a snapshot, clutching it in death. There was a woman in it, a pretty woman, and two little kids, and there was a handwritten inscription: *"Deine Dichliebende Frau, Hedi."* So I had made a widow and two orphans.

I had to secure the farmhouse and get a message back for a burial detail to come get our man. I had a lot to think about. But sooner or later, you know, there comes the time when a man has to face up to whatever it is that's hanging back there on the rim of his conscience. I never remembered that German's face, only his hand clutching the picture. For days I fought the image down, but it kept returning and, at last, when they pulled us back to a rest area, I went to see the Chaplain, Hiro Higuchi.

"How can I help you, Dan?" He looked as desolate as I felt.

"I don't know." I shrugged. "I guess I just wanted to talk to somebody."

"I know. I know how it must be."

We were quiet for a while, then I said, "The thing is, it's as though there were two Dan Inouyes, Chaplain. One of me is damn proud of the kind of soldier I am. I'm a good squad leader. I'm tough. I do my job."

"But?"

"But I can't get used to it, to killing other men. Chaplain, I was brought up in the kind of house where we had an obligation to a hungry dog or a sick cat. My parents are gentle people, they never lifted a hand to any of us kids. I *believe* that thou shalt not kill."

"Don't ever *stop* believing it, Dan," he said urgently. "Listen, this is not our way. We are fighting because we have to. Our enemy *does* believe in killing. He has killed millions of blameless people already, and he will kill us if we do not defend ourselves and our liberty. There is no making peace with madmen. This is what you must remember. You must fight—yes, and kill—to protect the kind of life that helped you grow up to hate killing."

I left his tent and walked in the darkness for a while. It was good to talk with someone about it. I felt better. And then, as I picked my way over the stony terrain toward my own area, I remembered my father sitting next to me on that crowded bus to Nuuanu, and the plea in his voice when he said, "Do not bring dishonor on our name." And if there was one thing I knew for sure, it was which side honor was on.

Few men fought in all of the 442nd's campaigns and battles. Our casualty rate was so high that eventually it took 12,000 men to fill the original 4,500 places in the regiment. But fewer men still missed a battle as long as they could stand up and hold an M1. The outfit had the lowest AWOL rate in the European theater of operations and the only men I ever heard about going over the hill had very special reasons. Depending on whose morning report you go by, it may be that I contributed to that AWOL rate.

In late August, 1944, as we were approaching the Arno River north of Rome, I came down with a severe case of ingrown toenails. It was something that had bothered me off and on for a long time, but now I was actually having trouble walking. One night, after we had settled into a bivouac area, I pulled my boots and socks off and, almost simultaneously, two things happened: the smell from my feet snapped my head back, and a medic walked by.

"Let me look at those!" he yelped, and squatted by my side.

I could tell that the big toes on both my feet were infected—nothing else could smell that bad—but I couldn't see that that was any reason for him to get so excited. He looked as though he had just discovered a terminal case of leprosy.

"How long have those toes been bothering you?" he said.

"I don't know . . . a couple of weeks."

"Do you know what those blue streaks are?"

"What blue streaks?" I leaned forward. I didn't see any blue streaks.

"Those, right there, on both ankles. Do you know what that is, soldier? That's blood poisoning."

I'll have to admit that that didn't sound too good. And neither did those ugly streaks, when I finally spotted them, make me feel any better. "Well what do you do for that?" I asked him. "You got some medicine or something?"

"Not me. That's a job for the battalion surgeon. Let's go."

He wouldn't let me put my boots back on so two guys carried me back to battalion headquarters, where the doc took one look, pumped a shot of sulfa into my behind and sent me back to regiment in a jeep. There *two* doctors took one look, more sulfa and boom! before I knew what was happening, I was on my way to the hospital in Rome. "Surgery," the major had said ominously, "and there's no time to lose. So it was that next morning, with shot-up GI's in every other bed on the ward, I found myself hospitalized for ingrown toenails, and feeling a little silly about the whole thing.

They operated on me that very morning. I sat up on a table, my back braced against the wall while they gave me a local anesthetic, and watched the whole messy thing. Then they mummified my feet in about 800 yards of bandages and wheeled me back to the ward. The whole job had taken twenty minutes, but it would be two weeks, the doctor said, before I could get back to my outfit.

I got plenty of sympathy. Guys came by my bed and whistled their commiseration at the melon-sized bandages around my toes. They offered me cigarettes and delicacies out of their packages from home. And finally, inevitably, they asked me how it had happened. "You step on a land mine or something?"

"No, no. It's . . . uh . . . ingrown toenails. They had to cut them out and . . ."

It was as though I had flicked a switch. The light of compassion went out of their eyes and in about ten seconds flat I was all alone. They simply turned around and went back to their beds without so much as a "See you around, pal." Nor in the two days that followed could I get another word out of any of them.

It was no mystery. It was the freeze and I understood it perfectly. I had seen it put to use in my own outfit. Right or wrong, combat troops have nothing but scorn for any GI who skips out on the fighting for anything less than a Purple Heart. And here, in a ward where guys had had limbs amputated and bullets fished out of their stomachs, a case of ingrown toenails was about as convincing a reason for hospitalization as athlete's foot. I think the only thing I got credit for was originality: these guys had heard lots of goof-off alibis, but ingrown toenails—that must have been a new one.

I didn't have much heart for defending myself. As far as I was concerned, they were dead right. So I had just come off two months on the line—big deal. The raw fact was that my outfit was catching hell on the Arno River while I was sleeping on clean sheets and eating fresh vegetables 150 miles from the front—because I had ingrown toenails. That would make a fine story to tell my children! That was a fine way to protect the honor of the Inouye name!

Maybe I could have stuck out the two weeks if they'd let me become one of them, those poor battered and beat-up guys on the surgery ward. But as it was, alone with thoughts that worked their way down and scoured my insides, I'm surprised I lasted through the second day. Be that as it may, by lights-out that night, I was ready to walk out on the Via dei Fori Imperiali in my pajamas. I flagged down the ward boy as he made bed-check: "Hey, buddy, will you bring me my things?"

"No," he said, "and pipe down: everybody's sleeping."

I grabbed his arm and pulled him close to the bed. "Look," I whispered urgently, "I'm not about to con you. I'm walking out of here tonight if I have to do it barefoot! Now why don't you be a nice guy and get me my uniform?"

"Jesus, man, I can't do that! If I got caught they'd ream me out and leave me for dead. That's a . . ."

"I got twenty-five bucks that says you won't get caught."

". . . court-martial offense." He stopped cold: the number had just registered on his brain. "How much?"

"Fifty bucks."

Ah, the venality of humankind. Where would we puritans be without it? In fifteen minutes, when he was sure everyone, including the floor nurse, was sound asleep, he was back with all my things. He had to go back again and sneak into the kitchen for a knife to slit my boots open so they would accommodate those bulbously bandaged feet, but then there was a silent exchange of greenbacks and a furtive trip down back corridors, and presto! I was limping along the sultry streets of Rome looking for a military vehicle bound north.

That part wasn't easy either. Without proper orders, I had to steer clear of the regular personnel convoys and command cars where I was almost sure to be challenged. Instead, I tried to thumb a ride with the odd supply truck, or a jeep with maybe a couple of guys traveling alone. And so, mile by mile, sleeping by the side of the road, buying meals at the occasional farmhouse still standing, I worked my way back toward Firenze, where the outfit had been bivouacked when I left. Only by this time, they were on the far side of the Arno, and it took me hours of hobbling around in the darkness among the units that were bedded down outside Castello—"Hey, anybody know where E Company is?"— before I finally found the 2nd Battalion and reported in to the C.O. It had taken me two days and three nights, and if I had wandered around searching for them for as little as two hours more, I'd have lost them for good: at 8 A.M. the whole battalion shoved off for Livorno, a Mediterranean port where a fleet of Liberty ships was waiting to take the 442nd to France.

"We got word that you took off, Inouye," Captain Akins said when I'd reported in. "What's the matter, didn't that hospital chow agree with you?"

"Nothing about that hospital agreed with me, sir. I figured this is where I belonged."

"I see. Well they've got you listed as AWOL back in Rome and they're hot to court-martial your fanny."

"Yes, sir," I said, relieved because he was grinning.

"Why don't I save them the trouble? We'll have our own little court martial here when we get a chance and find you not guilty. Meanwhile you can ship out with us."

"Yes, sir. Thank you, sir." I grinned back at him.

"And take it easy until those feet heal up. We don't want to have to carry you to Paris."

Nobody had to carry me, and we never got to Paris. But the thing is that everyone thought we could march right in. We thought the war was going to end any minute, that France would be a breeze after the unending battles for every hill in Italy. The 7th Army was driving up the Rhone

Valley. North, Patton's 3rd Army was slicing straight toward Germany. It didn't seem as though anything in the world could stop us. But the hard fact is that our very bitterest fighting lay ahead, and many of the men who looked forward to France as a lark and a lot of laughs died there without seeing anything but the port of debarkation and a couple of foxholes that didn't look a bit different from Italian foxholes.

We were trucked north into the Vosges Mountains and went into the line on October 14. A sense of nightmare hung darkly over the regiment. Almost from the day we landed gale winds had been driving the autumn rains into our faces, and when they died down an eerie fog rolled across the broken land, so that it seemed as though the sun and the sky had been wrenched forever from this bleak world into which they had dumped us. Ahead, curving toward the German border, lay a series of mountain towns—Bruyères, Belmont, Biffontaine, La Houssière—fiercely defended by the enemy from long-prepared positions, and with armor and artillery that was perfectly suited to that rocky, precipitous land. Their fire was timed to burst in the tops of the towering pines that darkened the terrain, and the men below, huddling small in slit trenches that suddenly provided no cover at all, were peppered with shell fragments and pine slivers that drove through skin and muscle and bone with all the force of steel. This is how "Americans," the official history of the 442nd Combat Team, describes the first eight days of the battle:

"The fighting had been something [the men] had never seen before. In Italy, the enemy had held hard for a day or two and then pulled a planned withdrawal . . . Here . . . there was no let-up. The enemy fought bitterly, fought until he was killed or driven back, fought with the terrible desperation of a man with his back to the wall . . . [He] had artillery—artillery and plenty of ammunition. Day or night the guns were never silent. Shells crashed in the tall pines by the hundreds and thousands. Our men had no houses to protect them from the fire and keep off the rain which poured down steadily night after night. Some of the GIs risked death in the open rather than spend a night in a hole half-filled with freezing water. The strain was beginning to tell . . . [Some men] were going back to the rear suffering from combat fatigue (which had never happened before) . . . This was no reflection on the courage of any man. Their nervous systems were simply not equipped to stand the terrible pounding and sudden shocks of this unceasing battle. That, coupled with the fact that many of them had not slept for eight days."

Finally, on October 23, we were pulled into reserve; although the Germans, zeroed in on the rest area with a battery of eight-inch howitzers, made sure that none of us got too much rest. Then we moved up again through sporadic artillery fire and air attack and by the morning of November 4 we were ready to lock horns with the Germans again. And this would be a big one: the famous battle to rescue the "Lost Battalion" was about to begin.

We had been given a preliminary briefing that morning and now, stripped down to combat packs, ammo and all the grenades we could carry, we waited to move up to the line of departure. I remember sitting on a stump writing a last letter home and trying to ignore the periodic whines and explosions of the 88s when someone stuck his face at mine and said the C.O. wanted to see me. I signed off with something smart like, "Time out, folks, the captain wants me to

come down and tell him how to win the war." Then I
grabbed my helmet and took off for the C.P. I suppose I
thought there was some change in plan, I don't know. I
certainly hadn't the vaguest idea that what was in store for
me was a stunning upheaval in my personal fortunes.

At the C.P., Captain Akins simply said that I was to report
to the adjutant at regimental headquarters immediately. Any
other time and place and I would have asked what was up—
I mean, that was an odd order to get an hour from jump-
off—but he was preoccupied with preparations, the jeep
driver was waiting and—well, odd or not, an order is an
order.

But I couldn't help thinking, and my thoughts were wild:
had there been a death in my family? was one of my men in
trouble? was I?

At regimental headquarters Master Sergeant Earl Kubo, a
former police lieutenant and an old buddy, was waiting for
me. But instead of the casual, "Hi, Dan," he jumped to his
feet and snapped off a salute. "Sir," he said, "this is for you."
And he handed me an envelope.

"Thank you, sir," I said, taking it, naturally assuming he
was relieving some of the pressure with a harmless little
joke.

"Begging your pardon, sir," he said, and there wasn't the
trace of a smile on his face, "but I believe I'm entitled to
have my salute returned."

Automatically I lifted my hand to my head in a lame
imitation of a salute. "You gone battle-happy, Earl?" I said.

"No, sir. And I think the contents of that envelope will
explain everything, *if the Lieutenant would open it.*"

Still staring at him, uncomprehending, I tore the thing

open and at last my eyes focused on the single sheet of paper: I had been awarded a battlefield commission; I was now a 2nd lieutenant in the Army of the United States.

"Congratulations, sir," Earl was saying, and now he *was* smiling, and I thanked him, numb, speechless with the sense of honor and a sudden overwhelming weight of responsibility. And Earl understood. Without another word, he led me to the battalion surgeon, who was to give me a physical before I was officially sworn in.

I must have been an imposing sight as I stood there in my birthday suit. My hair was long and tangled. Despite my best efforts at washing out of my helmet and in the occasional stream we came to, I was grimy with the stain and stink of the muddy terrain. The surgeon eyed me distastefully and commanded his medical orderlies to "Take this . . . officer . . . out and clean him up!"

They showered me and cut my hair. They got me a clean uniform. Next day they brought me back. Then I was tapped and thumped and listened to. And everything was fine, except my weight: I had lost 19 pounds eating K rations and fighting, and I weighed exactly 111 pounds.

"You don't qualify for a commission," the doctor said. "You're underweight." Then he sighed. "But, of course, by that standard, about 90 percent of the GIs in this outfit don't even qualify for the army." He entered 135 pounds on my physical report and the following day I was legally endowed as an officer and gentleman by order of the President of the United States. I was the youngest lieutenant in the entire regiment.

On November 6, I started back to rejoin my outfit. By the time I reached them, the bloody battle of the "Lost Battal-

ion" was over. My platoon, which had numbered 20 men
when I left them only three days before, now had eleven GIs
capable of carrying a weapon; and that included me.

What had happened was that the 1st Battalion of the
141st Infantry, part of the almost-all Texan 36th Division,
had driven down a ridge east of Biffontaine. Clearing the
enemy as it moved swiftly forward, the outfit had swept into
a narrow valley between Gerardmer and St. Die, and here
the Germans, having been rolled back on their own strong
support positions, turned to fight. Furthermore, enemy units
filtered in behind the unfortunate battalion and completely
cut it off from any contact with the American forces. Twice
the Texans tried to hammer their way out of the trap, and
twice they failed. Nearly 1,000 GIs were effectively surrounded and desperately short of supplies and ammunition.
That was when Major General John E. Dahlquist, C.O. of
the 36th Division, had ordered the 442nd to the relief of the
Lost Battalion.

They had jumped off right after I left. The bombardment
from the German defenders was unbelievable; endless
rounds of artillery and mortar shells, and at every roadblock
a withering hail of rifle and machine gun fire. The casualty
rate approached 50 percent and there were some companies
without an officer or platoon leader left standing. Days
passed and the men were still 1,000 yards short of the
trapped Texans, whose situation had grown critical. A few
planes had managed to drop some food and ammunition, but
they were in terrible need of water and medical supplies.

And then a kind of universal anger overtook the "Go for
broke" outfit. Without orders, without even a plan of attack,
men got up off the ground and began moving ahead, firing as
they went, rushing to the cover of a tree and lobbing a

grenade into a machine gun nest, closing with the Germans in deadly individual battles of bayonets and rifle butts and fists. And at last a platoon of B Company broke through the enemy line and made contact with the Texans. There were tears of relief and gratitude, a few exhausted embraces, but no time for cheers. The enemy was on the run and General Dahlquist ordered the 442nd to drive on. By the time I got back, the worst was over, but not until November 17, with St. Die firmly in our hands, were we relieved. The outfit had been engaged in the most desperate kind of fighting for 25 out of 27 days.

I lost even more weight in that time and looked like a scarecrow, but I had no complaints. I was alive. When General Dahlquist called the regiment out for a retreat parade to commend us personally, he is reported to have said to the C.O., "Colonel, I asked that the entire regiment be present for this occasion. Where are the rest of your men?"

And Colonel Charles W. Pence, as bone-weary as any dogface in the outfit, replied, "Sir, you are looking at the entire regiment. Except for two men on guard duty at each company, this is all that is left of the 442nd Combat Team."

And there we were, cooks, medics, band and a handful of riflemen, a ragged lot at rigid attention, without a single company at even half its normal strength. One had only 17 men and was commanded by a staff sergeant. My outfit, E Company, with a normal complement of 197 men, had exactly 40 soldiers able to march to the parade ground.

General Dahlquist looked at us for a long time. Twice he started to speak and choked on the overpowering feelings that took hold of him. And in the end, all he could manage was an emotional, "Thank you, men. Thank you from the bottom of my heart." And the saddest retreat parade in the history of the 442nd was over.

Next day, though, when we were detached from the 36th Division and shipped to Nice, the General sent an official letter of commendation:

"(1) The 36th Division regrets that the 442nd Combat Team must be detached and sent on other duties. The period during which you have served, October 14 to November 18, 1944, was one of hard, intense fighting through terrain as difficult as any army has ever encountered.

"(2) The courage, steadfastness, and willingness of your officers and men were equal to any ever displayed by United States Troops.

"(3) Every officer and man of the Division joins me in sending our best personal regards and good wishes to every member of your command, and we hope that we may be honored again by having you as a member of our Division."

Later, every survivor of that bloody battle was made an honorary Texan—which may have had something to do with my future closeness to Sam Rayburn and Lyndon B. Johnson.

Captain Akins had saved a pair of his gold bars to pin on me. I knew the commission had originated with him—he had to recommend me—and I thanked him and asked why it had been kept so secret.

"I was afraid that if you had too much time to think about it, you'd turn it down," he said. "I don't think you appreciate your ability enough, Dan. You've got a lot to offer and I hope to God you make it through this rat race in one piece."

"Thanks," I said wryly. "Same to you."

But he didn't hear me. His mood had turned quiet and dark, and when he spoke again, I listened as hard as I could:

"It's not easy to wear those bars, Dan. Some days you'll swear they weigh a ton. Which men do you pick for which dirty job? And what do you write to their people when they don't come back? That you're sorry? Everybody knows that. So what? They're still just as dead, aren't they?" He shuddered, then he looked at me. "You have no responsibility now that is as important as keeping your men alive. There will be times when you can't—men getting killed is what war is all about—but you have to give every GI in your outfit every last inch of the odds. Help them, teach them and, above all, command them, because if they believe in you and you're any good, that's the best protection there is. I could sit here all night, Dan, and still not tell you all there is to being an officer—this battlefield commission, you know, has to take the place of four years at West Point or ROTC, and even the officer factory at Fort Benning takes 90 days— but you'll catch on to it all if your luck holds out. The main thing I have to tell you is that you must begin thinking about your platoon as part of your body: the men are the arms and legs and guts, and you're the brains. The army is not a democracy, Dan. When the brain commands, the feet have to move. That's what close order drill is all about; so that the men get used to your voice giving commands, so that they learn to obey those commands automatically, instinctively, without so much as a second's pause to think it over. We don't have seconds to spare."

He sighed deeply, then slapped my knee and stood up. "One last thing. You'll have to do your gambling with us officers now, not with the men."

He was smiling at me, and I said, "It'll be a pleasure to take your money, Captain. And—thanks for everything you said tonight. It's a big help at a rough time in my life."

I did gamble with the officers after that, silly little poker games for a nickel and a dime and everything wild but the kitchen sink, but that was absolutely the least I learned from Tom Akins. I never forgot the things he said to me that night, and I never stopped learning from his example, and all of that was a big handhold up to my confidence when I took command of the 3rd platoon.

There were some things about being an officer that I never got used to, like being served on plates while the men lined up with messkits to wait their turn on the chow line, or watching them eat powdered eggs when I'd just had a couple of fresh ones. Nor did I care much for being called, "Sir," and "Lieutenant Inouye." I tolerated it when there were outsiders around, but in the privacy of the 3rd Platoon, it had to be, "Dan." And this went double in spades in combat situations. I didn't wear my bars because they were a dead giveaway, and I mean dead, and I surely didn't want some German sniper zeroing in on me because he *heard* me singled out as the platoon leader.

There was so much to learn. And of course what you learned, and how quickly you learned it, had a direct bearing on whether men lived or died, on whether *you* lived or died. At first I was horrified at having to censor my men's letters home. It was required of all junior officers, and I'm certain there were valid security reasons for it, but reading the personal mail of a man you knew only as a soldier was like being the third person in his bedroom. And they held nothing back. After a battle, they'd write as many as a dozen letters a day, losing themselves, I suppose, in memories of home, dreams of some far-off time of peace and the terrible longings that beset us all in a violent world, a world without a breath or whisper of comfort or quiet. A man would tell his wife how much and in precisely what ways he missed her, leaving out not a single detail. Another would tell his mother that he cried himself to sleep each night. A third would beg his girl friend to wait, to be faithful. And in every case, there you were, looking over his shoulder, gifted by the government with the legal right to be a peeping tom.

And then, gradually, I became detached from this aspect of my men's lives, this other world that was so far away and out of a past so long behind us as to seem unreal. I remember Captain Crowley, who cared so much about his people's yesterdays and tomorrows that he couldn't help them today. And finally I put those letters to work for me. I let them tell me what was in the writer's heart and mind. I read each one two and three times. I read between the lines. And I found out which men had suddenly grown battle weary and, to the best of my ability, I protected them, and so doing, protected us all.

If a man revealed classified information in a letter home, I didn't just slice the offending words out and pass the rest of the letter on. I went to the man; had it been just a slip, or was he getting careless, or foolish, or worst of all, apathetic, fed up? If a man's letters revealed some crisis back home, if I sensed that he was growing unnerved about an ailing child or an aging parent, I pulled every string I could grab hold of to get him a few days of rest in a rear area. And it was as much for me as for him. A shaky GI was less than useless; he could be a menace to every other man in the outfit. I didn't see that it was my job to give the Germans any extra advantages.

In one 60-day period, I led 72 patrols up to, and sometimes right through, the enemy lines, and not one of the men who went with me was a volunteer. I didn't believe in volunteers. That might work gloriously for John Wayne and Errol Flynn. But when the bullets are real, the men you want backing you up on a dangerous mission are the ones you have picked out yourself, guys who are psychologically sound and physically fit. Hero complexes aren't necessary, but steady nerves are. A guy with a to-hell-with-everything attitude may reach the objective, but he may also get half the patrol killed doing it. Far better the man with a healthy appreciation of the odds, a sensible respect for the enemy and a rational concern for his own life.

I made just one mistake in those two months and hurt only myself. Hurrying back from a Christmas Eve patrol, almost tasting the turkey dinner they'd promised us, I used the same return route as the one we'd gone out on. Meanwhile, the Germans had booby-trapped it and, in my haste to get back to our lines, I never saw the trip wire. Luckily it was hooked to a concussion grenade which blew most of its force into the mountain. I got off with a slight thigh wound and was so embarrassed about it I didn't even put in for a Purple Heart.

Sometimes I had to resort to a kind of benevolent treachery to do what I knew was right. One night I was to take four men out to locate a particularly harassing machine gun nest. That meant there was every chance we'd be fired on— we *wanted* to be fired on so we could pinpoint the emplacement for our artillery. It also meant it was no job for a guy who was liable to choke up, because we'd have to crawl out of there on our bellies as soon as the Germans opened up.

An hour or so before we were to jump off, I was censoring some mail and came across a letter from one of the men scheduled to go along. His wife was about to have a baby and he was swearing to her on tear-stained pages that nothing, absolutely nothing, was going to keep him from coming back to her.

Now a man in that state of mind I did not need on a tricky night patrol. He had been a good soldier but, like all of us, he was vulnerable. And the critical thing was that his tiny area of vulnerability had been pierced just before a dirty job, and I wasn't about to risk his life or mine pretending he was the same man. I could just picture him thinking about his baby when that machine gun began looking for us, freezing to the ground while the rest of us bellied out and, sooner or later, getting picked up by a burst of tracer bullets and dying there on the cold ground because he wasn't going to take any chances.

But how do you scrub a man from a mission to which he'd already been assigned and still leave him with a shred of self-respect?

Without knowing the answer but positive that, somehow, I had to find it, I walked over to his tent. He was getting his gear in shape and I asked him how things were going. Fine, he said, just fine, but he didn't look up at me. Then he took his glasses off and began cleaning them, and still not sure of just what I was going to do, I said, "Let's see those goggles, soldier. I think I'm getting a little near-sighted myself. Maybe . . ."

And as he passed them to me, I dropped them on the ground.

"Damn! I'm sorry," I muttered. "I just wanted to see if . . . here, I'll find them." And I went pawing over the dark earth with my hands and feet, edging him out of the way until I'd touched them. Then, carefully, deliberately, I ground them to splinters and slivers with my boots. I picked what was left of them up and we just stared at each other.

To this day I don't know if he realized what I'd done, but it didn't matter. I had found an out for both of us.

"Listen, I'm sorry as can be about this. I'm just a clumsy . . ."

"No, no. It was dark. You didn't mean . . ."

"No," I said. "I didn't mean it."

Of course I had to find a substitute for the patrol. Even better, my nervous GI got shipped back to be fitted for a new pair of glasses and when he returned to the outfit in a week or so, you just knew that he had grabbed hold of himself again. And so he eventually made it back to that new baby.

The war went endlessly on. We fought our way through the Maritime Alps until March 1945. Then, we had Top Secret orders for a major move. Every latrine had its own set of rumors, but I don't think anyone was greatly surprised when they shipped us back to Italy; that's the kind of luck the 442nd was running in. It was on this trip that I got a stunning insight into the navy way of wartime life.

As soon as we boarded the transports that were to carry us from France to Leghorn, officers and men were separated. Then a very proper naval type led the six of us from E Company to our own cabin—which only had five bunks. The C.O. and exec were no problem, but our host, in his crisp khakis, obviously had to get rid of one of us smelly 2nd lieutenants. "Gentlemen," he announced, "may I have your dates of rank?" And like a quartet of parrots we gave him the dates of our commissions, whereupon he turned with a sad, what-can-I-do? smile to our most junior member, the new leader of the 2nd platoon, and said, "I'm sorry, you'll have to make another arrangement."

That's not quite the way it worked out. The 2nd platoon leader may have been junior to me, but he was older, wearier, and infinitely more in need of a bed. So I told him to take mine and I found a place on deck to sack out. But we agreed not ever to mention our little subterfuge to the navy brass; we didn't want to upset them when they were trying to fight a war.

Mess was even funnier, or would have been if it weren't so sad. It happened to be Sunday and the naval officers, to a man, showed up in immaculate whites. There was white linen on every table, sparkling crystal and gleaming china, all of which tinkled when they sprang to their feet on the captain's entry. I have this mental image of the rest of us, the poor bedraggled officers of the 442nd in our unpressed ODs, battlefield mud on our boots, just sitting there gaping at the scene as though we'd stumbled onto a remake of *Andy Hardy Goes to Annapolis*. Nor was that the end, not hardly. The printed menu offered a choice of fowl or fish, wine and cognac. The conversation was properly low, the laughter subdued and the cigars heady with the sense of the good life. And all this right smack in the middle of World War II and not 20 yards from the galley where hundreds of GIs filed by, messkits extended, to get the usual wartime ration.

When we reached Leghorn, we were trucked north to an area in the sector of the 92nd Division, to which the 442nd was now attached. The 92nd was one of only two outfits in the army made up of Negro troops. They had fought hard and lost many men and the Germans seemed to take a fiendish delight in bombarding them with propaganda leaflets—a white man making love to a Negro girl, and the inevitable caption: "Is this your wife?" And the taunting questions: "What are you fighting for? To go back to slavery to your white masters?"

Our side didn't help much. The division officers' clubs

were segregated—this in the heart of a war zone—as was every other recreational facility. One of the first things our regimental C.O. did was send word through the 442nd that we were to steer clear of both the white and colored clubs. Since there was no way we could change a rotten situation, he wanted us to be as free of it as we could, and we kept very much to ourselves.

The mission of the 92nd was to breach the western anchor of the Gothic Line, a system of rock and concrete fortifications high in the mountains of northern Italy. Elaborate bunkers and fortified machine gun nests made it seem impenetrable. When the commanding general took our officers on a tour of the terrain and outlined the mission, he concentrated on its difficulty—the enemy's interlocking fields of fire and his unlimited observation down on our positions—and asked whether the 442nd could achieve its first objective, Mt. Folgorito, in a week's time.

"Yes, sir," our C.O. replied drily, "I think you can count on it."

Specifically, our job was to create a serious diversion on the extreme left flank. We wanted Mt. Folgorito because it commanded Highway 1 which led all the way north to La Spezia, but it was even more important for us to lure substantial German forces over from the central area where the main Allied effort was to take place.

We jumped off at midnight of April 5, two battalions moving through an unreconnoitered gorge and scaling the cliffs on the enemy's right. It was as eerily quiet as some other world. Later we learned that some men had slipped and bounced as much as 100 feet down the steep slopes— one fell to his death—but not one of them cried out and the soundless advance went on. We took the Germans by complete surprise. Most of them were lining up for chow when we hit them, and between 5:30 and 7:30 in the morning, all the high points were taken and the ridgeline secured. Barely forty-eight hours had elapsed since the commanding general had asked if we could do the job in a week—and this over terrain that had stymied the best efforts of Allied troops for fully five months.

Not that the Germans were finished. They had only lost the first round. Day after deadly day we were forced to throw ourselves against the bristling hills and ridges, gaining a few precious yards and perhaps a piece of high ground from which we could look across to the next ridge, the next line of fortifications. But we were moving. It was an area where the entire advance had been stopped cold in all the bloody months before, and even with the carnage and the bitter, slogging, inch-by-inch pace, there was a first cautious feeling throughout the 442nd that the end might be in sight. The Allies were nearing Berlin. If we could drive the Germans out of Italy, they would *have* to surrender.

Late one afternoon, Captain Akins called me to the C.P. to assign a mission to my platoon, a mission that I shall never forget. A German force of unknown strength had dug into the valley up ahead of us. A platoon from F Company was to drive on a little village to the left while my platoon moved up and took the village of Altanagna on the right. Then the German force would be caught between us and their position would become untenable. It sounded like a good plan.

I went directly back to brief my men and, with less than an hour of preparation, we moved out down the forward slope. I remember that it was just dusk, a quiet, spring-like evening that in another time and place would have been filled with peace and promise. We were halfway down when the Germans opened up with mortars and machine guns. We hit the dirt and kept inching forward, rushing from one bit of cover to the next, headed for a sad little cemetery just outside the village.

Then one of my men got hit. It wasn't much of a wound, a piece of shrapnel in the leg, and I told him to stay put until the medics came for him. The rest of us moved on. And that man became the only one I was to lose as an officer. Oh, my platoon suffered plenty of wounds, but only this single fatality, this man who must have become frightened alone on that slope and dragged himself into the next valley, and the next, and was found days later, dead from the loss of blood.

From the cemetery, I sent a scout up to have a look at Altanagna, a settlement so tiny that I've never found it on any map. He reported back that a full company of Germans was firmly anchored there and that an attack by our 14-man platoon would be sheer suicide. I radioed this information back to Captain Akins and got permission to stay put until sunup. But in the last light of day, we got a break: the German company, including two armored cars and a troop carrier, moved out across the valley toward the village on the left. I waved my men forward and we rushed in to begin a building-by-building search of Altanagna.

I found myself with two men in the basement of a solid stone structure just across from the church, kicking open doors and ready to throw a grenade at the first move or mutter of resistance. There was no one. Then, behind a heavy oak door in a dark corner, I heard the faintest semblance of a sound. It could have been a rat. It could have been a German. With the men covering me, I rammed a shoulder into the door, my other arm cocked to throw the grenade—and crashed into a room full of nuns. They stood there, hollow-eyed and frightened, some of them so en-trapped by the terror of this deadly entr'acte—one army fleeing, another bursting in—that they had forgotten to cover their shaven skulls. I tried to speak to them, to assure them that we meant them no harm, but even my few faltering words of Italian escaped me, and finally I just closed their door and went back to my men.

I suppose words weren't necessary. When they'd re-covered from the moments of shock, those nuns were a tower of strength. When the Germans counterattacked, they cared for the wounded townspeople, brought water to my men and moved through the village with courage and serenity, so that one could almost believe that the nightmare would pass.

The Germans hit at us twice, and they hit hard. Contrary to the rules of the Geneva convention, I used the tower of the church, the highest point in town, as an observation point—but gave my men strict orders to stay out of the sanctuary—and both times we drove the enemy back. Finally, caught in a crossfire between Altanagna and the village to the left of the valley, one of their armored cars a burning hulk, the decimated Germans fled and our mission was accomplished.

In the dead of night, oil lamps burning, a delegation of men and women of the village came to see me. You could see by their clothes that they were people of consequence in Altanagna, dark, formal suits and dresses, though shabby with age and streaked with the gray dust of war. They spoke through an interpreter and thanked me with Latin profusion for liberating their village, and they said it would be their great privilege if I accepted their humble offering to become the honorary mayor of the village.

I told them that the honor was mine, and that my men greatly appreciated the warmth of their welcome.

Then the interpreter turned back to me. He pointed to three young girls who had been hanging back in the shadows, and he said, "They ask me to tell you that they have brought these three maidens for your comfort, Lieutenant. They wish you a pleasant evening."

It took a little while for that to sink in. I could feel my men standing behind me and watching. I could see the three girls try to slink even further into the shadows. And I made what I suppose was the first speech of my career:

"Tell them, please, that I am horrified by their suggestion. Tell them that I understand that perhaps this was the German way, but that I hoped—we all hoped—they would know Americans to be different. We did not come here to take their women or their food or their lands. We came to bring peace and to take nothing. We are not conquerors, we are friends."

He must have gotten that across to them pretty much as I said it. The older ones sort of hung their heads—one of the women began to cry—then they came up to shake my hand. And the three girls, who must have been dreading a night of wild debauchery, kissed my cheek, the smiles on their faces almost, but not quite, overcoming the shame and the sorrow there.

We were relieved the next day and, having gone into reserve, marched out as the last platoon in line. The villagers lined the streets to wave goodbye to us, cheering for each platoon going by. Except for my platoon. For my platoon they threw flowers. Some day I mean to go back to Altanagna.

Our biggest single advance came on the day word reached us that President Roosevelt had died. Men just got up out of their holes and began fighting their way up. "Where the hell are they going?" the brass hollered at regimental head-quarters, and of course no one in the S-3 section knew. But down on the line, we knew. Every *nisei* who had been invested with first-class citizenship by virtue of the uniform he wore knew. We were moving up for FDR. He had given us our chance and we had a lot of aloha for that man.

Ahead of us now was Mount Nebbione, guarding the critical road center at Aulla and the La Spezia naval base. If we could take those two towns, the enemy's line of retreat to the Po Valley would be cut off. The 3rd Battalion poked at the outer edges of the German defenses on Nebbione and was thrown back. The 2nd Battalion tried circling them from the south and they flung everything they had back at us. We were dead beat now. For two weeks we had been fighting our way up and down 3,000-foot mountains and the men were walking zombies, marching, firing, hitting the ground, marching some more and hitting the ground again, only out of some instinctive memory of what they were supposed to do. The situation cried out for fresh troops, but there just were no such animals in northern Italy in mid-April of 1945.

And yet we could believe that we were close to the end. One day the regimental C.O. called the officers together and said that there was word of German peace feelers. "There's nothing we can tell the men," he said. "It might last another year and they have to be ready to fight on. But it might end next week and I'm telling you so that you won't take un-necessary chances, so that if it does end next week you won't have to blame yourself for some rash action that cost lives you might have saved."

We regrouped on the twentieth and made a new battle

plan. Our battalion was moved to the center of what was to be a three-pronged attack. E Company's objective was Colle Musatello, a high and heavily-defended ridge. In the early evening, Captain Akins called the platoon leaders together and gave us our orders. All three rifle platoons were to be deployed, two moving up in a frontal attack, with my platoon assigned to skirt the left flank and come in from the side. Whichever one reached the heights first was to secure them against counter-attack, for momentum was vital.

I went back to my area and briefed the men. I watched them move off in isolated clusters, seeking some last moments of solitude before committing their bodies again to the fates of war. Many pulled out talismans which they felt, or maybe only hoped had guarded them through all the bloody months past: a St. Christopher medal, a Buddhist charm, a rusted .30 calibre bullet. Some fingered their *sen ninbari*, a piece of white cloth with 1,000 stitches, each of which, in the Japanese tradition, protected the wearer against 1,000 misfortunes. I remember old ladies standing on the street corners of Honolulu with *sen ninbaris* destined for their sons in the army, asking total strangers to sew in a stitch.

Was it all nonsense, a throwback to some pagan time when men did not realize that they could invoke the protection of an almighty God? Who knows? I only know that God was not neglected on that night of April 20. We prayed, deeply, devoutly. And I don't believe you can fault a man who is asked to face sudden death if he seeks a small measure of comfort in some earthly amulet.

The fact is that I had carried two silver dollars, won during my gambling heyday in Camp Shelby, through every campaign. But perhaps I had special reason to regard them as a lucky charm. One was bent and the other cracked

almost in two from absorbing the impact of a German bullet
during the Battle of Bruyères. Since I carried them in a
breast pocket and wore a purple welt on my chest for two
weeks after the incident, I had some grounds for believing
they had done me some good.

And the further fact is that on this night of April 20, I was
suddenly and acutely troubled because they had mysteriously disappeared. I searched the area as best I could in the
darkness, and I asked around, but it was no use. Undoubtedly I had bent forward with my pocket unflapped and
the coins had slipped out, to be unknowingly ground into
the muddy earth by someone's boot. And I suppose they are
still there, in that narrow valley that once served as an
assembly area for the 442nd Combat Team.

I walked back to my tent, shivering a little for the night
had grown cold. I fumbled through my pack for my field
jacket, and *that* was gone. And I remembered: in the heat of
the afternoon, miles to the south, I had put it on the ground
beside me during a break, and when the break was over I
had marched off and left it. I can call to mind the sad,
sinking sensation that settled in the pit of my stomach. My
brain commanded me to be sensible; so I'd lost a field jacket
and two beat-up silver dollars; so what? But from the message center in my heart, I kept hearing forebodings of
disaster.

I went over to First Sergeant Dan Aoki's tent and borrowed his camouflaged parka. I knew he treasured it and I
promised to take good care of it. "But keep an eye on me," I
said. "I have a feeling that tomorrow is not going to be one
of my best days and you may have to peel it off my back."

He didn't laugh. He said, "You bring it back yourself or I
don't want it."

We jumped off at first light. Off to the right, we could

hear the crackle of rifle fire and an occasional machine gun burst as the 1st and 2nd platoons closed on the perimeter of the German defenses. For us, though, it was like a training manual exercise. Everything worked. I walked along directing artillery with my walkie-talkie. What little opposition we met, we outflanked or pinned down until someone could get close enough to finish them off with a grenade. We wiped out a patrol and a mortar observation post without really slowing down. As a result, we reached the western edges of the rise where the main line of resistance was anchored long before the frontal assault force. And we didn't mean to sit there and wait for them. We were right under the German guns, 40 yards from their bunkers and rocky defense positions, so close I had to call off our artillery. We had a choice of either moving up or getting the hell out of there.

We moved, hunching slowly up that slope that was so painfully devoid of cover, and almost at once three machine guns opened up on us. I can still smell that piece of unyielding ground under my face, and hear the *w-hisss* of the bullets tearing the air above my helmet. I lay there for a second, thinking about how neatly they had pinned us here and wondering how long it would take them to get us all if we just lay there hugging the earth. Then I pulled a grenade from my belt and got up. Sombeody punched me in the side, although there wasn't a soul near me, and I sort of fell backward. Then I counted off three seconds as I ran toward that angry splutter of flame at the mouth of the nearest machine gun. I threw the grenade and it cleared the log bunker and exploded in a shower of dust and dirt and metal, and when the gun crew staggered erect I cut them down with my tommy gun. I heard my men pounding up the hill behind me and I waved them toward the left where the other two nests were adjusting their field of fire to cover the whole slope.

"My God, Dan," someone yelled in my ear, "you're bleeding! Get down and I'll get an aid man!"

I looked down to where my right hand was clutching my stomach. Blood oozed wet between the fingers. I thought: *That was no punch, you dummy. You took a slug in the gut.*

I wanted to move on; we were pinned down now and the moment was crucial. Unless we stirred, unless we did something quickly, they'd pick us off one at a time. And I knew it was up to me. I lurched up the hill. I lobbed two grenades into the second emplacement before the riflemen guarding it ever saw me. But I had fallen to my knees. Somehow they wouldn't lock and I couldn't stand and I had to pull myself forward with one hand. Someone was hollering, "Come on, you guys, go for broke!" And hunched over, they charged up into the full fire of the third machine gun. And I was so fiercely proud of those guys I wanted to cry.

Then they had to drop and seek protection from the deadly stutter of that last gun. Some of them tried to crawl closer but hadn't a prayer. And all the time I was shuffling my painful way up on the flank of the emplacement, and at last I was close enough to pull the pin on my last grenade. And as I drew my arm back, all in a flash of light and dark I saw him, that faceless German, like a strip of motion picture film running through a projector that's gone berserk. One instant he was standing waist-high in the bunker, and the next he was aiming a rifle grenade at my face from a range of ten yards. And even as I cocked my arm to throw, he fired and his rifle grenade smashed into my right elbow and exploded and all but tore my arm off. I looked at it, stunned and unbelieving. It dangled there by a few bloody shreds of tissue, my grenade still clenched in a fist that suddenly didn't belong to me any more.

It was that grenade that burst into my consciousness, dispelling the unreality of that motion picture in my brain, and the shock of that astounding and spectral moment in time. The grenade mechanism was ticking off the seconds. In two, three or four, it would go off, finishing me and the good men who were rushing up to help me.

"Get back!" I screamed, and swung around to pry the grenade out of that dead fist with my left hand. Then I had it free and I turned to throw and the German was reloading his rifle. But this time I beat him. My grenade blew up in his face and I stumbled to my feet, closing on the bunker, firing my tommy gun left-handed, the useless right arm slapping red and wet against my side.

My men were running up on both sides of the emplacement. It was almost over. But some last German, in his terminal instant of life, squeezed off a final burst from the machine gun and a bullet caught me in the right leg and threw me to the ground and I rolled over and over down the hill.

For a while everything was quiet. Maybe I passed out. But soon I could hear the 1st and 2nd platoons firing as they moved up in front. I saw blood pulsing out of the nearly-severed arm in regular little geysers and I made a feeble attempt at putting a tourniquet on it. But there wasn't enough upper arm left to work with, so I just fumbled in that mass of muscle and bone until I found the artery and I pinched it closed.

There was a crowd of men around me and someone was

saying, "Let's carry him back," and they were grabbing at my legs but I kicked free.

"Get back up that hill!" I said in a voice that didn't sound remotely like mine. "Nobody called off the war! I want you to set up defensive positions and hold until the rest of the outfit gets here! Report back when you're all set. Get me a casualty report as soon as you can! Now get moving!"

And so they left me there, all alone with what used to be my arm, until the medic came. I asked him to cut the arm off, but he paled and said he couldn't. Instead, he gave me a shot of morphine so that soon I quit wanting to scream out in pain, and before I could stop him he'd slit the 1st sergeant's beautiful jacket clear up the side. Then he finally managed to get a tourniquet around the stump so I could let loose of that artery. "I'll get a couple of men and we'll carry you out of here," he said.

"I'm staying until the rest of the outfit gets here," I said. "I'm okay. You go look after some of the others."

It didn't take long. Captain Akins was among the first to find me. He said I'd be okay, I'd be fine, and I said sure I would, and realized for the first time that whatever else I was going to be, I was surely not going to be a doctor, not with one arm.

I sent for my platoon sergeant, Gordon Takasaki. "You're boss now, Gordie," I told him, "the new platoon leader. Now listen to me. This thing is going to be over soon—a week, a month, soon. Take care of yourself and take care of the men. Don't let anybody get knocked off so close to the end. Understand?"

Dan Aoki came by as they were loading me onto a litter. A lot of men were watching. "So long, Dan," they called.

"I'm sorry about your jacket, Sarge," I said.

"I'll take it out of your hide, Lieutenant." But I noticed that he was crying.

Then they carried me down off that hill. And all the way down I could hear men calling, "So long, Dan."

It was April 21. The German resistance in our sector ended on April 23. Nine days later, the war in Italy was over and a week after that, the enemy surrendered unconditionally.

Chapter VI

A Long Way Home

❀ It seemed to take a lifetime to get down off that hill. The Germans, preparing a counterattack, peppered the forward slope with shells and the two POWs Captain Akins had pressed into service as my litter-bearers had it pretty firmly fixed in their heads that they weren't going to get killed at this late date. With every round that screeched our way, they summarily dumped me to the ground and dove for the nearest shred of cover.

The fact is that between morphine and shock I was pretty well beyond pain. But it took a terrific effort for me to crawl back onto that blood-soaked litter each time and finally I said to the 3rd platoon man accompanying me back, "Let's see that they don't do that again, okay?"

"You bet, Dan," he said emotionally, and when they did, he leveled his carbine at them and would have shot them dead on the spot if I hadn't grabbed his arm.

"I appreciate your feelings," I mumbled weakly, "But they're the only transportation we've got. Just *tell* them."

"You bet, Dan." And starting with a strident, "Achtung!" he told them, and whether they understood his English or not, there was no mistaking that carbine swinging from one haggard face to the other. Thereafter we traveled on the double, barely even changing direction when the 88s whined close.

At the battalion aid station, they fished as much dirt and shrapnel as they could out of my arm and just whistled when they saw the body wound: the bullet had gone in near the right side and come out a slug's width from my spine. Then they put a "Morphine" tag on me, gave me another shot and trundled me into an ambulance for the trip to the field hospital.

I suppose I drifted in and out of coma. Some things stand crystal clear in my mind: somebody yelling to a medic as they were easing me out of the ambulance, "Hold that arm of his, soldier, or it'll fall off of its own weight!"; and a weary-eyed chaplain leaning over me and asking if there was anything I wanted to confess. But hours and whole days are lost in some dark void where I drifted with parched lips and a constant feeling of nausea and wildly-colored dreams of exploding grenades. I remember that first hospital, a tent big enough to house a circus, and all filled with men badly mangled in the machinery of war, all lying under glaring lights and waiting for the team of surgeons who went from table to table snipping and stitching and hadn't even the time to mutter, "Too bad," when they got to a man who was beyond help.

Then they were looming over me, sweaty foreheads and sad eyes peering out above the gauze masks. "Your people were too generous with the morphine, Lieutenant," someone was saying to me. "You might not wake up if we give you any more. You'll have to take this on guts."

I tried to shrug, but by the time I got the message to my good shoulder they'd already started and weren't paying any attention to me. And so I watched the beginning of that operation, the first of eight, and tried not to make any noise when they sliced away the ragged flesh, and wanted to ask them why they didn't just cut the whole damned thing off and be done with it. Then a nurse noticed my morbid interest in the proceedings and threw a towel over my face. Now all I had to occupy myself with was the pain and eavesdropping on the occasional mumbled communication from one doctor to another to the effect that my pulse and blood pressure were pretty rotten. I suppose I should have worked up some concern over that, but the raw truth was that the things they were doing to my arm hurt so badly that dying didn't seem like such an awful idea. As a matter of fact, it hurt so badly that by the time they were finished and started working on the wound in my side it was almost a pleasure.

Someone came around and showed me a bottle of blood. It had a name on it—Thomas Jefferson Smith, 92nd Division—and while they were rigging it for transfusion into my left arm, I thought how funny that was, showing me the blood, like a waiter displaying the label on a bottle of wine for your approval. And because I was to have 17 transfusions that first week, half of them whole blood, I had plenty of opportunity to find out that it wasn't funny at all. A lot of that blood was collected from the 92nd Division itself, and it was shown to the recipient, without comment, as silent evidence that fighting men did more than fight, that they cared enough about each other and the men assigned to their sector to donate their blood against that time when somebody, maybe the guy in the next foxhole, would need it to sustain life. And as I thought about the all-Negro 92nd

Division and looked at those names—Washington, Woodrow Wilson Peterson—it dawned on me that I was being pumped full of Negro blood. I am very, very grateful for it, and wish I could personally thank every man who donated it for me.

Sometime after that first transfusion, I guess they did give me a whiff of something because I remember floating off in that skyrocketing darkness for a long time. It must have been the next day before I checked in again. I was in an enormous ward and still another doctor was looking me over as though I were a fugitive from the law of averages. "How do you feel, Lieutenant?" he said in a melancholy tone. He was a very young captain.

"Not too bad. Did they cut my arm off?"

"No, no. They . . . uh . . . just . . ."

"You mean they're going to save it?" Now he looked as though he wanted to run off and hide. I tried twisting around for a look at my arm but it was under the covers and I hadn't the strength for an extended search. "Look, sir, I want you to tell me what the score is. Did they cut it off or not?"

You could just see him struggling to get a grip on himself. He was really very young. "They couldn't cut it off," he said. "It's turned gangrenous and they'll have to treat that and then sort of build up your strength before . . . they can proceed."

I closed my eyes. So that was that. From now on they could call me Lefty. I think that was the first moment I thought of myself as an amputee. But it's a funny thing— neither then, nor during all the long months of rehabilitation, did I consider myself a cripple or an invalid. It just never became part of my thinking. It isn't part of my thinking today.

"The wound in your side is coming along nicely," the doctor was saying. "No problem."

"Yeah, well, listen, Doc, I think I got hit in the leg, too. I think maybe they didn't notice that."

He turned a little green. But when he whipped back the sheets, there I lay on that immaculate bed in my dirty socks and dirty O.D. pants, an ugly cake of dried blood hardening below the right knee. "Damn!" he said, then bawled, "Nurse!"

"It's okay, Captain," I said. He was terribly angry and it seemed important, somehow, that I pacify him. "This is a pretty busy place."

"Yes," he said grimly, but in ten minutes I was back in that surgical circus tent and they were cutting my pants off and clucking over me like a bunch of nervous hens. This time they did give me a shot of something and when they wheeled me back to the ward, my leg in a fat cast, I felt as though I were midway on a three-day bender. The pain came back, of course, but it came slowly and I could sort of brace myself for it.

It was around this time that I found out Gordon Takasaki hadn't made it. They wheeled some of the boys from my platoon in and I knew there was bad trouble just from the look of them. "What happened?" I muttered.

"Day after you got hit we were ordered to take over some little town up the valley. We got caught in a crossfire. There were a lot of wounded and . . ."

"And?"

"And Takasaki and two others got killed."

I lay back on my pillow trying to breathe normally. I couldn't get it through my head that though the fighting was over three of my men were dead. I thought of Takasaki's parents—he was an only son—rejoicing that the combat was ended; and then getting that telegram—when would it come? today? tomorrow? next day?—that their Gordon was dead.

"He did good, Dan," one of the men was saying. "He was up front, leading us in, when he got it."

"Sure," I said, still a prisoner of the gloomy realization that we had come to within hours of the end without losing a man and then had lost three. It just didn't seem to be fair.

In a few days, I suppose when they became reasonably convinced that I wasn't going to die after all, I was transferred back to the general hospital at Leghorn. And it was there, on May 1, Lei Day in Hawaii, that the gangrene was sufficiently checked so that they could amputate my right arm. It wasn't an emotionally big deal for me. I knew it was coming off and, in fact, had stopped thinking of it as belonging to me for some time. But acceptance and rehabilitation are entirely different things. I had adjusted to the shock *before* the operation. My rehabilitation began almost immediately afterward.

I was staring at the ceiling in the afternoon of my first day as an amputee when a nurse came by and asked if I needed anything. "A cigarette would go pretty good," I said.

"Yes, surely." She smiled and walked off, returning in a few minutes with a fresh pack of Camels. "Here you are, Lieutenant," she said, still smiling, and neatly placed the whole pack on my chest and went on her merry way.

For a while I just stared at it. Then I fingered it with my left hand, trying to decide how I'd go about it if I *did* decide to have a fling at opening it with one hand. I mean, have *you* ever tried opening a pack of cigarettes with one hand?

I sneaked a look around the ward to see if there was

anyone in shape to help me, but everyone seemed to be at least as badly off as I was: this was obviously *not* the ward reserved for officers afflicted with athlete's foot and charley horses. Then I began pawing at that cursed pack, holding it under my chin and trying to rip it open with my fingernails. It kept slipping away from me and I kept trying again, sweating in my fury and frustration as freely as if I'd been on a forced march. In fifteen minutes, I'd torn the pack and half the cigarettes in it to shreds, but I'd finally gotten one between my lips. Which is when I realized that that bitch of a nurse hadn't brought me any matches.

I rang the bell and she came sashaying in, still smiling, still trailing that aura of good cheer that made me want to clout her one. "I need a light," I said.

"Oh," she said prettily. "Of course you do." She pulled a pack of matches out of her pocket—she had had them all the time, the dumb broad!—and carefully put them in my hand. And she strolled off again!

If I had obeyed my first instinct I'd have bellowed after her with rage. If I'd obeyed my second instinct, I'd have burst out crying. But let's face it, I was a big boy now, an officer, and I just couldn't let some female Sadsack get the best of me. I just couldn't.

So I started fooling around with the matches. I clutched them and pulled them and twisted them and dropped them, and I never came remotely close to tearing one free, let alone getting it lit. But by this time I had decided that I'd sooner boil in oil before asking *her* for anything again. So I just lay there, fuming silently, and having extremely un-Christian thoughts about that angel of mercy, Miss Whatever-the-hell-her-name-was.

I was on the verge of dozing off when she came around

again, *still smiling.* "What's the matter, Lieutenant?" she purred. "Have you decided to quit smoking? It's just as well . . . cigarettes make you cough and . . ."

"I couldn't get the damned thing lit."

She tsk-tsked at her thoughtlessness and sat gracefully on the edge of my bed. "I should have realized," she said, taking the mangled matches from me. "Some amputees like to figure it out for themselves. It gives them a feeling of—well, accomplishment. You know. But it doesn't matter. There'll be lots of things you'll be learning for yourself. We only give you the start."

I just gaped at her. I didn't even know what she was talking about. A start on what? Who needed her? "Look," I growled, "just light the cigarette, will you? I've been three hours trying to get this thing smoked."

"Yes, I know." Nothing ruffled her. Absolutely nothing. "But you see, I won't be around to light your cigarette all the time. You can't depend on other people. Now you have only one hand with which to do all the things that you used to do with two hands. And you have to learn how. We'll start with the matches, all right?"

And damned if she didn't open the cover, bend a match forward, close the cover, flick the match down and light it—all with one hand, all in a split second.

"See?" she said.

"Yes," I whispered.

"Now let's see you do it."

I did it. I lit the cigarette. And all at once her smile wasn't objectionable at all. It was lovely. I wish I could remember her name—I'll never forget her face—but all I remember is that she came from Eagle Pass, Texas, and as far as I was concerned she was the best damn nurse in the United States

Army. In a single moment she had made me see the job that lay ahead of me, and in all the weeks that followed she found a thousand subtle ways to help me master it. And in the year and a half that it took me to become a fully functioning citizen again, no one ever did anything more important for me than that nurse did on that afternoon in Leghorn when she showed me how to light a cigarette, the afternoon my rehabilitation began.

There was no whooping and hollering in the hospital on V-E Day. We were glad, of course, but too played out and still too close to our grim memories to feel like celebrating. Besides, if you thought about it—and the men who left a piece of themselves on the battlefield thought about it hard —what was there to yell about? We had beaten off the dictators and the killing had stopped. But for a lot of good guys it was all over, and the rest of us were only halfway home. All day after the news that the Germans had signed the surrender document finally came through I kept thinking about Captain Ensminger and those powerfully prophetic words he'd spoken to us in Hattiesburg, Mississippi, when we were just a bunch of raw recruits:

"The first battle will be bloody. But those who survive it will have a chance to make a world where every man is a free man, and the equal of his neighbor."

So now, at frightful price, the first battle was over. And I had lived enough in the past two years to know that the second battle, though not so bloody, would be just as hard.

The 442nd had run up an awesome record. There were those who called us the most decorated outfit in the U.S. Army. We won ten unit citations and 3,915 individual decorations, including 47 Distinguished Service Crosses and a

Congressional Medal of Honor. But the price was catastrophic. Nearly 700 men were dead, 1,700 maimed and critically wounded, and 3,600 in all had become casualties. The only men in the outfit ever captured by the Germans were a handful of wounded and the medics who refused to leave them even as the enemy closed in.

Captain Akins had promoted me to first lieutenant the day I was hit and recommended me for a Congressional Medal. I guess they only give that to you when you're dead, which is, maybe, the way it should be; instead, I got the D.S.C. to go with my three Purple Hearts. I was proud of them all, of course—and am now—but somehow they didn't seem terribly important at the time. I was concentrating as hard as I could on pulling my mind and body together, and if my nurse from Eagle Pass had given me an award for learning to write left-handed, now that would have been a decoration!

She had all sorts of sly ways of fending off those massive cases of self-pity that some guys used as an alibi not to put out. And she didn't care who she used as her catspaw, or what glaring lies she told with that perfectly straight Texas face. One day she came huffing and puffing up to me and said, "I really need your help this morning. Would you mind taking temperatures for me?"

Now, really, she needed my help about as badly as she needed a second head. The place was crawling with GIs who'd recovered from their wounds while their outfits were pulling out and now served as ward boys while waiting reassignment. Besides which, I hadn't even been out of bed to go to the latrine yet. So she needed *me?* But I had made up my mind never to argue with that gal again. Not after that first time. "Where are the thermometers?" I asked, starting to get up.

She pushed me back down. "Oh, you can't *walk* yet," she laughed. "I'm having them bring you a wheelchair."

"A wheelchair!" I promptly broke my resolution about never arguing with her. "Listen, a pogo stick would be better. I've only got one arm! How the h . . . I mean, how am I supposed to steer a wheelchair?"

"Why, with the other arm, of course. Silly!"

It was another one of those hipper-dipper deals. All of a sudden the wheelchair was there and she had maneuvered me into it—man, for a girl she was a strong one!—deposited a glass of thermometers and a batch of temperature charts in my lap and wished me luck. And there I was, about to take my solo flight in a wheelchair—without so much as a single lesson!

Actually, it wasn't too bad. Oh, I creamed a couple of tables and at least one doctor and spilled the temperature charts—but not the thermometers!—but I got the job done. In fact, toward the last, I was whipping along like an old pro, my left hand swinging from wheel to wheel to coax a little more speed out of the thing, and to steer me out of at least half a dozen disastrous collisions. For a while that morning I felt as though I could take on the world, one arm, as the expression goes, tied behind my back.

But it wasn't for me that that magnificent gal had conjured up this little charade. Although I was as badly beat up as anybody on the ward, I was making a pretty fair adjustment. But some of the others just lay there all day long, gazing uselessly and silently and pathetically up at the ceiling, having long ago surrendered to their pain or their disability and determined to make no effort to fight it. And what a shock the new temperature-taker must have been to *those* guys on that fateful morning when I did my wheelchair solo. There I was in all my loveliness—an ugly stump where my right arm should have been, my right leg in a hefty cast, and a swath of bandages under my GI bathrobe that made me look six months pregnant.

"Here, stick this under your tongue," I'd snap out in my best no-nonsense medical manner as I handed each one a thermometer. "I'll be back to read it in a few minutes." And around I'd wheel to the next bed. In a couple of days I was delivering meal trays!

Now I'm not saying that my antics made new men out of every wounded officer in the ward. But I did notice a couple of zombie types sort of straighten up, their eyes following me as if to say, "Well, hell, if that ground-up refugee from a pine box can tool around here in a wheelchair, the least I can do is *look* alive." And one guy who hadn't shaved himself since he'd been brought in asked me to have the ward boy bring him his razor.

Sometimes my scheming little nurse wasn't subtle at all. "You *must* get through to your friend in the next bed before the operation," she announced to me one day.

"Oh, come on," I pleaded. "I've been trying for a week and now he's due to go up on Wednesday and . . ."

"And if you don't succeed he'll probably never hear again."

And she looked at me in that way, as though in all the wide world only I could help her, and I'd have gotten down on my one good leg and scrubbed floors with my one arm for that blond Machiavelli, and I finally grumbled, "I'll try." And, oh, how I tried.

He was a second lieutenant, a young, blond kid, and I guess they put him next to me because our injuries were so similar—a grenade had just about blown his right arm off.

They'd brought him in the week before, after days of fooling around in the field hospital trying to save the arm. But there just wasn't enough left to put together, and so they'd sent him here for the amputation—and the moment they'd tucked him into bed he'd gone stone deaf.

The doctors talked to him. The nurse talked to him. I talked to him. Everybody had a whack at it. And though he looked as though he *was* trying to hear you, you just knew that not a single sound was registering on his brain. One night my nurse got me on the sunporch and explained all the psychological mumbo-jumbo about how the fact of the amputation was so unbearable to the kid that, in a sense, his mind had forbidden him to *hear* the doctors tell him what they must do. So now, on top of all his other troubles, he was deaf.

"Do you understand how that can happen?" she asked me.

"Sure, I understand," I said, remembering men without a mark on them who couldn't move toward the enemy because they were literally paralyzed with terror.

"Well, then, you must also understand that if the surgery is performed when he's in this state it may never again be possible to help him hear again, or certainly not without deep and extended psychotherapy. And the surgery can't be postponed."

Two days before the operation, I wheeled myself close to his bed. I went through the whole routine again, how they'd cut off my arm, too, and it wasn't so bad. I was managing and he'd manage, and anyhow he was alive and a lot of guys weren't. I said it, I whispered it, I wrote it—and all I got back was that empty-eyed stare and the four words he scrawled on the pad: "It's not my fault."

Somehow that got me mad. I mean, the way he put it, it was as though it were someone else's fault—mine maybe. I took a quick look around the ward, some of the guys were listening to the radio; some others were engaged in a six-bed conversation; but no one was paying any attention to us— and I put my mouth close to his ear and yelled, "Goddam it, it *is* your fault!"

And he heard me. He couldn't even pretend that he hadn't. His head jerked clear over to the other side of the pillow and his face went white and the empty look went out of his eyes—sheer hate was in them now—and he said, "You son of a bitch! You dirty son of a bitch!"

And then he began to cry. I hunched myself up close so no one would see him, and I held his good hand with my good hand, and he cried for a long time. And then he said, "God I'm scared. I'd rather have them shooting at me again than go through with it. But at least I can think about it now. Maybe I can even live with it. Thanks, whoever you are."

"I'm Dan Inouye," I said, and my voice was pretty husky, too. "And I'm telling you that I know damn well you can live with it!"

And he did, too. The time would come when I would teach him how to use two pencils for chopsticks—left-handed, yet!—and he beat me at learning to tie shoelaces. We went on to the hospital at Naples together and only lost track of each other when I was shipped back to the States. But by then he didn't need me. There wasn't any question any more about whether that young lieutenant was going to make it or not.

It was the Red Cross girls who gave us most of the actual therapy. Even in Leghorn, which was not a rehabilitation center, they were on hand just as soon as we were medically ready, fifteen minutes a day, an hour a day, two hours a day, however long our physical stamina permitted us to work our way up that long road back to self-reliance.

I already had a soft spot in my heart for those Red Cross gals. On the first day I was coherent I'd called one to my bedside and explained that I wanted to write a letter home about my wounds, and that, furthermore, I wanted to be certain my letter got there before that grim telegram from the War Department. Could she see to that?

She not only saw to it, but she put my stumbling dictation on paper exactly as I said it so that my mother and father would never have any doubts that it was really me writing, and that though I'd been pretty badly beat up, what was left of me was in one piece. That meant a lot to me. Having to tell my folks that I'd lost an arm was tough enough; telling it in my own way, I could at least soften the blow. It was certainly a lot better than that curt official notification: "The War Department regrets to inform you . . ."

And in all the long months ahead, the Red Cross was forever on hand when I needed them. I'd be less than candid now if I didn't say that I am aware of certain GI resentments against them, stories whose substance I have never been able to track down. I am not here to judge those stories or to judge the Red Cross. I am simply saying that for me, Dan Inouye, in a time of real trouble, they were there.

As soon as I'd learned to look after my personal needs, they taught me to use a knife and fork with my left hand. They taught me how to write with my left hand. And most important of all, they helped me to believe that there wasn't a thing in the world I couldn't do with my left hand, if I wanted to do it badly enough.

One day not long after the end of the war, one of the

platoon sergeants came to see me. He said I was looking great and I asked him about all the men in the outfit, and then he pulled a bulky envelope out of his pocket and tossed it on the bed. "The guys wanted me to bring you this," he said, his eyes having trouble finding a place to light. "It's . . . uh . . . your cut."

"My cut of what?" I asked, fumbling the thing open. Out cascaded a flood of Bank of Italy lira—$500 worth, I quickly counted. "So what else is new?" I said, starting to stuff the money back in the envolope. I wan't about to have anybody taking up a collection for me.

He pulled the envelope out of my reach. "Now take it easy, Dan. It's strictly legitimate. Well, almost legitimate. A couple of days after you got hit, see, we were moving up toward Aulla, or someplace else, I don't remember—man, was that 3rd Platoon of yours a mess after you left . . ."

"Get to the point!"

"Okay, okay. What happened was that we captured this German pay train. I mean it was a whole damn train, six cars, all full of money. Can you imagine that?"

I whistled between my teeth. I was impressed. "So?"

"Well, naturally we couldn't keep it all. Although Ralph said we should. You know the trouble with that guy, Dan, is he . . ."

"*Will you get to the point!*"

"Oh, yeah. Well, they knew at Regiment that we had this thing, I mean, we had all these train guards, prisoners, you know, and we had to take them to Regiment. Although Ralph said—okay, okay, I'm finishing! So we turned the money in, too, along with the prisoners."

There was a pause.

The picture of my father and mother taken in Waikiki soon after their engagement to be married.

Grandmother Moyo Inouye—taken in 1928.

Grandfather Asakichi Inouye—taken in 1928.

DKI, sister Mae Masako, brother John, brother Robert —(from left to right)—taken in 1934.

The Reverend and Mrs. Klinefelter—foster parents of my mother.

Picture of my mother, Lyndon B. Johnson and myself taken in June of 1961 in Honolulu.

Daniel K. Inouye—March 1, 1925 (six months old).

Daniel K. Inouye—June 11, 1926.

Daniel K. Inouye—September 22, 1928—with "ceremonial haircut."

Father and son—December 1946—return from war.

November 1962—Daniel K. Inouye and John A. Burns— election victory night. Burns was elected Governor of the State of Hawaii and Daniel K. Inouye United States Senator.

Honolulu Advertiser photo by Jerry Chong

January 1963—From left to right: John F. Kennedy, brother Robert, brother John, father Hyotaro, Daniel K. Inouye and Maggie. Taken in the Oval Room of the White House.

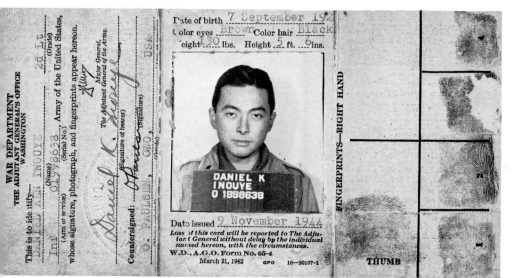

Identification photo, November 9, 1944, taken in France four days after I received my field commission as a lieutenant.

Maggie, Dan and Daniel K. Inouye, Jr.—September 1964. Son was two months old.

John F. Kennedy, Daniel K. Inouye and Lyndon B. Johnson. Taken at the Democratic National Convention of 1960 in Los Angeles.

Official portrait.

"Well, it was all in Bank of Italy lira, see? You could use it anywhere."

There was another pause.

"So we kept a little. Not much, honest. I mean, you should have seen that loot! Six cars full of it. And we divided up the little bit we kept and . . . and this is your cut."

My mind was staggered at the "little bit" they kept, considering that my "cut" alone came to $500. But all I said was, "Thanks, Sarge, it was real thoughtful of the guys." And I made up my mind to unload that money as quickly and as honorably as I could!

A couple of days later, while I was working on my writing with a Red Cross aide, a sudden thought occurred to me. "Say, are you people permitted to accept contributions from servicemen?" I asked her.

"Only the Allies," she said, then grinned. "Listen, we accept contributions from anybody."

"Swell! Get my wallet out of the drawer there, will you, and fish out some money. I want to make a contribution."

She found the wallet and took out a bill, a five, I think. "Thanks so much, Lieutenant. You're very . . ."

"No, look, there's a hidden flap in back. Just pull it out. I want you to have what's in *there*."

And so she found the secret compartment and the $500 and just about keeled over in a dead faint. She flushed beet red. She stuttered. Then suddenly she let out a little yelp and went running down the ward as fast as those high heels would take her. Ten minutes later she was back with the regional director, a distinguished-looking man who acted as though he'd just won the Irish sweepstakes but couldn't find his ticket. He made me a little speech about how grateful the Red Cross was, but that sometimes soldiers far from home made emotional decisions that everyone later regretted. "Now you've worked hard for this money, Lieutenant," he said solemnly. "If you can put it to good use . . ."

"Sir," I said, "excuse me for interrupting. But that money was a . . . a sort of inheritance. I'm positive the Red Cross can put it to better use than what it was intended for. Please take it."

Well darned if he didn't get all choked up trying to thank me and I was never so embarrassed in my life. At least not until that afternoon when he came back with a *Stars and Stripes* photographer! "I think this may be the largest single contribution ever made in the ETO," he proclaimed, beaming. "We must record this for posterity."

And they made me pose with the aide and staged pictures of me handing over the $500, and I squirmed and grimaced and whispered to her, "If I'd known they were going to make all this fuss I'd have let you take the five."

My "contribution" had another interesting consequence. The hospital C.O., a chicken colonel, came around to see me and we got pretty friendly. Which, a few days after they took the cast off my leg, inspired me with a brilliant notion. "Colonel," I said one morning in his office, "I'd like to have a pass to fly up and visit my outfit."

His response was typical of unimaginative men. "Are you crazy?" he roared. "Your arm is still draining, your stomach wound isn't healed and you've only been walking for two days."

"Yes, sir," I said, "but have you noticed now well I'm walking?"

"You're a wild man, Inouye. Where is your outfit?"

"I don't know. Up north somewhere. But I figure I'll hitch a flight to Milan and ask around. I'll find them."

He groaned. "Now see here, Dan, I couldn't possibly issue you a pass. Not a doctor on the staff would countersign it. I've never even heard of anything like this. You're a physical wreck. You haven't any idea where your outfit is. But you want to take off. Have I stated the case correctly?"

"Yes, sir."

"Well all I can tell you is that you've never asked me for a pass and I've never heard a word about any of this. But you damn well better be back here by bedcheck tonight. Do I make myself clear?"

"Yes, sir!" I said, smiling as I gave him a smart left-handed salute.

"And, Dan—good luck."

I had no trouble getting to Milan, which, incidentally, was off limits except for occupation troops. I hitched a jeep ride to the airfield, wandered around until I found a beat-up transport flying north with a load of rations, and persuaded the pilot to put me down in Milan. Those Air Corps types would do anything for you, as long as it was against the rules. Shortly after noon I was wandering around the ghostly city, asking every GI who wasn't wearing an MP armband if he knew where the 442nd was. None of them did, for the very basic reason that the outfit was nowhere near Milan. As I later learned, they had been sent north to Cuneo, near the French border, to man roadblocks and run motorized patrols, so I never did make contact with them. But the trip was far from wasted. It was to give me a last grisly look at the ever-changing, ever-the-same face of war.

It was mid-afternoon and I had been picking my way through the gray streets for some time, long enough, anyway, to become thoroughly depressed. The 442nd was apparently well beyond my reach and Milan, once one of the world's truly civilized cities, echoed disaster and reflected tragedy. Children darted out of the bleak buildings to beg for chocolate, but the handful of adults I saw scurried along the streets as though anxious to be gone from the sight of humankind. And then, as I was beginning to retrace my steps to the airport, I heard a commotion beyond a stone promenade at the end of a narrow street, the growling, raucous sound of a mob, sometimes pierced by the hysterical cry of a woman.

I made my way up the steps and looked out on the incredible scene that stretched beneath me. At the far end of a great stone square, a crowd of ragged men and women was venting its spleen, all the fury and anguish of all the years of bitter defeat, on three corpses. The bodies hung, head down, from the rafters of what looked like a bombed out gasoline station. Men fought to get close enough to stone them, or kick at the shapeless heads, and women held their children high to see.

I turned away, sickened. But I didn't leave that place, not right away. I wanted to *feel* the cries of that mob in my bones. I wanted to know, beyond any possibility of ever forgetting, that the tides of war are violent tides, indeed, not alone for soldiers, but for every human being swept into their tug and haul, tormented beyond endurance by war's cruel and impersonal use of them.

I stood there for a long time, my back to that mob, remembering the ghastly pictures of Mussolini and his mistress, executed and brought to this very city, perhaps to that very spot behind me—it had been less than a month before—their pitiful remains to be beaten and spat upon. And now the same awful act was being played out again. And perhaps all over Italy it was the same, the people wreaking their terrible revenge on the fascist idolaters who had deluded them with visions of glory, leading them down into those dark places of history from which escape had to be measured in shattered lives and shattered dreams. And at last I started down the steps and went back to the airfield.

In early July, I was checked out of the hospital at Leghorn. The next stop was Naples and some more fancy surgery to close up the flap on my arm. Since I was still officially listed as a bed patient, I had to be carried out on a litter, although once we cleared the hospital I persuaded the bearers to put me down until we got to the hospital at Naples, when I climbed aboard again.

The next weeks flew by. When the doctors weren't cutting and molding that poor stump of mine, I was free to go out on pass, and I took full advantage of the opportunity. By this time the worst of the city's ruins had been cleaned up and a small beginning had been made on reconstruction. In any event, Naples certainly looked a lot better than it did on that day, a lifetime ago, when the 442nd had landed there. I went to the opera and the great cathedrals and the good restaurants. I visited Sorrento and Pompeii. And little by little I began to feel that the war was really over, that the world was getting back to normal again.

Two or three operations later—it was the end of July—I was ready to go back to the States, destination: Miami, Florida. It was a great thrill, that moment when they told me, but it wasn't the same as it must have been for other GIs. Home for me was Hawaii, and I knew that I faced more surgery and many months of rehabilitation before I could go home. Still, it was a long step in the right direction and every new tangible token of the U.S.A. went straight to my heart.

One came in Casablanca, our first stop. They piled us into a big ward-like room for the night and at 10:30, just after lights-out, a captain came to the door and stood in the pale light from the corridor and said, "Men, there's somebody here with a message from home for you."

And a slim young fellow moved out of the shadows, although you could still barely make out his face, and he started to sing, "I'll Walk Alone."

"Who is it?" someone whispered, and someone else said, "Frank Sinatra."

And then they were all quiet, and when he was finished there wasn't a sound in all that huge room. Here were men who had been through hell, and had the scars to show for it, and all in one hypnotic moment a singer and a song had reached them so deeply with an image of home that they were incapable of a word or a movement. Who knows, maybe to this day Frank Sinatra wonders how come he laid such an egg in that hospital ward in Casablanca that summer night in 1945. If he does, if he remembers, this is to tell him that that silence was the most profound applause he'll ever receive.

Our next stop was the Azores where everyone lined up at the airport cafeteria and edged anxiously toward a radiant sign that said, "Fresh milk from the U.S. flown in daily, courtesy United States Army Air Corps." Man, did we eat: hamburgers with the works, apple pie à la mode, and enough milk to float us home on.

And at last our plane was lining up with the runway at the Miami airport, and then we were gliding close, and every man was lost in his own thoughts, uttering his own silent thanks in his own way to see again a piece of that blessed green land for which he had put his life on the line.

They took us to Coral Gables, just outside Miami, and the first thing they told us was that the Red Cross had arranged a free long distance call home for every man. There were rebel yells and Brooklyn yippees, but once the guys started taking their turns in those four phone booths, everything grew still again. We were all nervous and deeply preoccupied with what we were going to say, what we were going to hear.

Then they called my name and I went into the phone booth and told the operator I wanted to call Honolulu, and she did a sort of vocal double-take—"You mean, Honolulu, Hawaii?"—and I guess I must have won the prize for the longest long distance call of all. I could feel the perspiration gathering on my forehead as a fantastic network of telephone lines reached out toward that little house in Moiliili— Miami to Philadelphia, Philadelphia to Chicago, Chicago to Los Angeles, Los Angeles to Honolulu. And then my mother was saying hello, and she sounded so terribly near, and for a terrifying moment I couldn't bring myself to speak.

"Hello?"

"One moment please. Your party is on the line. Go ahead, sir."

"Hello? Who is it?"

"Mama?" I whispered, then finally found voice. "Mama, it's me, Dan—Ken."

"Ken!" I could see her at that instant. She would be looking up, raising her eyes in thanks to the Lord, and one hand would be clenched to her breast. "Ken, where are you? Are you all right?"

"Mama, I . . . I'm not allowed to tell you where I am. But I'm back in the States and I'm fine. I'm just fine, Mama."

"Thank God! Ken . . ."

"Please don't cry, Mama. I only have three minutes."

"No, no, I won't cry. Tell me, when will you be home?"

"I don't know. It'll be a while yet. They have to teach me how to . . . to get along with one arm, see?"

"Yes," she said, and there was a long silence.

I asked to speak to my father, but she said he wasn't allowed to place or receive any long distance calls, he was an alien and Hawaii was still a war zone. I asked how he was, and how the kids were, and she said they were all fine, but I could see that something had gone out of her. I suppose that in those few seconds after she heard my voice, she'd fixed it in her mind that I'd be along in the flesh right behind the telephone call. So I told her I would write and not to worry and then, crying, I hung up.

I stayed in Coral Gables only a short time. It was basically a relocation center, from which they funneled guys out to hospitals all over the country. I had a nice time—well-to-do families took us out to dinner and Florida, after all, is Florida—but I was anxious to get on with it. I didn't resent the time they'd told me it would take to get my arm and attitude in shape to face the world—two years they said it might be—but I was restless. I didn't want to dilly-dally. There was a job I had to do and I wanted to get started.

So I was a happy guy when they finally called me in for my permanent assignment. And they were nice about it. They said they liked to place the men in hospitals close to their homes, but since Hawaii was in a war zone that was, of course, impossible for me. "But you can choose just about any city in the continental U.S., Lieutenant," the personnel officer said. "Do you have any favorites?"

"The only one I've ever really seen is Hattiesburg, Mississippi, and the answer is no. How about New York?"

"We can put you in Atlantic City, less than 100 miles away."

"It's a deal!"

And a few weeks later I was aboard a train bound north, about to begin twenty of the most important months of my life.

Atlantic City was wonderful. I suppose the fact that it was so near the ocean gave it a special appeal to me. And beyond that, there was hardly anything you could tell the people who ran the place about the care and feeding of human beings. And there was a lot to be said for the facilities. Instead of a hospital, we were installed in one of those luxury hotels taken over by the government early in the war. Instead of a ward, we were assigned three-man suites. All in all, it beat the stuffing out of a slit trench on Mt. Nebbione in the Italian Apennines.

But of course it wasn't the opulence of the quarters that made this time in my life so meaningful. Nor was it the fact that I learned to function, to be as self-sufficient with one arm as I'd been with two. It was, quite simply, that over the next twenty months this bristle-edged roughneck of an infantry officer was transformed into something resembling a gentleman. Me, a gentleman!

And it was no accident. I was a Pygmalion project, Operation Eliza Doolittle. Some of my new *haole* buddies at the hospital decided they were going to buff the jagged corners off the kid from Moiliili who pretended to know all there was to know about anything worth knowing—but still broke into pidgin-English when he got excited; who had been in some of the best restaurants in the world's most sophisticated cities—and was still more comfortable with chopsticks than with a knife and fork; whose idea of a stimulating evening was a high stakes crap game; and whose favorite before-, during-, and after-dinner beverage was 3.2 beer, and keep it coming! As you can see, there was a lot of raw material to work with and any civilizing contribution my new mentors could make had to be a distinct improvement.

It didn't begin the first day. For one thing, I was much too sensitive about my minority background to even admit that I was anything short of a perfect specimen, let alone express a willingness to learn from a bunch of *haoles*. And for another thing, we didn't really get to know each other until one of our ward mates died.

He was a tall, dreamy-looking first lieutenant from the Midwest somewhere, one of those guys who rarely said much, but if you were in a group you looked for him, and were disappointed if he wasn't there. We'd sit around drinking beer in those early days, just getting to know each other and concentrating on not gaping at each other's missing arms and legs. This guy had all his limbs, but he'd taken a shred of shrapnel across the spinal cord and was paralyzed from the hips down. He got around in a wheelchair, was developing a massive set of arm and chest muscles—and would be dead within a matter of months because his kidneys were ruined.

Everybody knew it. It was one of those pieces of miscellaneous information you pick up about a person, like the name of his hometown or the baseball team he roots for. He very casually told us about it one night—"The docs did their best but there's just no more they can do," was the way he put it—and then never mentioned it again. And darned if he didn't make *us* forget about it. Oh, you knew he had an incurable disease. You even knew he was going to die pretty soon. But you never brooded about it, and surely not when he was around. He was just too *alive*. In that quiet, good-hearted way, he made of us, a bunch of strangers, friends, real friends. If there was a card game, he'd give up his seat to any newcomer. If we were going into town, he'd wheel himself from room to room spreading the word so no one would feel left out.

He seldom talked about his wife. He kept her picture by his bed—a cute little thing who didn't look old enough to date, let alone marry—but only referred to her in response to direct questions. She was going to some teachers' college and still lived at home with her folks. Beyond that, nothing.

Then they took him to the hospital for some treatments, and when he came back he didn't seem like the same guy. He stuck close to his room and if you went around to roust him out he pretended to be napping. One early evening, after dinner, I fell in with his rolling wheelchair—he didn't like you to push him—and asked where he'd been hiding.

"In the sand, like an ostrich," he said.

We kept on going through the lobby and out to the boardwalk. It was one of those autumn nights when summer seems to have forgotten it's six weeks gone; the sky was soft and the trees were still and the breakers sounded for all the world as though they were rolling up on the beach at Waikiki. I was pretty sure he wanted to talk, and I wasn't about to chase him back into his shell with some clumsy question. So I just kept walking, and waiting. In a little while he looked over at me and said, "I run out of steam a lot sooner these days. Would you . . . mind pushing, Dan?"

I stepped around to the back of the chair and leaned against it. On we rolled, past the boardwalk lights and into the darkness, and at last he said, "Do you know, I've never told my wife that I'm not leaving this place alive."

"I didn't know that," I said.

"I couldn't figure out how. She's just a kid. Twenty. It was hard enough to write and tell her I couldn't walk. But I was still overseas then. It was as though we weren't in the same world. But now she's—what?—600 miles away. She could be here in time for breakfast."

"I sort of wondered how come she hasn't been here yet."

"I told her—I keep telling her—to wait. I tell her I may be getting a leave soon. I tell her she can't spare the time from school. I tell her . . . anything that comes into my head."

"And now you're running out of time?"

He looked straight ahead into the dark. "When I was in the hospital I made them give it to me straight. They said I wouldn't make it to Christmas."

"I'm sorry." I put my hand on his shoulder, but he didn't seem to notice.

"I think I can get through it okay. I went through D-Day and then the Bulge, and you know you can only stay scared for so long. But I've got to tell her. I've got to see her and . . . well, I don't know."

"You think it's your fault? You think you're letting her down?"

"Let's face it, it's a dirty trick to play on a nice kid."

"Suppose you got killed in France?"

"It'd be over with, quick. Lots of guys get killed in war. But to make it back home and then die, to know that she's going to be thinking about me dying . . ."

"Can I tell you something? What I think? Quit worrying about her. So she's young, that's all to the good. She'll bounce back. She's got fifty years ahead of her and you've got two months. What you have to do, you have to get yourself through those two months the best way for you. You've got to let her help you. Call her up and tell her to get her fanny down here—for breakfast!—and the hell with her school. Do you understand?"

I was very angry. I didn't understand why. It had nothing to do with the girl, I'm sure, just the rotten unfairness of it all, that this guy should be dying and spending his last days worrying, not about himself, but about somebody he'd been married to for six weeks and hadn't seen in two years.

We walked along a little farther, then he asked me to take him back. I left him downstairs, near the telephone booths, and though his wife didn't show up for breakfast, she was there, by God, at dinnertime.

She was prettier than her picture, with all the freshness of a girl and the beginning warmth of womanhood. And in the next weeks she spent at Atlantic City I never saw her without her man and, when I saw them together, her eyes always seemed to be on him. No one ever knew when he told her, maybe that first day, but she obviously took it like the lady she was, no wailing, no hysterics. Her only concern was him, and so she did help him through those last days.

Toward the end, they threw a little party for us. "It's really for me," he said, "a farewell party," and he absolutely refused to let it sag down in gloom. When one of the guys got bagged on martinis and began drunkenly moaning about what a lousy shame it all was, our dying friend hushed him up. "This is a party," he said, "not a wake." He went through the long evening perfectly composed and did everything that could be done to maintain a party mood. Once he wheeled himself over to where a small group of us were brooding in our beer. "Look at it this way," he said, "I'm just the first to go. All the rest of you will be along sooner or later, and no matter which way they send me chances are I'll see half of you eventually."

Not two weeks later they took him to the hospital in a coma, and by morning he was dead. But he had left his mark on every one of us. We had come there as strangers, a bunch of hard-bitten combat vets with only our grisly war wounds in common. But sharing that great guy was such a powerful emotional experience that it was almost as though we had all been in the same outfit together. We were more than friends. Each of us was deeply concerned with how everyone else was making out. Each of us was ready to help out in any way we could.

For the first time I really came to understand *haoles* as people. I mean, let's face it, you eat and sleep and learn with a bunch of guys, and help change the dressings on their amputated arms and legs, and pretty soon you don't even notice that their eyes are shaped differently from yours. What you do notice is that they're people, the same as you are, with a set of worries and joys that pretty much match your own.

And then, of course, they went to work ironing out those irritating little differences that I'd brought from Moiliili. Like the fact that I couldn't make a "th" sound to save myself. "Hey dere," I'd say, "what's dat?"

One officer who had his M.S. in English once held a mirror up to my little idiosyncrasies of pronunciation, and I didn't like what I saw. "Dat," he said to me, bearing down heavily on each word, "is a thoy thurtle for my son Thom." But long before I could get sore, he'd sat me down on his bed and commanded, "Now put your tongue just under your top teeth and blow. That's how you make a 'th' sound. Come on—try!"

I tried. And I kept trying, not only to straighten out that damned "th" but to untangle my pidgin-English gibberish.

Calmly, patiently, he showed me the way, even writing out exercises for me to practice at night: "A man who aspires to life's heights begins to climb by expressing himself in clear, correct English." The old Dan Inouye would have put it something like this: "Guy who want to get ahead better talk good."

Up until then, the only books I'd ever read were pot-boilers and what was on the required list at school. Now I was eased into Joseph Conrad, Henry James, Stephen Crane, Hemingway and Thomas Wolfe. I didn't like them all, but I could sure see the difference between good writing and *The Mystery of the Beheaded Blonde*. And those I did like, I liked very much, and learned from, and felt uplifted for having read.

Where one friend left off, others began. One man-about-town from Boston showed me how to handle silverware. Another instructed me on wines—"When in doubt, order champagne"—and a third taught me to play bridge, a game I'd always associated with the absolute upper class. I'll have to admit that bridge never gave me the gut-tightening excitement of a good crap game, but on the other hand, these days I sometimes wonder how many people a United States Senator could round up for a crap game. But make it bridge and there's no problem.

I owe a great deal to those men. More than any single grace or amenity, they taught me to feel relaxed and at home among people of all sorts. They helped me to aspire to all that is meant by good and gracious living. You might even say that by washing the grime from my poor boy's face and straightening my *nisei* necktie, they made it possible for me to think seriously about trying for political office. But maybe the most important thing they did was to inspire a kind of awed compliment from my mother. "This is what you learned in the war?" she said when I first came home. "To talk like a *haole* and behave like a gentleman?"

At one of our early orientation lectures at the hospital, a medical officer told us, "We can't make you as sound a civilian as you used to be. For all the advances in orthopedic surgery, no one has yet figured out a way to replace an arm or a leg with anything resembling the real thing. But we're going to do our best, and our best is pretty good, to send you home healed in body and mind, and able to do a few things that maybe you never knew anything about before you came here."

He wasn't kidding. One of the first things they taught me to do was drive a car. "With one arm?" I said doubtfully when they suggested it.

"Wait until you see your instructor," was the reply.

He was an enlisted man and he was missing both hands and both feet. "Frostbite," he said matter-of-factly.

Fitted with a pair of hooks and artificial feet, he could walk, light a match—and drive a car like Barney Oldfield. In no time at all he had taken all the mystery out of driving for me and pretty soon I was tooling along down Atlantic Avenue as though I'd been born behind the wheel, and with only one arm, at that! "Hey, Lieutenant," he said, grinning with real pleasure, "you're terrific. You ought to take up flying next."

"Too easy. The next thing I'm going to learn is brain surgery."

Actually, the next thing I learned was to blow a respectable scale on the trumpet. You'd never confuse me with Harry James—I guess my lips weren't strong enough or something—but it was another small achievement. And once I'd gone as far as I could with *that,* I was content to get back to some serious piano study. This time my teacher was a one-armed former jazz man who could play with the best of them. He also had a wonderfully invigorating attitude about his handicap. "Big deal," he shrugged. "I've had handicaps all my life—I'm colored. What's another one, more or less?" He must have been a good teacher: later on, when some of us gave a little recital, there were those who were kind enough to say that I'd played the best one-handed *Danny Boy* they'd ever heard.

I swam and played basketball and picked up some knowledge of carpentry and plumbing and electricity. They weren't trying to train us in any particular trade or occupation. But without pressure and at a nice leisurely pace, they were giving us the feel of many different skills, some of which we might consider as a means of future livelihood, but most of which were only intended to demonstrate to us that an amputee could *do* things. He could function and required neither pity nor special dispensations.

We had lectures and seminars on every conceivable aspect of adjustment to civilian life. Sex? Naturally. One such session I particularly remember had a doctor, a nurse, a psychologist and an occupational therapist on the panel. We asked questions, some of them quite frank, and each one was answered by the appropriate panel member, with an occasional contribution from the floor by someone personally acquainted with the problem under discussion. It seems to me that we were about finished—I was certainly more enlightened than I'd ever been—when a nice-looking young lieutenant got shyly to his feet.

"I'm . . . uh . . . getting married in two weeks," he said

reddening. "I'm a little . . . uh . . . worried because my . . . uh . . . girl has never seen me without something . . . uh . . . covering this." And he pointed to his empty shirtsleeve.

"Nothing to worry about," the psychologist assured him. "If your attitude toward your loss is healthy, so will your wife's be, and soon you'll both forget it."

One by one the "experts" solemnly informed him that his behavior need be no different from anyone else's, that he was fully qualified to carry out every responsibility of husband and father. It was all topped off by the nurse, a captain, who flatly stated that the young lieutenant had to make absolutely no adjustments in order to lead a complete sex life.

"Now just a minute! *Just one darned minute!*" The voice came from the back of the room and belonged to one of us, a grizzled major with one arm, who planted himself solidly on his feet and had every eye in the place riveted on him when he said, "Captain, Nurse, honey . . . whatever you want me to call you . . . would you mind if I just offered the lieutenant here a word or two of *practical* advice? I mean, I'm sure you know all about this medical science stuff, but when it comes to the sex life of an amputee . . . well, may I?"

The nurse, who didn't know whether to laugh or flee, said, "By all means, sir."

"Son," said the major, speaking directly to the thoroughly embarrassed lieutenant while the rest of us listened breathlessly, "I'll boil it all down to one rule: just be sure she sleeps on your bad side."

"My bad side?" The lieutenant looked appalled. "But, why?"

"Because if she sleeps on your good side, the only hand you've got is, shall we say, neutralized. Which means that unless you've got educated toes, you're both going to miss a lot of the good things in married life."

There was a moment of stunned silence, then a spontaneous burst of applause for the old major who'd apparently done some solid research and come up with "the school solution" to a problem many of us would face. Even the redfaced lieutenant joined in the handclapping after a mortified second, grinning sheepishly, and so did the one-upped nurse.

Of course the thing I had the most of in those months was time to think. And the thing I thought about most was what was to become of me. What was I going to do with my life now that my dream of being a surgeon had evaporated?

I had taken a whole battery of aptitude tests at the rehabilitation center and they showed pretty conclusively that my strengths were not in the applied sciences. I seemed to have a bent for working with people and that suggested a career in social work, teaching or the ministry. In turn, I locked each one in my mind and spent long hours cataloguing the pros and cons. In some ways, they all appealed to me. Yet deep down I knew that I'd never be completely happy at any of them. I had this vague, just-beginning urge to be at the center of things, to strike out in directions never before imagined by my people. What directions? How? I didn't know.

In all that big converted hotel, I was one of only two *nisei*. The other was somewhat older, a captain named Sakae Takahashi. He had been a teacher in civilian life and maybe the important thing that drew me to him was that he, too, was groping toward a more direct participation in the affairs of men, toward that high place where the action was. We'd walk the boardwalk or sit in his room until the small hours of morning talking of home and of our hopes for Hawaii and ourselves.

I made all the usual, uninspired observations—how proud I was of our people, how lucky it was that we were Americans. Sakae agreed, but he was more thoughtful. What kind of Americans were we? As good as all the others? Certainly the 442nd had fought as hard as any outfit in the Army, and the folks back home had been fully as loyal as Americans anywhere.

We were walking that particular night and when I asked, "What are you getting at?" Sakae stopped and looked at me:

"I want to know why I don't *feel* as good as all the others. I want to know why all those *nisei* in California were locked up. And most of all I want to know why there has to be a limit to our hopes."

"Who says there is?"

"Suppose you want to join the Pacific Club."

"Big deal."

"Suppose you want to be Territorial Governor of Hawaii."

We turned and started walking again. I said, "We ought to have that right."

"We ought to have every single right that every single other American has! Man, we shed a lot of blood in this war. What was that all about? Was it all wasted? Dan, I'm not looking to put the blame on anybody. I don't even really care about all that stuff that happened before. What I'm interested in is tomorrow. I want my kids to have every break. I demand it!"

And little by little I began to appreciate what he was talking about. There seemed to be inherent in every American of Oriental descent a certain subtle sense of inferiority.

If they had enough to eat they were satisfied, and never mind that they had to live crammed together in Honolulu's ghettos. If they found work as clerks or shopkeepers, that was as lofty a goal as they dared aspire to. Oh, a handful had become doctors and teachers, but they were the brilliant exceptions, and even they had to know their place.

What Sakae was saying, and what I came to believe with all my heart and soul, was that the time had come for us to step forward. We had fought for that right with all the furious patriotism in our bodies and now we didn't want to go back to the plantation. Times were changing. The old patterns were breaking down. We wanted to take our full place in society, to make the greatest contribution of which we were capable, not for Hawaii's Japanese-Americans, but for Hawaii.

In time, I came to think that I could direct my best effort toward these ends as a lawyer. Nor did I ever envision myself studying law so I could defend the needy and protect the rights of the hard-pressed. From the first, I thought about the law in its purest sense, the law of the land. I wanted to help make the laws. I wanted to become a lawyer so I could go into politics.

Nothing I can possibly say would be an exaggeration of the importance of those talks Sakae and I had. In my mind, there came a gradual gathering together of past and future. History was no longer a catalogue of old heroes and stirring events. It was the shape and real problems and the concern of the very human men who wrestled with them. The things that happened in Hawaii in these next years of promise and change would be the history my children learned in school, and it would mark their lives, and their children's lives, for better or for worse.

Sakae and I became very close. He had a passion for the theater and we often went to New York to see the latest plays. On one such trip, he met and fell in love with a Caucasian girl and an incredibly short time later I was best man at their wedding. We would meet again, Sakae Takahashi and I, fighting side by side in those political battles foreshadowed by our long talks in Atlantic City. He was to become the first Oriental in the Territorial cabinet and is now majority leader in the State Senate. But I still remember him most vividly as an intense and earnest young man, gathering strength to fight that second battle for democracy. When he was discharged and left to go to law school, I felt absolutely bereft and, for weeks afterward, at loose ends.

I worked hard at my rehabilitation. I felt that I had to get everything I could out of it because I was incapable of allowing anyone's sympathy to make things easier for me. Therefore, handicap and all, I'd have to be ready to do whatever a two-armed man could do, and I wanted to stock up on all the training I could get. I didn't even make an exception for the artificial arm they fitted me with, although I hated it from the instant it touched me. It was an ingenious device, a prosthetic appliance that, once mastered, could do almost as much as a human hand. I can't say exactly why it repelled me; maybe it was the hook on the end of it, or maybe it was simply that it wasn't really part of me. But hate it or not I learned to use it. I could eat with it, pick up a checker with it, even shoot pool with it, although I must say that eventually I learned to play a better game with just my one arm. Anyway, once I got the hang of the thing, I took it off and put it away and haven't worn it at all since I returned home.

I left Atlantic City in the summer of 1946 for the final phase of my rehabilitation, nine months of study and training at Battle Creek, Michigan. Nor was it all work. I won a swimming medal, went ice-fishing and whooped it up at more parties than I'd ever have the stamina for today.

It was in Battle Creek, too, that I was indoctrinated into the subleties of discrimination, Mainland-style. In Hawaii, every white man was a *haole*, which, incidentally, is not a derogatory term; it has no racial connotation, and simply means white. Here, though, I noticed the formation of what you might call "secondary" relationships. In combat, a man's primary obligation was to the outfit, so everyone in it was his buddy. Essentially the same thing was true in Atlantic City: we'd all shared a traumatic experience and we were all mending together. But by the time we got to Battle Creek, the worst of our wartime memories and experiences were behind us. The strong and straightforward tie that bound together different men from different places was frayed by the pressures of the moment and they began to clique off according to their ethnic background: the Irish in one group, the Jews in another and the Italians in still another. The Negroes were particularly isolated.

This was no personal hardship on me. I was a kind of freak in their little charade—not black, not white, not Irish, not Jewish—and they all made me welcome. Please note the psychology here. Was I irresistible, such a prince of a fellow that they all wanted me for a friend? Nonsense! I'm a nice enough guy, I guess, but I'm also smart enough to realize that my big attraction was my singleness; as the only *nisei* in the whole place, I represented a minority so small as to pose absolutely no threat to any of the others, so they all welcomed me with open arms.

Still, the whole thing irritated the daylights out of me. I suppose it reminded me of the kinds of discrimination I'd come up against. Anyway, I found myself heavily engaged in a one-man campaign to get them to knock it off. If the conversation got around to race and religion, I'd tell them that all kinds of GIs had gone to war for the U.S.A., and when they got hit they all bled red. If Reilly and Geoghan and Callahan wanted me to go to town with them, I'd say, "Let's take Berman. He's not doing anything."

They'd fight it. They'd say, "Ah, who needs Berman? You want to come or not?"

"I don't think so," I'd tell them. "You guys go ahead. Have fun."

And forced to feel and finger their guilt, they'd yell across the barracks, "Hey, Berman, want to go to town?" And we'd *all* have fun.

Little by little the invisible barriers came down. It wasn't that hard; there were only thirty in our barracks and I can be very persistent. Except that neither I nor anyone else could make the slightest dent in the stubborn shield, composed half of suspicion, half of an inborn sense of rejection, with which the colored contingent protected themselves. Outside of some casual conversation, they mixed with no one, stayed away from the officers' club and even went to the PX in a body. Nor did this insularity have anything to do with a sense of intellectual inferiority. Every one of those men had been to college—a Negro pretty well had to have been to become an officer in the World War II army. It was—what was it?—two centuries of the white man's disdain.

I got to know them as well as anybody, but we were far from close. I did go into Chicago and Detroit with them.

They even got me a couple of dates with Negro girls. But they would let you only so far into their lives, and they froze if you probed their hopes and feelings, as though you were chafing an unhealed wound. Once the brightest and most articulate of the group asked me if I considered myself colored, and I said no.

"Well, are you white, then?"

"No, I'm Oriental, Asian, yellow, if you have to have a particular shade." He seemed to be worrying this around in his mind, so I said, "Would it make you feel better if I told you that I suppose not being white makes me colored?"

He looked at me sharply then. "It wouldn't make me feel anything," he said. "You want to be friends? That's okay with me. But let's both understand that we're different breeds of cat, and let's keep it that way." He made that single "Ha!" kind of laugh. "Man, don't be colored for my sake. If you need somebody to call you nigger, that's your headache. I got plenty of my own."

It saddened me deeply. But it has helped me, in 1967, to understand the Negro's impatience with platitudes and pro-testations of friendship—if only he'll wait for equality until tomorrow, or the day after. He has already waited such a long time.

I was finally discharged, as fully restored as the army's best efforts could make me, in May 1947. But as far as I'm concerned my true homecoming happened a year earlier, when I'd gotten a 60-day leave and wangled myself a plane ride back to Hawaii. I was *still* not supposed to leave the mainland, you understand, but if you've read this far you probably understand, too, that I can't bring myself to do everything by the numbers. I mean, I did have 60 days of free time; there were military aircraft flying between the

West Coast and Hawaii every day of the week; I'd have no trouble hitching a ride. Well, you can see the inevitable line of reasoning that led me home.

But if the idea was mine, I'll always be convinced that the credit for getting me there alive belongs to God. I'd telephoned the air base at Fort Dix and gotten a line on a flight to San Francisco that afternoon. But by the time I'd found my way to Flight Control, about 50 GIs headed west for Christmas were signed in ahead of me. "Sorry, Lieutenant," the man said, "we've got a full load and a waiting list."

I cursed my luck and tried scrounging for something else. The best I could manage was a puddle-jumper to Kansas City—five stops, which would make it an all-night trip, and a good chance of bucking a snowstorm just brewing over Pennsylvania. I took it. We hit the snowstorm, all right, a beauty that bounced us 500 feet with each gust, and we had to come down someplace in Ohio and hole up until it blew over, so that we didn't make it to Kansas City until late afternoon. But at least we made it; ten minutes after landing I picked up a newspaper and learned that the flight I'd missed to San Francisco had cracked up while landing, injuring most of the passengers, though no one died.

Well, that'll shake a man. But you have to figure that those are the odds—luck, chance, fate, call it what you like. My problem was getting to the coast, so I tossed the newspaper aside and went to work. For a while it looked promising. Yes, Flight Control said, they had an Army Air Corps plane coming through for Los Angeles, due any minute, as a matter of fact, and with a couple of GIs from the 442nd aboard! Full of hope, I said, "Any chance of me hitching a ride?"

"You traveling with a priority, Lieutenant?" he asked.

"A priority? No, I'm just going home on leave. I . . ."

"Sorry. That flight's reserved for passengers with special orders and military business. No telling how many will be waiting in Denver."

"I'll take a chance," I pleaded. "If I get bumped in Denver I'll . . ."

But he shook his head sadly and moved to other business, and I was standing there like an idiot talking to myself. So I watched *that* flight take off after only the briefest stop, bound west toward the promised land without me, and I plunked myself down in that dingy lounge with visions of sitting out my whole leave right there, waiting for a seat on a plane home. And in case you're reading this faster than I can put it down, you're absolutely right, *that* plane went down, too! It cracked up in the Rockies with only a handful of survivors, one of whom was one of the *nisei*—who lost a leg in the accident.

It was a special irony. I really wanted to see those 442nd guys and even considered stowing away. Anyway, if escaping death once by such a quirk was chance, I couldn't help feeling that pulling it off twice was something more. And if God kept me off those flights because He has some particular task in mind for me, He'll find a willing worker.

In the end, of course, I did get to the coast, but still had to wangle a flight on that last, long trans-Pacific leg. I managed to hitch a jeep ride from San Francisco to the Air Corps base at Hamilton Field, and promptly ran into fresh trouble. As I checked through the guard post at the entrance, a captain—I suppose he was officer of the day—noticed that I returned the M.P. sentry's salute with a nod of my head, and he came storming through the door.

"Where'd you learn your military courtesy, Lieutenant?"

he bellowed at me. "That guard is entitled to a salute. It's officers like you that make it so tough to maintain any sense of discipline in this man's army . . ."

He ranted on and on while, in the narrow confines of the jeep seat, I tried to get my overcoat open. Then he noticed what I was doing:

"Listen, don't show me your ribbons. They don't excuse . . ."

"Captain," I finally broke in, "you haven't given me a chance to say anything so I was trying to show you, not my ribbons"—here I finally got my coat open and pulled my hook out—"but the fact that I don't have an arm to salute with. I don't think you'd want me doing it with a hook, would you?"

I thought the poor man was going to burst into tears. He started to apologize, couldn't make it, leaned close and just touched my shoulder. "I didn't know," he whispered at last. "I . . . didn't know."

"Forget it, sir. No harm done."

"No, listen, where are you bound? Is there anything I can do for you?"

Well, that's how I got my ride home. I told that captain my problem and he just about broke his back to get me a seat on a troop carrier flight bound for Hickam Field that very day. That's what I call really atoning for an error.

And sometimes when your luck changes, it really changes. I had to wait to board the plane, since it was done by rank and I was very nearly the most junior passenger. And somewhere in the lounge, the most senior officer, a brigadier general, noticed me. Anyway, once we were aboard, he sent his aide back to my seat to ask if I'd like to join him up forward. And so he was my seatmate on the trip, and given his rank, the service was as good as the company. We chatted about Hawaii—this was to be his first visit—and I told him a little about the ins and outs of Honolulu. He asked if this was my first trip back and I said yes. He asked if I had a ride home and I said no, and thought no more about it until we bumped down at Hickam, just past midnight. No sooner had the props stopped spinning than a staff car with a gleaming single star on the front bumper came tearing up under the wing.

"There's your ride, Lieutenant," the general said with a smile. "Just tell the sergeant where to take you."

"But . . . but that's your car, sir," I stammered. "How will you . . ."

"Oh, I imagine I'll get a lift somehow. But I want you to take my car tonight." And he didn't look at my hook when he said, "It's little enough for what you've given."

And so Dan Inouye, who'd barely made it into the army and had gone off to war with a uniform that didn't fit and high hopes of making corporal, came home in a general's car, a staff sergeant carrying his bag. I had called from the terminal—"Hello, Papa, I'm sorry to wake you up, but I'm at Hickam Field and I'll be there in twenty minutes"—and now as I stood outside the house in the still, deserted street I suddenly couldn't believe it. Was I really home? Had all those incredible things happened to me in the more than two and a half years that had passed since I last saw this place? Then the door opened and light poured into the dark street and my mother was saying, "Ken?"

I had my arm around her and felt her tears. I had my arm around all of them, my father, my sister May who had been a child when I left and was now grown and beautiful, my brothers John and Robert flushing with embarrassment and the pride plain in their faces. It was a sublimely happy moment, that homecoming, those few first minutes when we dispelled the long years with our joy and gratitude.

John took my bag from the sergeant, who saluted smartly as he left. Robert took my coat and May brought me a chair. "Shall I bring you something?" my mother whispered. "Tea? You're hungry! I'll make . . ."

"No, no Mama. I'm fine."

I was. I looked around the house, my home, suddenly grown smaller and yet just the same. There was the picture of President Roosevelt on the wall, with one of me next to it. A blue star hung in the window. When I turned back, they were all looking at me, at my uniform and the ribbons on my chest, and, of course, at the hook. Now there had come that moment of awkward silence, the fumbling for a thought after the first heedless and loving greeting.

I lit a cigarette—tense, stomach tight—and had taken a deep-down drag before I realized what I was doing. May's eyes widened. My father, who must have had a pretty clear idea about my little vices—he'd once sent me a cigarette lighter, cautioning me never to mention it to my mother—tried to pretend he was in another city. And Mother came to her feet as though pinched.

"Daniel Ken Inouye!" she said in exactly the old way.

I looked sheepishly at the cigarette, then at her, then at the rest of them. And then we all began to laugh, my mother, too, and I knew that I was home.

Chapter VII

No Man Is an Island

※ In 1924, the year I was born, Americans of Japanese ancestry made up a bare five percent sliver of Hawaii's voting population. Less than twenty-three years later, when I was finally discharged from the army and came home to stay, the *nisei* were the largest single voting bloc in the islands, having accounted for three out of every ten ballots cast in the previous year's election. They spurred no social upheaval with their votes then, the usual comfortable Republican majorities were returned to the Territorial legislature, but one could hardly help feeling a certain stir in that postwar spring. There were more Oriental names in the House of Representatives. Good solid Chinese and Japanese families were moving into the better neighborhoods, and the *haoles* were making room for them without a murmur. Hawaii seemed at a turning point in history, gathering breath as it made ready to push off in directions never before imagined. One could almost feel the ferment of impending change. A quiet revolution was brewing and it was an exciting time to be alive.

201

The 442nd was very much a part of what was happening. Nor was it only that we had fought valiantly for our country and wanted now to taste the fruits of victory. It was more subtle. For all our Anglo-Saxon first names, we had gone off to war as the sons and grandsons of immigrants, heirs of an alien culture and very much expected—and, I suppose, expecting—to resume our unobtrusive minority status if and when we returned. But the army had given us a taste of full citizenship, and an appetite for more of the same. We were the "can-do" outfit and we were heady with a sense of ourselves: all those medals and citations proved something, didn't they?

The feeling was infectious. It spread to the old folks, and those were jubilant, heartwarming days for them. The 442nd was toasted and paraded and written about, but our mothers and fathers were the ones who understood, better than any homecoming GI, what we'd brought back with us. They walked tall and proud then, and it was a far cry from the bitter "Speak American!" days.

And if you were young in Hawaii in that pivotal year, if you were ambitious and believed implicitly in the promise of the Declaration of Independence, what did it matter that you had only one arm? You had given it for America and America, at last, was yours.

There was, of course, the great wild spree of homecoming celebrations. There were boys I hadn't seen in years, and we toasted each other in boilermakers; and there were so many others I would never see again, and those of us who had survived toasted them, too. There were weddings, long delayed, and parties, long promised, and they seemed to run one into the other, and every time two 442nd vets met on the street that was reason enough to start some fresh drinking. And, inevitably, there was the time my buddies brought me home reeling and roaring, three sheets to the wind, gloriously stoned. Inevitably, my mother was waiting up for me. If she said anything in those first fuzzy hours I am the last person to ask about it. I remember only her constant scurrying to my bed through the night bearing a pan and a damp cloth, and in the early morning her heartbroken sigh, "Ken, Ken," less in rebuke than in the stunning realization that her oldest boy was mysteriously, and in some ways, not very satisfactorily, grown up. Nor did she ever acknowledge the episode again, except to quit the Women's Christian Temperance Union, a group in which she had been active all her adult years. Naturally I didn't mention it, either, but I certainly acknowledged it; once those exuberant homecoming days were behind me, so, too, was my brief and stormy romance with the cup that cheers. I like an occasional cocktail before dinner now, and perhaps a nice wine with it—but that's it!

Once I was back to normal living, the first thing I did was register for classes at the University. I remember talking with my old friend and teacher Dr. Hamre, and how hard it was for him to accept the fact that I was giving up my dream of medicine. "You'd make a fine internist, Dan," he said, "or a radiologist. There are any number of branches of medicine in which you don't need . . ."

The poor man's voice trailed off in embarrassment and I had to help him: ". . . two hands? Sure, you're right, sir, but you know how it's always been for me. A surgeon or nothing." We stood there awkwardly for a moment, then I said, "Anyway, I feel compensated. I *want* to be a lawyer. When I was a kid I used to go to sleep thinking about all the sick people I was going to help. Now I think about *all* the people and *all* their problems, and I'm not worried about not having enough to do."

I worked hard at my pre-law courses and got good, though not spectacular grades. I was elected to the Student Council and was active in the 442nd Veterans Club and eventually served as a two-term commander of the Disabled American Veterans Oahu chapter. And I promptly became involved in a great controversy over, of all things, the grave markers in the national cemetery at Punchbowl.

Ever since the GIs who had fallen in World War II were returned to the Islands, their graves had been marked with temporary wooden crosses. Slowly, however, pressure had been building up, especially among the religious leaders of the Hawaiian community, for a system of permanent markers. Finally, in 1949, the Quartermaster Corps, charged with maintaining the cemetery, announced that it would begin replacing the temporary crosses with permanent markers, and it was universally assumed that these would be the traditional crosses. People had an image of the crosses in the military cemetery of Flanders Field and orators invariably referred to ours as a Christian nation.

And so it might have been, if some of us hadn't objected. The first logical question is what business was it of mine? And the answer is that the Territorial legislature, desiring to pass a resolution indicating to the Congress of the United States what kind of memorial markers it favored for the national cemetery at Punchbowl, was holding a hearing on the subject and I, as the local commander of the Disabled

American Veterans, had requested the opportunity to make a statement. The next question—why my statement opposed the crosses—has a more subtle answer.

The cross, a hallowed symbol to me personally, represents Christianity. But I knew that many of the men who had fought beside me in Italy, some of whom now rested forever in Punchbowl, and some others who had died on Guadalcanal and Iwo Jima and in other long forgotten Pacific Islands, were Buddhist or Jewish or had no formal religious beliefs at all. They were surely in no position to speak up for themselves. Who, then, would defend their right to lie in death with the same spiritual convictions they had borne in life? In the case of the *nisei* of Buddhist faith, certainly not their aged parents, so long taught to hold their peace and suffer their indignities in silence. And though it was no secret that not every grave in Punchbowl was occupied by a Christian, neither was it a matter of much concern to the vast majority of Hawaiians who, without malice or prejudice, simply wanted a lovely memorial for their boys with row on dramatic row of silent white crosses. And so, since there seemed to be no one else ready to speak up for the dead, I took on the job. I did it reluctantly and with misgivings, but they were my buddies and I believed it was what they would have wanted.

I made my position clear in the statement to the legislative committee considering the cross resolution. I spoke to them, I said, as a local commander of the Disabled American Veterans. I reminded them that the dead in the national cemetery represented different religions—and that a few claimed no religion at all. What happened to our vaunted freedom of religion if, by government edict, we marked them all as Christians? Where was the fairness, the simple respect, owed to those who had given up their lives for this country?

There was the kind of reflective quiet I had learned to recognize as that moment when a point of view is on the very brink of prevailing, and into that moment I threw my counter-proposal. Instead of rows of standing crosses, why not create a true memorial park by placing a flat marker at each grave, to be inscribed with the name, dates of birth and death and religious symbol of each man—a cross for Christians, star of David for Jews, wheel for Buddhists and nothing at all for non-believers.

So it was. I am gratified that Punchbowl today is a tranquil and lovely resting place for thousands of brave men, unmarred by a subtle, unintentional religious bigotry. Not that the matter was closed insofar as I was concerned. To the chagrin of everyone who felt that the legislature had evolved a fair and reasonable solution to a knotty problem, I was hailed before a board meeting of our council of churches and called on to explain how I, as a good Christian, could have fought against Christian interests.

"Gentlemen," I said, "that is simply not an accurate statement of the facts. I have never acted against the good interests of my church. As a Christian, I am called upon to uphold and propagate my faith, and I have done so. But as an American, I am taught to believe—and *do* believe—that the religious faiths of others call for my full tolerance and respect. It may be that such tolerance and compassion will some day persuade our friends of differing faiths that ours is God's way. But surely we will never achieve that goal—or any measure of mutual understanding—by forcing them to bend to our will on the grounds that we outnumber them."

Not another word was said. The battle of the crosses was over. But I suppose there remain yet some devout churchmen who consider me a heretic, or, at the very least, a misguided radical.

In the summer of 1947, I was signed up as a member of the Democratic party by that onetime police captain, John Burns, who, in those dangerously tense days after Pearl Harbor, had publicly expressed his confidence in Hawaii's Japanese-American community. In a time when most people —and many officials—were loudly worrying about the Islands' security because of the "foreign" element in our midst, Jack Burns wrote a letter to the newspaper declaring that he wasn't worried at all. In his capacity as a police officer, he said, and as the man charged with responsibility for civilian intelligence matters, he had yet to see or hear anything that would lessen his full faith in the loyalty of Hawaii's Americans of Japanese descent. It is difficult now to fully understand how much courage it took for an official to make such a statement in those nervous days after Pearl Harbor was bombed. But the *nisei* understood, and they remembered, and their feeling of aloha for Jack Burns runs strong to this day.

For each of us, you see, bore our private and rankling hurts at the hands of *haoles* who didn't understand. Mine happened in the doorway of a barbershop outside San Francisco. I had been discharged from Percy Jones General Hospital in Battle Creek and was on my way home for good. Naturally I wanted to look my spruced-up best and a day or so before the troopship left, I went to this barbershop in one of the towns ringing San Francisco—and got as far as the door.

"Are you Chinese?" the man said to me.

I looked past him at the three empty chairs, the other two barbers watching us closely. "I'm an American," I said.

"Are you Chinese?"

"I think what you want to know is where my father was born. My father was born in Japan. I'm an American." Deep in my gut I knew what was coming.

"Don't give me that American stuff," he said swiftly. "You're a Jap and we don't cut Jap hair."

I wanted to hit him. I could see myself—it was as though I were standing in front of a mirror. There I stood, in full uniform, the new captain's bars bright on my shoulders, four rows of ribbons on my chest, the combat infantry badge, the distinguished unit citations—and a hook where my hand was supposed to be. And he didn't cut Jap hair. To think that I had gone through a war to save his skin—and he didn't cut Jap hair.

I said, "I'm sorry. I'm sorry for you and the likes of you." And I went back to my ship.

Now it was 1948 and Jack Burns, who did understand, was retired from the police force and active in politics. In fourteen years he would be Governor of the State of Hawaii, but anyone who might have made such a prediction in 1948 would have been led off to have his head examined. Apart from the Republicans' customary prosperity at the polls, the Democratic Party seemed in an unusually bleak state of disrepair.

Even my more broad-minded friends were concerned when they heard I'd cast my lot with this ragtag outfit. "Think about your future, Dan," they said. "If you have to get involved in politics, why don't you join the Republicans?"

"Because I don't believe in their principles."

"Oh, come on, buddy, what's the difference between them, except that the Republicans are in and the Democrats never will be?"

This argument always irritates me. I happen to believe that there is a deep and fundamental difference between the two major parties in our country, and I don't think I've ever crystallized it better than when I told my friends, "The difference between them is that the Republicans' chief concern is property, things, what we own; the Democrats worry about people—what we are."

I don't know if I convinced them, but I didn't much care. Politics was all new to me, supercharged with excitement—a real-life game in which the stakes were the ideas and people you believed in—and I knew from the very beginning that I was in it to stay.

Before the war, the Republican grip on the territorial legislature had been ironclad. Economic power was still hard-held by the few dominant Caucasian families descended from the missionaries and traders who had organized the Islands' commerce 100 years before and created moneyed empires in banking, wholesaling and shipping—the Castles, Cookes, Baldwins, Damons, Athertons, Robinsons and, most pervasively powerful of all, the Dillinghams. Their economic interests were best defended by the Republican party and their newspapers diligently preached the Republican message and their plantation supervisors hustled the Republican vote. In 1941 they were still tying the ballot pencil in such a way that, even in the privacy of the curtained booth, a field hand voting for a Democrat might just as well shout it from the top of a palm tree. Not surprisingly, few did.

Now it was 1947 and there was a war behind us and John Burns and a handful of others wanted to change all that. I became their willing disciple. We believed that the Democratic party was the natural home of the *nisei,* and of all the disadvantaged multitudes whose labor helped to build the great fortunes.

We started out by aiming for the moon. In 1948, there was to be an election to choose a delegate to the United States Congress. This was the most important office the people of Hawaii had it in their power to offer. The incumbent and already avowed Republican candidate for re-election was Joseph Farrington, a man who had everything on God's green earth going for him. His father had been governor. A highway and a high school were named for the Farringtons, and Joe, politically attractive and personally popular, was president and publisher of Honolulu's largest daily, the *Star-Bulletin.*

Go fight City Hall.

Well, we decided we were going to. Nobody, though, was expecting miracles. As a matter of fact, we would have been happy to come up with a reasonable candidate. In the summer of 1948, whenever two Democrats got together, the first question they asked each other was who the party could put up to run against Joe Farrington. And the days grew longer and hotter and still there was no answer. Then reading the paper one afternoon, I came across an article in the back pages, so small the proofreader might have missed it, that said that John A. Burns, chairman of the Oahu County Committee of the Democratic party of Hawaii, had announced his intention to run for the Delegateship. That was all.

I knew Jack Burns, but not well enough, not then, to do

what I did. But I was such an amateur in the professionals' ballpark that I picked up the telephone, asked for Burns, told him I'd read the article and asked him if he thought he could win.

Now Jack's political hallmark is absolute honesty. And he gave me an absolutely straight answer. "No," he said, "but that's not going to keep me from trying my hardest."

"But if you did win, you'd give it everything you had, right? You'd be a good Delegate?"

"I think I'd be a good Delegate," he said slowly, "Yes. I have strong feelings about Hawaii and its people. I think I know their problems. And I think I can express to Congress our great desire for statehood."

"Jack, do you need some help?"

He laughed. "No one ever needed it more. Can I count on you?"

"For anything at all."

When I hung up, I sat back to do some hard thinking. I had committed myself to a candidate. That Jack Burns was to become my political godfather, that we would fight for the same things and work closely together over the next twenty years, I then had no idea, of course. But I did know that I admired and greatly respected him and I felt good about being on his side. Nothing that has happened in all the years since has ever changed that feeling in the slightest. And because Jack Burns has loomed large in my life, I think there are things about him that I ought to tell.

For instance, when he spoke of Hawaii's desire for statehood, it was with special feeling. Most people wanted it, yes, and it was certainly a popular political issue. So the politicians talked about it—and did nothing. Someday, they said, but the day was always in the far, far future. Jack Burns, though, felt the statehood issue deep in his heart. He believed it to be a sheer injustice that it was denied to us, and he chafed under the second-class citizenship inflicted on all of us because Hawaii remained in territorial status. Therefore when he said that he could express to Congress the people's great desire for statehood, I believed him.

His formal education consisted of one year at the University of Hawaii. Then he had to go out and earn a living. But he is one of the most intelligent and best-read men I know, and he has done it all on his own, finding genuine pleasure in erudite works of philosophy and history, able to quote sections from St. Thomas Aquinas, Jefferson and Jackson. Not unnaturally, his great love was the history of the Hawaiian people.

He left the police force because he felt he could do more for Hawaii if he became fully active in politics. It was a great financial sacrifice. He and his wife opened a little store to support themselves, but what small profit they made was usually sacrificed in gifts of food to the poor and needy.

And they shared a great personal tragedy. Burns was still a member of the Honolulu police department in the 1930s when his wife was suddenly stricken with a particularly virulent form of polio. There was nothing to be done, said the doctors, no cure, no treatment, and Mrs. Burns was destined to spend the rest of her life in a wheelchair. It was a turning point, as much for Jack Burns as for his courageous wife. Until that time, he had not been very different from most men: he enjoyed an occasional evening out and a drink or two, and what was not accomplished today could surely be done tomorrow. Now, though, he saw himself as mother *and* father to his son and daughter, as well as an unfailing companion to his wife, and without fanfare or dramatic announcement he never took another sip of liquor. To this

day, though the demands of his office may call for a toast to
government officials and foreign dignitaries, he does it in
water. Always a devout Catholic, he became a daily com-
municant, going to mass every morning no matter how great
the temptation to sleep in. Many times during our long
friendship we have gone together to conventions and caucuses that lasted as late as four in the morning—and at 5:30
Jack Burns is up and about, preparing to be at church for
the 6 A.M. mass.

Some time later, Mrs. Burns became pregnant. The doctors were horrified. There was every chance that neither she
nor the child would survive the birth, they warned, and
assured her that the church would certainly sanction a
therapeutic abortion in the dangerous circumstances. But
Bea Burns had a character to match her man's, strong-
willed, unbelievably high-principled, and she simply said
that she wanted that child and meant to bear it.

Among the Burns' close friends in the Japanese-American
community was an able masseur, Professor Seishiro Okazaki.
From the pall of worry and gloom settled on those who knew
the Burns' best, he stepped forward with a hopeful and
concrete suggestion. Skilled massage, he said to Jack, had
been known to strengthen seemingly dead muscles. If Bea
were willing, he would treat her every day, and though he
promised nothing, his words were gratefully received after
the leaden pessimism of the doctors. And so the Burns'
moved from their home in Kailua on the far side of Oahu to
a small flat in Honolulu to be near Professor Okazaki's office,
and every day, for hours at a time, he massaged her lifeless
limbs. And the baby, a boy, was born in perfect health and
there wasn't a happier couple in the Islands than Jack Burns
and his wife Beatrice.

"I have no money," Jack told his friend Seishiro Okazaki,

"so it may take me a lifetime. But I'm going to pay for what you've given me. You've filled Bea's life and you've given me something beyond what money can buy, another son."

Okazaki smiled. "John," he said, "if I were interested in money I'd have found a rich patient. I did this because you are my friend."

Jack and Bea talked that over. And they decided that if money was not the answer, they would have to show their gratitude another way. And so the boy was named James Seishiro Burns. Today he is a successful Honolulu attorney, and probably the only Irishman in Hawaii with a Japanese name.

Until the day she became first lady of the state, Bea Burns never had a maid or servant in her house. Sitting in her wheelchair, she did all the family's cooking and housework. Though a virtual prisoner in the house, which had steep steps, she never uttered a word of complaint, nor did her husband; nor did they ever find anything but the highest happiness in each other's company. Those are the kind of people the Burnses are, and I'm proud they are my friends.

A few days after I'd called Jack with my offer of help, he asked me to come to a meeting of his campaign committee. It consisted of six people, including himself, and the total campaign fund came to $300. I wound up on the executive board of the campaign committee. I made speeches, raised funds, sat up night after night plotting strategy and searching for some magic ingredient to persuade the voters that after decades of Republican rule, the Democrats deserved a chance to move Hawaii into the sunshine of full equality—social equality for all the people on the Islands, political and economic equality for the territory with all the 48 states of the mainland. My first speech was to a compact and re-strained little group on the island of Hawaii—I paid my own way there—and failed to start a stampede for the Burns bandwagon. As for campaign expense, most of the money we raised came from the pockets of the executive board. But I did contribute to a breakthrough that would have a lasting effect in campaigns to come.

In those early postwar days, most veterans of the 442nd were about as political-minded as a three-year-old stretching for the cookie jar. They wanted a broader and better life for themselves and their families, but as a baby doesn't realize that someone has to help him reach the cookie jar, so had it so far failed to occur to the returning GIs that the good things they aspired to might be available through their elected representatives in the territorial legislature and the U.S. Congress. And the few who had good things to say about politicians, from force of habit, usually said them about Republican politicians.

About this time, I was elected to the Board of Directors of the 442nd Veterans Club, then in the full warm flush of its popularity. We had grossed $250,000 at our first fund-raising affair and were everybody's favorites. But as it happened, Joe Farrington was the club's favorite. This was hardly surprising, since he'd kept in touch with many of the men during the war and even visited us during training at Camp Shelby. But it certainly made things tough for John Burns. Farrington was invited to address the club and was guest of honor at a big birthday party, but Burns—although an honorary member of the 442nd because of his courageous stand on behalf of the *nisei*—was left out in the cold.

I raised this question at a board meeting and was told that politics had no place in the club. "I agree with you," I told them. "But you are the ones who are giving this whole situation political overtones. You offer Farrington a forum and you give Burns the air. What do you suppose people are thinking?"

They got the hint. The upshot of the matter was that both Farrington and Burns were invited to address us, three minutes each and no politics. But the real result was to show the world that the 442nd Veterans Club took a Democratic candidate for high office seriously.

I wish I could go on to say that Jack Burns won the election. He didn't. The time was almost, but not quite, ripe. But that campaign did demonstrate that the Democratic party welcomed and cared about the returning GIs. In the years just ahead, the *nisei* flocked to sign up with us and, inevitably, the balance of political power turned. Eventually John Burns did become the delegate to Congress—and helped Hawaii achieve statehood. Ever-growing numbers of 442nd vets were elected to the legislature and town councils. And that seemingly fruitless campaign of 1948 was to have a very profound effect on my own future. Meanwhile, there was yet some groundwork for me to cover, and it was to take me back to the mainland.

There was a girl. My parents knew her parents and I had seen her around college—she was an instructor or something—but I hadn't ever met her. Then in the winter of 1947, a week before Thanksgiving, someone introduced us and, in the unlikeliest circumstances, I promptly decided that I was going to marry her. I don't think the possibility of marriage had ever even occurred to me before that moment, but afterward it never left my mind. Everything I had and wanted to have suddenly became absolutely meaningless unless Margaret Awamura would share it with me.

We had been to a football game, five or six of us, and had driven back to Waikiki to get something to eat. As we were walking up to the restaurant, dressed as we were for the game—sandals, denim pants, plaid shirt—a fellow I knew casually, a dentist, called to me from across the parking lot, then began walking purposefully toward me, leading a girl by the arm. I thought this was a little odd—I mean, I really barely knew the guy—until he came close enough so that we could all see the girl. Then I understood. He was showing her off, and I didn't blame him.

I recognized her, of course, but somehow it was as though I were seeing her for the first time. She was pretty, but it was more than that. There was a kind of warmth about her, a quiet, contained exuberance that made you feel good about just being in the same city with her. She was smiling at me and I hope I had the good sense to smile back.

"I want you to meet my girl friend, Dan," the guy was saying, "Margaret Awamura."

I don't remember what I said. It was hard to refocus my brain in the backwash of his insanely shattering statement. *His* girl friend? His girl friend, indeed! How the hell could she be his girl friend when *I* was going to marry her?

Somehow the evening ended. My heart was certainly not in it once Margaret Awamura said goodnight and disappeared into the darkness, and it was a relief to get back home, alone and able to think about her without worrying that the wide world was reading every thought on my face, as though it were printed there in capital letters.

I had never felt anything remotely like this before. I had

gone out with lots of girls, liked some better than others and enjoyed myself with all of them. That's what girls are all about, right? To laugh with and dance with and kiss good-night. But this one, this Margaret Awamura—well, I wasn't laughing.

I went through a couple of bad days. I wanted to call her—and that's the understatement of the half-century—but honorable young men just don't telephone a girl they are introduced to by a guy who sounds serious about her. Or at least they aren't supposed to. But the time finally came when I'd argued the pros and cons out with myself to the point where I didn't know which end was up, let alone what was right and wrong. I didn't know what I was going to say to her, but I was going to call. I didn't even know if she'd talk to me, but I was going to call. I didn't know anything, only that I was going to call.

So I called, five days after we'd met.

"May I please speak with Miss Awamura?" I said. It didn't even sound like me.

"Which one?"

"I beg your pardon?"

"Which Miss Awamura do you want to speak to? There are six of us."

"Oh. I want to speak to Miss Margaret Awamura." My courage was fading fast. If I'd run into one more stumbling block I think I'd have hung up.

"This is Margaret."

"Oh. I . . . uh . . . I hope you'll forgive me for calling you. This is Dan Inouye. I don't know if you remember . . ."

"Yes, I remember. We met a few days ago." She sounded as though she was smiling.

"Yes, yes, that's it!" I had been ready with a big speech

about how we'd met—she'd been with so-and-so, I was with so-and-so—and now I didn't quite know what to say. She saved the day.

"Why should I forgive you for calling?" she asked.

"Well, I don't know. I . . . I, I mean we only just met and I don't know if . . . well, if it's the right thing, to call, I mean."

"Then why did you call?" The smile was still there.

I laughed. "I'm a hopeless victim of my emotions," I said. I felt confident again. I felt marvelous. "Look, my old outfit is having a Thanksgiving dinner-dance at the Fort Shafter Officers Club next Saturday night. I'd be honored if you went with me."

"I'd be happy to."

"Seven o'clock?"

"Fine."

There was a little pause, then I said, "Are you what's-his-name's girl friend?"

"I'm not anybody's girl friend," she said sweetly, and hung up.

I wasn't about to push it any harder—I knew when I was well off. Besides, I had more important things on my mind. The only clothes I owned were a sport jacket and some slacks, which might have been all right for any other girl, but not for a date with Margaret Awamura. I cornered my buddy Tom Hirai, who was about my size, and made him lend me his navy blue double-breasted suit. At 6:30 that Saturday night, driving my father's car, I was cruising around her block, suffering each painfully-passing minute until 7 P.M.

I don't think I quite made it. Margaret was playing the piano when I came in. She looked like a Dresden doll. In a moment, though, I was surrounded by her family. I shook hands with her father, bowed to her mother, paid my formal respects to her grandparents and said hello to each of her five sisters. I felt nine pairs of eyes on me even after we'd closed the door behind us and walked out to the car, and I had the unsettling feeling that they weren't regarding me with what you'd call open admiration.

But Margaret was wonderful. She made small talk all the way to Fort Shafter and I was vividly conscious of her presence beside me, and by the time we got there I was so in love that there was a soft golden glow over the whole world. It was an enchanted evening. Everything seemed to go exactly right. She loved to dance, and so do I. She ate heartily, and good food is one of my little addictions. And I could tell by the way the other boys found some excuse to come over to our table, or worked their way close to us to chat on the dance floor, that I wasn't the only one smitten by her charm.

We left around midnight and I began a small debate with myself as to the propriety of asking her if she wanted to drive up to Diamond Head and look at the ocean. It was a beautiful night. "What are your plans for the future, Dan?" she asked me.

I told her that I planned to finish up at the University of Hawaii and then go to one of the Stateside schools, maybe the University of Colorado, for an accelerated law course. "I'm about four years behind," I said. "I can't afford to dawdle."

We talked about her. She had studied for her master's degree at Columbia in New York, and now she was a speech instructor at the University. "I could use another speech course," I said, only half-joking. "Maybe I'll enroll in your class next year."

She laughed. "I don't think that would work out."

I don't know why that tickled me so. Maybe because it implied that there was already something between us more personal than a student-teacher relationship. Anyway, I decided not to ask her to drive up to Diamond Head. I didn't want to risk straying out of bounds, not even by a half-inch.

When we said goodnight, I told her how much I'd enjoyed myself. "I hope we can do it again," I said, "and often."

"Perhaps," she said, and went inside.

Man, she was a cool one. I drove home in a quandary. What did that "perhaps" mean? Where did I stand?

I called her the next day. It was all I could do to keep from calling her in the middle of the night. I said, "Look, will you have dinner with me Saturday night?"

"I'd love to."

I heaved a sign of relief that she must surely have heard. That afternoon, I went into town and bought my first suit, shirts, ties and a new pair of shoes. I was leaving nothing to chance.

Naturally Saturday took forever to arrive. By the time it did I had a pretty good case of jangled nerves which my reception in the Awamura household did nothing to soothe. Margaret's father attempted some polite conversation, but her mother sat there, stiff and formal, as though the less said the better. I could almost feel her thinking that if she endured this with silent good grace, I might go away, like a bad dream. I could hardly blame her. By this time, I knew that Maggie—infinitely attractive and impressively educated—had a list of suitors whose prospects were stunningly more promising than mine. I was still in college and all I had to offer anyone was high hopes.

I felt distracted all through dinner. There seemed to be something I wanted to say, but I couldn't quite close in on it.

So I listened politely as Maggie talked, made all the proper responses and kept fumbling around for that elusive something that was prickling at my mind. Afterward we drove to Ala Moana and walked to the sea wall where we could see the torch fishermen casting soft circles of light on the water. Now neither of us spoke, but we held hands and were very conscious of each other. Then, as we turned to walk back to the car, she asked me what was the matter.

"Nothing," I said. "Why?"

We were in the car. She was watching me. She said something about how hard I was puffing on my cigarette. And then, all at once, the something that had been flitting around in my brain clicked into place. I knew what it was I wanted to say, and without prelude or amenities I said it:

"Maggie, I want you to marry me. Will you?"

Of course when the words were out I felt like an idiot. Where did I come off asking a girl like this to marry me? On our second date? And yet I understood myself well enough to know that I had had to do it. It was still another challenge, perhaps my greatest, and whether I got my ears pinned back or not, I had to let her know how I felt before she committed herself to one of those other guys.

I could see her eyes in the dark, and her mouth. She was smiling. Only then did it dawn on me that she had already spoken and that the word she'd said was, "Yes."

I took her hand again, not daring to speak because I didn't know what to say. I would have been better prepared for anything—"Oh, this is so sudden, Mr. Inouye. I shall have to think it over." Or, "You honor me, dear sir, but my heart belongs to another"—than for her simple, straightforward, beautiful "Yes."

I said, "Let's go home, Maggie." It was December 6, that

second date of ours. I know because we have celebrated it together ever since.

We had a long and happy courtship. It was a rare day when we didn't see each other and no day passed without at least one long telephone conversation between us. The most insignificant happenings took on a certain importance when we talked about them—*because* we talked about them—and in sudden innocence we unraveled our innermost thoughts and memories so that the experiences of one became a part of the other. We never formally announced our intentions to our parents. Mine became first to know when I asked Maggie to go to church with us one Sunday. All the family had their turn at sneaking sideways looks at her, all but my mother who paid strict attention, as always, to the service. But later, when I had taken Maggie home, it was Mother who put their speculation into words.

"It is one thing to take a girl dancing," she said. "It is another to take her to church. You must be serious about her."

"I am. I'm going to marry her, Mother."

Her eyes crinkled with gladness and she reached up to hug me. "May you both have long days, and happy ones," she said. "She is a lovely girl."

My father shook my hand, there were some jokes from my brothers and sister. Then they got down to brass tacks. Was Margaret a Methodist? Mother wanted to know. Had I spoken to her father? Had we chosen a wedding date?

I began working my way through the answers: Margaret had been raised a Congregationalist, but would be happy to become a member of my church. I had not spoken to her father; the Awamuras, in fact, had no knowledge of our intentions. As for a wedding date, we had decided to wait until I finished my junior year the following June.

Now my father took over: "In order for this to be done properly, we must choose someone to discuss the terms of the marriage with a representative of the Awamura house."

"You mean a . . . a go-between?" I yelped, horrified.

"Of course. It would be considered insulting for you to presume to ask for her hand directly." He firmly shushed my agitated protest before I got it out fully. "Daniel, this is a tradition among our people. It does you no harm and it will please the Awamuras and the Inouyes. Shall we consider it settled?"

"Yes, sure," I muttered and sank back in my chair. I was thinking that if it really did please the Awamuras, it might well be the first time I had done something right as far as they were concerned.

That had been the one jarring note in the wonderfully happy world Maggie and I had woven around ourselves in the past months. No matter how hard I tried to please her folks—and, oh, how I tried, minding my speech and manners and dress and barely breathing in their presence—they were plainly cool to the whole idea of my coming around and monopolizing their daughter's time. I was pretty sure her father secretly liked me—he would introduce me to people as *Captain* Inouye, the rank I was promoted to when I was discharged. But Mrs. Awamura, who made no bones about wanting the very best for her daughter, obviously didn't think I was it. To me she was polite, but restrained. And Maggie had some bad moments. There were times when, from her quiet, from a certain sadness, I could tell that she and her mother had had another of those "serious" talks.

It was just another obstacle to overcome as far as I was

concerned. But seeing Maggie unhappy was sometimes more than I could take. Once I said to her, "What made you say yes to me? My future is anybody's guess. But what's-his-name?—he's a professional man, and there were others . . ."

"I'm not in love with the others!" she said angrily. "And I'm not in love with what's-his-name either. And I believe your future will be greater than all of them put together. Does that answer your question?"

"Yes, Ma'am," I said quietly, and never brought it up again.

I wish I could say that there was some dramatic turning point, that some clever strategem of mine finally won Mrs. Awamura over. The fact is that by the time Maggie and I were married, she was my biggest booster, but exactly how it happened, I'll never know. Maybe I just grew on her. Or maybe my regard for the old traditions in the matter of the go-between convinced her that I wasn't the wild and irresponsible young buck she had dreaded.

I'll say this about the ultra-formal and stylized way of arranging a wedding among people of Japanese descent: they must be doing something right, for their divorce rate is among the world's lowest. For our go-between—called *nakaodo* in Japanese—we chose the Yasumoris, pillars of the church and dear old family friends. The Awamuras choices were also eminently respected members of the community, Dr. and Mrs. Kohatsu. On the appointed evening, the Inouye team—and we were quite a contingent, Mr. and Mrs. Yasumori, my parents and myself—appeared at the Awamuras' home on the stroke of eight. We brought the traditional gifts of rice, sake and fish, and we took our places on the floor in the traditional way, the Yasumoris and the Kohatsus facing each other from opposite sides of a low table. Behind their respective *nakaodos* sat the Inouyes and the Awamuras, and farthest away from the action, as though we were only incidental onlookers, sat Maggie and I. Now and then I caught her eye and we smiled secretly. Only the *nakaodos* spoke.

First the gifts were exchanged. Then Mr. Yasumori began to extol the virtues of one Daniel Ken Inouye—he was a fine, upstanding young man from a good family, a war hero now studying very hard for an honorable profession—and I had to concentrate to remember that he was talking about me.

The Kohatsus accepted this intelligence impassively—the Awamuras looked as though they were pretending not to have heard—and then our side listened to the recitation of Maggie's qualities: she had earned a master's degree, was so accomplished a seamstress that she made all her own clothes, and her family's reputation for honor was unimpeachable. I wanted very much to add that on top of all that she was beautiful, but I held my peace.

Now the *nakaodos* consulted briefly with their clients, presumably recommending that the engagement be made. Then Mr. Yasumori passed to Dr. Kohatsu the ring I had bought wrapped in plain paper. "We would like to offer this as a gift," he said solemnly.

Dr. Kohatsu nodded, took the ring and passed back a small gift that represented the dowry. Glasses were filled, a toast was drunk—and Maggie and I were officially engaged!

The wedding date was set for June 12 so that Maggie and I could take advantage of the semester break for our honeymoon. Two nights before, the boys from the 442nd threw me a bachelor dinner that—naturally—wound up in a crap game. Now the fact is that I had sworn off and hadn't gambled for as long as I'd been home. And since I was absolutely sure the pressure would be on me to get into a game this night, I'd left temptation behind me—all my money, except for the change in my pocket, maybe 35 cents.

But I hadn't reckoned on my buddies' power of persuasion. After a marvelous teahouse meal and happy good fellowship, somebody broke out the ivories and there they all were, down on their knees and begging for that new pair of shoes just as though we were back in the day room at Camp Shelby. Then they started on me: "Come on, Dan, for old times' sake. Don't be chicken."

Well, to make a long, sad story very short, I ran my 35 cents into $125 and then promptly went to the nearest telephone to call Maggie and try to purge myself of guilt.

"Oh, I'm so glad you called, dear," she said. "Did you have a nice time?"

"Yes, I had a very nice time. Maggie, I . . ."

"Who was there?"

"Oh, all the guys. Listen, honey, I have to tell you . . ."

"Well, you'd better get to bed. It's late and . . ."

"Maggie!"

"Yes, dear?"

"Listen, I . . . uh . . . got into a crap game. I mean, all the guys were shooting and . . ."

"Oh, Dan! I thought . . ."

"I know, but . . ."

"How much did you lose?"

"Lose? Who said anything about losing? I won $125."

There was a pause while she mulled that one over. Then necessity won out over principle. "Bring it right over here," she said crisply. "It will just pay for a nice set of china for us."

So ended the short, illustrious career of Dan Inouye, crapshooter.

We invited 300 people to the wedding and 450 showed up.

This surprised nobody since, in Japanese custom, an invitation addressed to the head of the household automatically included the whole family. Many of our friends were too poor to own suits and came in sport shirts and slacks. But that did absolutely nothing to mar the dignity of the ceremony or the happiness of the reception. The Reverend Hiro Higuchi who, as a chaplain in 442nd had been so close to me in the war, officiated. That took a little doing since he was a Congregationalist and Maggie and I wanted to be married in the Harris Memorial Methodist Church. But a talk with the church fathers straightened that out and Reverend Higuchi was able to marry us.

Late in the afternoon, Maggie and I fled in a shower of rice and good wishes and slipped away to a honeymoon cottage at the Niumalu Hotel in Waikiki, just about in the middle of the site now occupied by the Hilton Hawaiian Village. And next day we drove to Punaluu on the north side of Oahu where, for seven dollars, we had rented a beach shack for our five-day honeymoon. We did our own cooking, sunned ourselves and swam and went to country movies in the evening. It was an enchanted time and ended all too soon. So much did we remember and love that time and place that as soon as we could afford it, we built our own beach cottage just three doors away. But our paths take strange turnings and the pressures grow and the demands on our time are ever present; since 1959, Maggie and I have spent a total of seven days in that cottage.

When our honeymoon was over, we came back to a little apartment and settled down to the hard work of getting me educated and lined up for a law degree. That had absolutely top priority. But although I was only able to contribute $33 to our joint savings account, the GI Bill of Rights and my army retirement pay made me almost a self-supporting husband. Of course it was Maggie's salary as a teacher at the university that saw us through those years, and quite a few to follow.

Our life was full but not placid. Politics became an integral part of it almost from the day we returned from our honeymoon. I went to weekly political meetings, meetings that went on for hour after interminable hour, and came tiptoeing home at two or three in the morning. I don't say it was fair, but Maggie understood, bless her, that for me, it was necessary. "But why does it always take so long?" she once asked me. "Can't you all just decide what you want to do and then come home?"

How to answer that? How to explain that we were still feeling our way, throwing out ideas that had been locked in our secret hearts until this moment in history, weighing strategy that had never before been tested, dreaming a dream that sometimes shook us by its very audacity?

"Listen, why don't you come along tonight?" I finally said. "I think if you sat in with us . . ."

She stayed with it until around midnight. As always, the eight or ten of us who were present at the meeting that night started with a discussion of our aims and aspirations, the party philosophy, you might call it. Then we got down to cases—tactics, candidates, precincts, votes—the raw material of politics, so little understood by the nonprofessional. Once, when I looked up from a heated conversation about the importance of block captains, Maggie lay curled up in a corner of the sofa, sound asleep. She never complained again.

Our immediate objective in those months was the party convention and control of the Democratic Oahu County

Committee. Those of us who met night after night with our plans and dreams for the rehabilitation of the Democratic party—men like Jack Burns, Dan Aoki, my old hospital friend Sakae Takahashi—were agreed on this much: any chance we had for winning the territorial legislature would go glimmering as long as we were cursed with the I.L.W.U.'s kiss of death.

The International Longshoremen's and Warehousemen's Union had dominated the postwar Democratic party. Its members and friends held down most of the county committee seats. And as it flexed its muscles in those chaotic months when Hawaii was shifting from a war to a peace economy, it quite naturally attracted the oratorical notice of Republicans and not a few conservative Democrats. Inevitably the union was accused of being dominated by communists and, by logical extension, so were the good Democrats struggling to build a political force out of a handful of volunteers and some passionate ideas about equality of opportunity.

No one with any sense of political reality denied that there were probably some communists in the I.L.W.U. But the important fight as far as our little group was concerned had to do with forcing an end to the union tail wagging the party dog. All of us were sympathetic to organized labor, but how far could we go as a party if we were dominated by the tight little leadership of a single union?

To free ourselves from this stigma, to assert full control over our political destiny, we chose candidates for the county committee who were beholden to no one and bound by no ideology but the principals of Democracy. I was nominated for secretary—amid considerable sympathetic head-shaking, for a simple head count showed that I didn't have enough votes to win. But the head-shakers overlooked two magic ingredients: hard work and the secret ballot. When the votes were counted, Jack Burns was elected chairman of the county committee, and I was the secretary.

We had won a vitally important victory. We had recaptured control of our party. Now it remained to be seen if in the near future we could persuade the people of Hawaii to entrust us with the stewardship of the territorial government.

By the time I graduated in 1950, I had pretty well decided that I wanted to study law at George Washington University. It had a certain ring to it, and two years in the nation's capital, the ultimate goal of all political activity, would surely enrich my understanding of the profession to which I meant to dedicate my life. To satisfy my ego, I made application, too, to Harvard, Michigan and Columbia law schools. Since I was definitely going to George Washington if they'd have me, that was a lot of extra work. But when I got letters of acceptance from all four, I felt it was worth all the work. Man's ego is like that.

In late summer, Maggie and I sailed for the mainland on the *Lurline*, the same proud ship that had carried a couple of thousand jammed-together, wide-eyed *nisei* to their great adventure—was it already eight years ago? This trip was considerably different. Although we could afford only a small cabin, the warm present and the promise of what lay ahead were very much with us and we savored every hour.

From Los Angeles, we flew to New York, then took the train to Washington, where a room was waiting for us in a boarding house run by a charming lady known to the generations of students from Hawaii who boarded with her as Auntie Code. Every morning, briefcase tucked under my arm, I took the bus to school, and every evening I hurried home to Maggie, hours of homework, then more hours of lively conversation with the other students. In a month or so, however, as we grew accustomed to our surroundings and some of the stardust was brushed away from our eyes, Maggie and I decided that for all of Auntie Code's vivacity and the friendliness of the other roomers, in the interests of privacy, we'd better make a change.

We found a neat little apartment in Arlington, furnished it sparely but to our taste and splurged on a green Plymouth that was only a year old. As a matter of financial fact, I don't think many students could have matched the income that, between us, Maggie and I brought home. I had my pension as a retired Army Captain, about $200, my GI education benefits came to $115, and Maggie soon had a job with the Navy Bureau of Yards and Docks. She started as a file clerk, though she had never done that sort of work before, and within three months had been promoted to administrative secretary, though she had never done that sort of work either. Together we were grossing something in the neighborhood of $800 a month, and it went to my head to the extent that I spent more for my suits then than I do now.

I was working very hard. After a semester or two of planting my feet firmly in the good solid ground of the law, I even pulled down a couple of A grades and became a member of the board of editors of the *Law Review* and had some of my briefs published. Soon I was invited to join Phi Delta Phi, an international legal fraternity which counted among its members supreme court justices and most of the faculty of the law school. It was a signal honor, heightened a year later when I was elected exchequer of the George Washington chapter.

Meanwhile, I engaged in a couple of extracurricular activities that in ways large and small I hoped would contribute to my political career. For a period of three months, two hours every week, I attended a school for bartenders. I have already explained how my days as a two-fisted drinker ended, and I had no intention of starting anew. But I did feel that if I was to be mixing socially and entertaining people from all walks of life, I ought to gain more than just a fumbling knowledge of how to mix a variety of cocktails and highballs. And I did. When I had acquired sufficient know-how for my limited purpose, I quit. This was somewhat before certificates of completion were awarded to my class of neophyte bartenders, but I arranged a sort of graduation exercise of my own. I invited the members of my class to a party at our apartment and mixed them an awesome variety of drinks. Early on, Maggie cornered me at the refrigerator and nervously whispered, "Dan, what on earth are you doing? You don't know how to mix any of those . . ."

I took a quick look around, kissed her behind the ear and hastily confessed what I'd been doing for those two hours every Thursday. She nearly fainted.

My second venturing from the classroom was somewhat more directly related to the world of politics. One day I went to the office of the Democratic National Committee and volunteered my services in any capacity they felt might be useful. I told them I wanted no pay, only the experience of working close to the grass roots, of learning enough so that when I went back to Hawaii I could bring something more than just my amateur standing and a brand new law degree. I remember that it took a long time for their initial astonishment to melt into curiosity, and finally into real interest.

"You mean," one of them said, "that you want to go back and rebuild the Democratic party?"

"Not quite," I said. "There was never anything to rebuild. All we're trying to do for a starter is to give Hawaii some semblance of a two-party system."

They took me on, and from that day until I graduated and left Washington I haunted that place. I was there almost every hour I could spare, making charts, writing reports, running out for coffee and listening, always listening. After a couple of months, they realized that unlike most "volunteers," I didn't get bored or discouraged by the pettiness of some of the jobs that needed doing, that I made no complaints and that I really had come to learn. And so, little by little, they worked me into the second echelon of the hierarchy, permitting me to sit in on strategy meetings, publicity planning meetings, fund-raising meetings. Still I listened, said very little and learned a great deal. The principles were the same—like the number of plots that can be used in a novel, there are only so many basic political tactics—but the refinements of those principles! The refinements were the difference between the winners and the candidates who also ran.

Once, as part of my larger education, they asked me to sit in on a meeting involving a local election in Maryland. The matter at hand seemed elementary: the candidate was popular, seemed way ahead in the polls, yet was in real danger of losing. Why? Because complacency had set in among his workers and supporters, and while his opponents' people were out beating the bushes for votes, everyone on our side seemed content to sit home and make plans for *after* the election.

The old pros ran that meeting, men who could feel a trend in their guts, and who could cut through the verbiage, inflated vote estimates and apologies with a single—sometimes obscene—word. As soon as the preliminaries were done with, the chairman said, "Send a dozen men out to tear down our signs."

"*Our* signs?" This was the voice of amazement and, as I came to understand, the voice of the well-meaning amateur.

"Exactly. Our signs. Then spread the word among our people that *they're* doing it." There was a babble of confused chatter, then a smart rap on the table by the chairman. He said, "You're up against a disease—complacency, overoptimism—and there isn't anything that can kill a candidate deader faster. You need strong medicine and I've just prescribed it. Now get going."

I suppose the medicine worked—our candidate won—but even then it seemed a little *too* strong for me. I learned the lesson that nothing is more deadly to a campaign than complacency, but I've always preferred to try heading it off *before* it was too late for anything less drastic than sign-smashers.

In my last year, I divided my free time equally between political headquarters and the Congressional galleries. I was fascinated by the Hill, by the intricacies of parliamentary procedure and debate. There, right in front of me, were the elected representatives of all the people of this land, the stars, the duds, the tacticians, the operators, the statesmen, each in his own way going about the business of attending to the legislative business of the United States. I never saw myself down on the floor of the House or the Senate in those days; the limit of my ambition then was a seat in the Territorial legislature, I suppose. But I think that even then I understood the political process and its application to our democracy, for those men to me represented not the sordid machinations of the backroom bosses, but the end result of our representative form of government. Some states were represented by abler men than other states, and this was because some people cared more and worked harder.

In this year, too, I faced a personal crisis, a decision I didn't want to be forced to make, but was. The Phi Delta Phis who were members of the graduating class were asked to submit names of men thought to be worthy of an invitation to join the fraternity. It seemed to me that the two men I proposed were eminently qualified. They were both on the *Law Review,* sound students and thoroughly honorable. And so I was stunned and sickened when on the first ballot both were blackballed. Eight Phi Delta Phis had written "No" on their paper ballots.

I started to say something, then realized that by the rules of this little charade I was not permitted to speak. There would be an automatic second ballot. If the results were still the same, and if I insisted on the privilege, I would be allowed to make an appeal on behalf of my candidates. And so I waited, for the second ballot, for the same eight secret blackballs, and then I got to my feet. I realize now that this had seldom happened before: in keeping with the way the game was rigged, sponsors whose candidates were rejected were supposed to pretend acquiescence in their brothers' judgment, out of embarrassment if for no other reason. But I kept thinking about the Pacific Club back home, and about a thousand other abrasions of the human spirit on the grounds of race and religion, and I asked for the floor.

"Gentlemen, I want to say a few words about the two men

I have proposed for membership in this fraternity. I will say no more about their qualifications except that they are fine students and they are gentlemen. What I want to put into words, so that none of us can pretend ignorance, is that these men are being turned down here because they are Jews. I know it, the eight men who have blackballed them know it, and I want to be perfectly sure that everyone in this room knows it.

"Now according to the rules, you will all have one more opportunity to walk up here and drop your little pieces of paper in the ballot box. But when you do, please consider that you will be voting, not only on these two men, but on Dan Inouye, as well. You see, I'm not an Anglo-Saxon, and if these men don't belong in this fraternity, neither do I."

You go along—everyone does—month after month, year after year, taking certain facts of life for granted. You don't ask questions because the questions don't occur to you. Then something unexpected happens and suddenly there is the truth, right in front of you, and often it is ugly.

That's what happened to me. Never in history had the Marshall Inn of the Phi Delta Phi accepted a Jew, and I didn't know it. But the same thing happened to all the other members, too. Oh, they knew about the taboo—only they never questioned it. It was there, a tradition as old as the fraternity. But no one had ever tested it or made a fuss about it, and so they never thought about it. Until this day.

Now they marked their ballots and marched up to the box, avoiding my eyes and returning to their seats in the kind of soundless tension where your heartbeat feels like thunder. And the box was open and the ballots read, and there wasn't a single No.

I felt a mixture of things, relief and pride among them.

But mostly I felt happy because I didn't want to think I had misjudged these men who were my fraternity brothers, happy to have affirmed my belief that they *were* basically decent, happy to have played some small part in opening their eyes to the cruel injustice they had come close to perpetrating because they hadn't thought, hadn't questioned.

Afterward, at least three of them came up to me and admitted that they had been among those casting blackballs, and expressed appreciation to me for forcing their eyes open. All of them, I know, are happy about their ultimate decision, for I have heard them express deep pride in the fact that the two men in question were their fraternity brothers. For one of the two is Bruce Phillipson, now an eminently successful Washington attorney and certified public accountant, and the other is Sheldon Cohen, the United States Commissioner of Internal Revenue.

I was graduated in September 1952, with a J.D. degree, different from the usual LL.B. in that it marked some extra courses I had taken and my service on the *Law Review*. Unfortunately, I wasn't able to wait for the graduation exercises. As a matter of fact I left before the final grades were posted because now the important thing for me was to get back to Hawaii and begin studying for my bar examinations.

My mother, who had flown to Washington—her first trip to the mainland—joined Maggie and me for the trip home, as did a classmate, John Ushijima. We took a full month to drive across the country because it was important, too, for me to see my United States. North to New England and across the Mohawk Trail we went, west to Chicago, then up to Canada, and back through the plains of Iowa and Kansas and on through the desert to Las Vegas and across the mountains to the coast. Never before had I really understood the immensity and diversity and great promise of this land of ours.

I returned to Hawaii armed with a law degree—although it wouldn't be worth much until I'd passed the Territorial bar exam—a little practical experience in stateside politics and a fierce desire to get back to work for the Democratic party and the people of Hawaii. And there was plenty to do. Besides the day-in, day-out job of recruiting new members and maintaining the enthusiasm of the old ones, a group of us—John Burns, Sakae Takahashi and a few others—had come to the conclusion that one of the ways we could give meaningful help to Hawaii's small shopkeepers and wage-earners was to organize a new bank. Of the four banks then doing business in the Islands, two were run by the big companies and were hardly sympathetic to the needs of the plain people, while the other two were so small that they were in no real position to offer assistance.

We set it all out on paper. The bank would be capitalized at $1 million, with no single shareholder permitted to own more than $10,000 worth of stock, so we'd never face the problem of having bank policy dictated by one man or a tight little group of men in control. We proceeded to line up some really solid people—*haoles, nisei,* Hawaiians, Filipinos, Chinese: it didn't matter to us what they were so long as they saw the importance of it as we did and were willing to go along.

And then we got a taste of racial discrimination—in reverse! The law said that to establish a new bank, one had to demonstrate that there was a need for it. "We already have four banks meeting general requirements," said the examiner. "What would your bank do that they aren't?"

We meant to serve the *little* people, we told him excitedly, the working men and women who were cold-shouldered when they went elsewhere for a loan.

"You mean the Japanese community?" he asked.

Yes, the Japanese community, we told him, and all the other underprivileged enclaves, as well.

But he heard only what he wanted to hear. If we went into business to cater to the *nisei,* if our board of directors was made up of Japanese-Americans, he would approve our application. Otherwise . . .

We were bitterly resentful at this turn of events. Every one of us was opposed to any purely ethnic approach, either to politics or to business. But there seemed to be no other way. Now we had to go out and raise the required capital from the older and more conservative members of the Japanese community, and their terms were stiff: they wanted control of the board. We debated and argued and pleaded, and finally agreed on an even split—half the board to be chosen from the oldsters, half from among the eager young *nisei* who had had a glimpse of the future and liked it.

All this time I was supposed to be studying for my bar exams. Maggie was concerned at all the hours I was spending *away* from my books—and there were moments when I was pretty worried, too. As it happened, the exams fell on the same day that we potential bank directors were to appear at hearings which would determine whether or not our application would be granted. I remember rushing from the examination—and it was tough!—to the hearing room, perfectly aware that two vitally important decisions in my life were being made this day, and yet, strangely, almost unnaturally calm. I had done all I could. The rest was in the lap of God, and I trusted Him.

My trust was not misplaced. The bank application was

approved and that scrawny little infant we brought into the world that spring of 1953 is now a robust $72 million giant, and still dedicated to the original principle: helping the man who needs, not a couple of million dollars to finance a merger, but enough to buy a few hundred dollars worth of stock for a new store, or to tide him over between jobs. Althought I have suggested resigning from the board of directors because, as a public official, I cannot participate in the bank's business, I have always been cheerfully refused.

As for the bar exam, Maggie and I received the happy word in August: I had passed and was free to hang out my shingle and begin practicing the law. But of course my heart was in politics. I had studied law to help me be a better practicing politician. In a sense, everything I had done in life pointed me toward that goal. I saw it—and still see it— as a thoroughly decent and worthwhile profession, a chance for men of goodwill to offer genuine service. I have often expressed the wish that our universities institute courses in the art of practical politics so that men of high caliber are attracted to this vital area of government service, and so that the bleak picture of the hack and the ward heeler are erased from the American consciousness.

Not that images mattered to me. I knew then, as I know now, that as long as I could walk, as long as I could talk, and as long as people wanted me, I was in politics to stay. Nor did I even have a chance to hang out a shingle. The day after I passed the bar exam, Mayor Johnny Wilson, one of a handful of exceptional Democrats to succeed at the polls, called me into his office and appointed me assistant prosecutor for the city and county of Honolulu. I took charge of my first case that very afternoon.

Chapter VIII

A Reckoning in Ballots

✿ We believed there was a chance that 1954 could be our year. Ever since the war we had been whittling away at the absolute dominance of the huge Republican majority in the legislature. Now there was a certain promise in the air, a secret and contagious spirit that whispered, "Go for broke!" This year. Now!

Again we nominated John Burns for Delegate. I was named his campaign chairman and my first statement to our people was a request for anybody who thought we were just going through the motions again to roll up their voters list and sit this one out. We meant to win this time, I said, not only the Delegateship, but control of the Territorial House and Senate, as well.

That summer, at a meeting at Dan Aoki's house, Jack Burns dropped his bombshell. We were discussing likely candidates and overall strategy when Burns, who usually sits quietly absorbing every word and intonation—but has only to clear his throat to gain everyone's attention—suddenly spoke up: "Dan, I think it's time for you to run."

I tried to brush him off politely—the idea seemed that outlandish to me—but everyone went quiet, staring at me as though my shirt were on backward. "Listen," I said, "why me? There are other guys who have been around longer, better qualified . . ."

"Because you can win," Burns said.

"In the Fourth District?" I thought he was kidding or crazy. In Hawaii's whole experience with representative government, only two Democrats had ever been elected from the old Fourth District, where I lived.

But he wasn't crazy, and he certainly wasn't kidding. "Who was it that made the big speech about going through the motions?" he asked quietly. "Who is it that keeps saying times are changing and that the people want a chance to come out from under 54 years of Republican rule? That was you, Dan, and this is your chance to prove you believe it."

I looked around at the impassive faces. I wanted to tell them that I did believe it, that my only concern was me: who would vote for Dan Inouye? I wasn't even thirty years old, had never been a candidate for an elective office and felt numbingly unready. I wanted to run, sure—but now?

Dan Aoki spoke up. I respected Dan. Everyone did. He had been a 442nd first sergeant, was now president of the Veterans Club and knew as much about the needs and hopes of the ex-GIs as anyone around. "They'll go for you, Dan," he said. You've got the right combination—a war hero, a fresh face. If we want the vets to come into the Democratic party, we've got to give them somebody they care about, one of their own. You."

"You're on," I said to them. "I'll do it. And I'll give it everything I've got."

There was no cheering or back-slapping. For one thing, we had nothing to cheer about—yet—and for another every one of us took the whole thing as a deadly serious challenge.

That night I discussed it all with Maggie. "Go ahead, Dan," she said. "If you think you're ready for this, I'll be happy to be on your side and working for your election."

Next morning I walked over to Benny's Photo Shop— where, to this day, I have all my official pictures taken—and said to my old friend stooping behind the camera, "Make this a good one, Benny. It could have some bearing on my future."

When the prints were ready, I took them around to the newspapers with a short statement I had scrawled while I waited. The next day, there I was, on the front page of the Honolulu *Advertiser,* announcing to the world that it was going to be different this time, that the tide was coming in strong for the Democratic party in Hawaii and that we meant to ride it to victory. In the next several weeks, I had plenty of professional head-shakers bemoaning my fool-hardiness. They told Maggie, they told my father—they even told me!—that I was a nice guy, but absolutely crazy if I really thought I had a chance against the Republicans. "Do you *like* beating your head against a stone wall?" someone asked me.

But the stone wall was crumbling. If you had a feel for the political mood of the people, you could sense it that summer and autumn of 1954, like a fresh breeze off the Pacific. For one thing, we were getting some topnotch candidates. Un-like past years when a sort of Democratic suicide squad— loyal workers but something less than inspiring candidates— ventured forth to have their brains beaten in by Republican opponents, 1954 was the year of the eager young hopefuls, better-educated, thanks to the G.I. Bill, unscarred by past election defeats, and all abrim with vigorous, forward-looking ideas about the management of the Territorial government. In the Fourth District, until this campaign a permanent graveyard for Democratic hopes, four of our six candidates were veterans and included persons of Japanese, Portuguese, Caucasian and Hawaiian descent. Let me say a word about them:

Spark Matsunaga, war hero with the 100th Battalion, lawyer and now the senior member of the Hawaiian delegation to the U.S. House of Representatives.

Masato Doi, member of the 442nd, soon to become chairman of the city council for the city and county of Honolulu, then to be appointed a circuit judge by Jack Burns.

Russell Kono, a war vet who fought in the China-Burma-India theater with Merrill's Marauders, a successful lawyer and now a magistrate.

Anna Kahanamoku, sister-in-law of Hawaii's beloved swimming champion, Duke Kahanamoku, had been a physical education instructor at Washington Intermediate School when I went there, a beautiful, gracious woman of Hawaiian-Portuguese-Caucasian ancestry who has since been chairman of the board of education and served in the Hawaiian state senate.

Daniel K. Inouye, now a United States Senator.

William Crozier, a long-time Democrat and one of the only two ever elected from the old Fourth District, the only one among the six of us who would fail to win in that crucial election.

This gives some indication of the caliber of our team. There were other straws in the wind. In one speech, I suggested that the best way for the electorate to make a judgment between the two parties was for every Republican candidate to get up on the platform with his Democratic

opponent and debate the issues face to face. I even took a
deep breath and said we'd foot the bill for radio time,
although our treasury still suffered from chronic anemia.
This, of course, was six years before the Kennedy-Nixon
debates revived interest in this time-honored style of campaigning—and the point was that the Republicans didn't
even respond to the invitation. Even if some of our own
people hadn't yet realized it, our opponents had grown
acutely aware that the day of the halfhearted Democratic
way of battle—hula dancers, luaus, pretty balloons—had
ended. We understood the issues and were prepared to talk
about them—education, economic development, the kind of
future Hawaii ought to aim for—and, more than anything
else, this shook the Republicans' confidence. And as we
slashed away at them, our audiences growing in size and
enthusiasm, many a beseiged G.O.P. candidate must have
sadly wondered what ever happened to the good old Democratic patsies who used to roll over and play dead for them,
election after election.

The six of us running from the Fourth District campaigned as a team. Each of us had a particular issue—mine
was education—on which we spent many after-midnight
hours of study, but our central theme was progress, for all
the people. We had played a small but vital part in the great
war and now that it was won we were not about to go back
to the plantation. We wanted our place in the sun, the right
to participate in decisions that affected us. Day after day, at
rally after rally, we hammered home the point that there
must be no more second-class citizens in the Hawaii of
tomorrow.

Then came the meeting at Ainahaina. Once again we had
challenged the Republicans to a radio debate. Once again

their reply was dead silence. But somewhere, at some strategy meeting, they must have faced up to the grim fact that we Democrats had a chance to win, and their reaction was that well-worn, John Wayne-to-the-rescue ploy, the "Truth Squad." So it was that the first of our speakers had been talking for about five minutes when, with a great flourish and determined air, in charged the "Truth Squad," their chairman grabbing the microphone to announce that they could no longer stand idly by while "these so-called Democrats" went on deceiving the people. He went right to the heart of what the "Truth Squad" had come to say: the Democratic party had been captured by the I.L.W.U., we were the willing tools of I.L.W.U. leaders Harry Bridges and Jack Hall and hence, at the very least, soft on communism.

For a long and electric moment I just sat there, the words ringing in my ears, and the realization that this infamy was going out over the air numbing me: in the space of three minutes we had been lumped with Bridges and Hall, made out to be either fools or traitors, and I could see all our high hopes, all our back-breaking effort, going out the window. True or false, a political charge travels with the speed of light, while a denial moves at a snail's pace and most often doesn't catch up until the day after the polls close.

I remember getting to my feet and moving to the microphone. It wasn't my turn to speak and, truthfully, I had no idea in that instant what I meant to say or do. As a matter of fact, until I actually began talking, everything blurred in my eyes. But Maggie was in the audience, and she remembers vividly:

"I was afraid," she told me later. "The skin on your face was all tightened up and you looked as though you were going to kill somebody. You said something under your breath to the moderator, then you just took the microphone out of his hand and you looked straight ahead and began to speak."

Once I heard the sound of my voice, all the ripples of faces in front of me stiffened into focus and became people. It was like the first instant of combat: one second you're scared to death, and the next you set out to do what needs to be done. I knew how desperately important it was that I win these people back, here and now, not tomorrow or next week when the smear had hardened to fact in their minds.

I put the notes for my speech into my clenched teeth and tore them in two with my only hand. I said that in my view the danger to our democratic institutions was less from communism than from the social conditions on which communists fed and flourished—poverty, slums, inequality of opportunity. These were the evils, the very real evils, that my fellow candidates and I were pledged to fight. If our opponents wanted to wage a shadow war, a smear campaign, that was their sad privilege.

"But I cannot help wondering," I said, "whether the people of Hawaii will not think it strange that the only weapon in the Republican arsenal is to label as communists men so recently returned from defending liberty on the firing lines in Italy and France. Let me speak for those of us who didn't come back—I *know* I speak for my colleagues on this platform, and for good Democratic candidates everywhere in these Islands—when I say that we bitterly resent having our loyalty and patriotism questioned by cynical political hacks who lack the courage to debate the real issues in this campaign."

I had never before called attention to my disability for the simple reason that I didn't consider it a qualification for public office. But at that moment, blinded with fury, coldly aware that I was engaging in a bit of demogoguery, I held up my empty right sleeve and shook it: "I gave this arm to fight fascists. If my country wants the other one to fight communists, it can have it!"

There was a moment of stunned silence, then a crashing of applause. A man ran to the edge of the platform and cried up at me: "It's about time somebody stood up to them!"

Arms waved, and handkerchieves, and sometime during that tumult, the Republican "Truth Squad" skulked off the platform—and with them went any chance they had to win the election. That was the turning point, and when the votes were counted a few weeks later, five of the six Democratic candidates running from the Fourth District were elected, a victory beyond our wildest imaginations. We had won 22 of the 30 seats in the House, and 10 of 15 in the Senate, besides gaining control of most of the city and county councils. My name led the ticket.

We had one disappointment, but it was a big one. Jack Burns lost the Delegateship to Elizabeth Farrington, widow of Joe and daughter-in-law of the onetime Governor. A mark of how far we'd come was that of 140,000 votes cast, Mrs. Farrington's winning margin was less than 1,000—and she could thank the heavily *haole* districts for those.

Jack moved slowly among the winners that night, congratulating us all. And whenever anyone offered him words of sympathy, the tough ex-cop shrugged them off: " 'Fifty-six is another election," he said. "I'll be back."

And he was.

Even today, there are some good Democrats in Hawaii who would just as soon forget the session of the Territorial legislature that was called to order in February of 1955. It was wild, full of sound, fury and confusion and, if you were looking for a log of solid legislative achievement—well, I'd have to concede that you'd come to the wrong place.

Of the 22 members of the Democratic majority, only 8 had any legislative experience whatever. Most were young, burning to set right out redressing evil. We were convinced that our zeal would see us through, that because our hearts were pure and our aspirations lofty we would prevail. We believed in ourselves. Thanks to the GI Bill and the fact that most of us were vets, few legislative bodies anywhere in the country could boast the level of professional and educational competence that we brought to our task. But when it came to the ways and means, the give and take of practical politics, we were pretty much in the dark.

Our first problem was organizing the House, a job that had been regularly and routinely handled by the opposition for all the years anyone could remember. We went at it with gusto, emotion and crossed fingers. Meetings and caucuses were held all over the Territory, nearly all of them concerned with the best way to conduct this first Democratic-controlled legislature. Since we five winners from the Fourth District represented an important block of votes, I was designated to express our preferences for the leadership posts to be assigned in the House. In order of importance, they were speaker, vice-speaker, majority leader and then the various committee chairmanships.

When the final choices were to be made, a group of us sat down for a long session of debate, discussion and decision. The selection of our speaker reflected a kind of idealism rarely found around statehouse caucuses. Though most of the Democratic members were *nisei*, we promptly decided that the Speakership should go to Charles Ernest Kauhane, a Hawaiian. Why? For reasons that most political practitioners would think laughable: because as a member of the minority in the past he had carried the ball for us through many lean years; and because short as we were on experience, Kauhane had as much of it as we could lay claim to.

We agreed on Elmer Cravalho as assistant speaker—which must have been a sound choice because he is now speaker—and then came the chore of assigning committee chairmen. It was a monumental task because, traditionally, each member of the majority party was to be given a committee to chair. On and on the meeting went—finance committee, judiciary, Oahu County—and so intent was I in getting the right people in the right places that when we were done and Charles Kauhane said, "Well, we've done a good job except that there's no committee left for you, Dan," all I could manage was a small, "Oh."

"The only thing left," Kauhane said, "is majority leader. Do you want to be majority leader?"

I shrugged. "Why not?"

And that's how it happened, which will come as news to some people who are convinced that I connived for the post. The fact is that it was a job with limited powers, small staff and still seeking definition, having been created only a few years before by the Republicans.

And still I took it very seriously. My personal problem was clear-cut: I had only the vaguest possible notion of what responsibilities were entailed in my new post as majority leader. And so, seeking guidance and moral support I took what I considered to be the most direct possible action. I wrote a letter to Sam Rayburn, who in 1955 had already served as majority leader of the U.S. House of Representa-

tives longer than any man in history, and I told him how in
more or less haphazard fashion I had been named to this
important post. I had been studying everything I could find
about a majority leader's responsibilities—which wasn't
much—and asked if he could give me some basic human
guidelines that would at least get me through this first
session. And bless Mr. Sam's big Texas heart, he took sympathetic notice of this obscure Hawaiian legislator of whom he
had never heard and whose name he wouldn't learn to
pronounce for six years, and he said essentially this:

Though the rules of legislative bodies differed, it was
generally true that a majority leader had few constitutional
powers; that he knew of no constitution, including that of
the United States, which made any reference to a majority
leader; that the post, like others within the internal frame-
work of the governing party, was a convenience and a tool to
help keep the legislative business moving.

There would be further strictures, not only on my powers,
but on my freedom of choice. Wrote Rayburn, if, for example, my personal convictions led me in direction A, but the
clear-cut sentiment of the majority was toward B, I was duty-
bound as leader to press for B, and if in good conscience I
could not, I was obliged to resign as a party functionary, for
at that point I could no longer represent the will of the
majority.

What, then, makes a good majority leader? The understanding, appreciation and practice of good human relations,
said Mr. Sam, and the Golden Rule was as good a guide as
he'd ever encountered.

I don't think I have ever had better advice, and the days
were upon us when I needed it desperately.

The thing is that most of us felt that we had an undiluted mandate from the people to wade right in and pass into law those wide-ranging reforms on which we'd campaigned and which were written into the Democratic platform. With the Republican minority shrieking as though mortally wounded, we passed a graduated income tax bill for the first time in history. We tackled Hawaii's archaic and restrictive land laws, tried to effect broad new approaches to economic development. Taking on the problems of education, in which I had a specific interest, we doubled the appropriation for the University of Hawaii and greatly increased the budget for the Department of Public Instruction.

But of course we had reckoned without the Republicans' entrenched power. Though we could outvote them in the legislature, we couldn't override the veto of Governor Samuel Wilder King, President Eisenhower's appointee. He made plain his conviction that Hawaii was far from ready for the drastic social and economic innovations we had proposed by vetoing no fewer than 72 pieces of Democratic-inspired legislation, a record of nullification never before approached.

And still we tried, although the frustrations of the hour grated on us and spurred bitter exchanges, not only with our political adversaries, but within our own ranks as well. When we reached the sixtieth day of the session—mandated by the organic act of the Territory as the limit of the legislative period—we simply stopped the clock and kept right on going.

The results were far from happy. An eager gang of idealistic freshman had collided head-on with a hard core of practical oldtimers and there was generated more heat than light and, to this day, some of the wounds have not yet healed; one sad outcome is that our speaker, Charles Kauhane, left the Democratic party and became a Republican.

But if we didn't achieve the legislative revolution we were after, we did learn the greatest lesson of all—that politics is the art of the possible. And so armed we were infinitely more capable of writing a significantly progressive record in the days ahead. Nor was that first session a total legislative loss. For me, it was not only a training ground, but a means of bringing influence to bear on some matters that, though they would never change the world, did correct some injustices that rankled many of us emotionally.

As majority leader, my name appeared in the press more frequently than that of the average member. And despite my political differences with Governor King, I liked him personally and respected the integrity with which he fought for his beliefs. Not infrequently, I would stop in to see him late at night, and we would discuss the legislative doings of the day, always striving toward some area of accommodation, a position we could both support. We didn't reach it often, but when we did, it was a cause for genuine celebration.

In any event, these advantages, plus some suggestions I had made to soothe our internal frictions, put me in a sound position to make a few recommendations to the Democratic caucus. One of the first had to do with the usual practice of choosing the chaplain of the House.

Until then, the chaplain had traditionally been appointed by the majority party and was, without exception, a Protestant. Both these practices bothered me. Why? Because I deeply believed in the sanctity of our constitution which expressly guaranteed our freedom of religion; it protected all religious denominations and recognized none as an "official" church. So why should that body involve itself in religious matters to the extent of choosing a chaplain?

I think I have made my devotion to the Methodist Church plain enough so that I can hardly be accused of anti-Protestant bias. But in a land where people of all creeds and beliefs mixed on virtually every level of life, I felt strongly that there ought to be room for the prayers of all denominations in our legislative halls. And this was my suggestion to my fellow legislators, that we call on all the religious bodies in the Islands—Catholics, Protestants, Jews, Mormons and Buddhists—and invite them to participate in a rotating program that would enable all of them to be represented in the House. The only stipulation we laid down was that the invocation be given in English or Hawaiian, our two official languages.

I tried hard to keep this from being publicized—I wasn't advocating it out of political motivations, and I didn't want it thought that I was—and my friends in the legislature, some of whom were pretty dubious about the whole scheme, were happy enough to keep it quiet. My great gratification came not from any newspaper stories, but from the visit I paid to the senior bishop of the Bishops Council of the Buddhist Church of Honolulu. I had been designated to notify him of our plan and thought it best to take an interpreter with me. Still when we tried to explain what we wanted to do, he turned obviously angry.

"He thinks you're joking," the interpreter said. "He says he never heard of such a thing."

I started all over again. "Tell him there never has been such a thing before. But times are changing. We are a mixed people and we want every religious group—Buddhists,

Protestants, Catholics—to be fully represented, to participate in the opening and closing prayers of our legislative
sessions."

And then he understood very well. And he began to cry.
"My son," he said through the interpreter, "do you know
that this is the first time that a Buddhist has been asked to
represent his faith in any American legislature?"

I said I hadn't known that, but that I hoped it would not
be the last.

My only regret is that since he was unable to speak
English or Hawaiian, he had to send another priest to
represent him. Still, the effect was the same and I am proud
that this practice we instituted in 1955 is carried on to this
day in Hawaii's House of Representatives.

I had less luck with another proposal in which, again, I
had an emotional involvement. Iolani Palace, the seat of the
legislature, is the only royal palace in the United States. The
Territorial House of Representatives met in the throne room
and the Senate met in the royal dining room. The Governor's
office, on the floor above, was once the private quarters of
the King.

By training and education and intense personal feeling, I
felt all this to be a near-sacrilege. I kept remembering
Hawaiian history and how, thanks in part to my mother's
teaching, I had developed a high regard for Hawaii's royal
rulers. And I remembered, too, that on the day of annexation, when the Stars and Stripes was raised and the Hawaiian flag brought down, some of the officials, seeking souvenirs of the historic day, cut up the honored old Hawaiian
flag and passed the pieces out among themselves. In World
War II, our country avoided destroying treasured art centers
or seats of government. American pilots were told not to
bomb the imperial palace of Japan, and during the long

occupation General MacArthur did not take over the Emperor's quarters.

Yet here we were, the duly elected legislature of the Territory, moved lock, stock and gavel into Iolani Palace, the speaker sitting on the royal throne itself! I didn't like it and I tried hard to change it. I suggested to the Democratic caucus that we should simply refuse to meet in the throne room and thereby dramatize the issue so that more suitable quarters could be found for us.

"If we have to," I said, "let's pitch a tent outside and meet there!"

No, that would be undignified, they said. And to someone else's proposal that we meet in a schoolroom, they said, no, it was too far away and would be inconvenient. So we stayed in the throne room, much to my constant discomfort. But the tale does have a happy ending. A new State capitol building is in the works for Hawaii, and before long the old palace will be restored to the people.

From the start of my political career, I seemed to have developed a knack for upholding some surprising positions. I was not tilting at windmills. I am no Don Quixote. But uncomfortable as I sometimes felt up on the firing line of an unpopular issue, I felt even more strongly that somebody had to speak up. When no one else did, well, I was elected, in more ways than one.

There are, for instance, some veterans who are still convinced that I betrayed their best interests thanks to my stand on various special benefits bills. When I was still commander of the DAV, the legislature was considering a proposal to award a $300 bonus to every ex-GI who had suffered a service-connected disability. This struck me as extremely unfair and wasteful, and I said so. On the one hand, you might have a man who served a few months and broke an arm in a jeep accident, or came down with a case of ulcers. On the other, you had thousands who'd fought the enemy with everything they had to give and were lucky enough to return without permanent injury. Who deserved the $300? And what about the families of those who'd died in battle? Their men had suffered the most permanent injury of all, yet they got nothing. And anyway, who said that the state or nation owed anyone anything for coming to their defense? It was *their* state, *their* nation, wasn't it?

But in this instance, nothing I said helped. The bill passed, and in due course veterans of the Korean and Viet Nam conflicts were included, with the result that many are still waiting for their bonus money.

Not long before, President Truman had vetoed a bill providing free cars for blind vets and those who had lost an arm. I thought such a measure was insane—why did I deserve a free car?—and, as DAV commander and one who would directly benefit, I wrote to the President and commended him for his courageous act. He promptly replied, thanking me for my unselfish attitude, but in the end all either of us got on this issue was a lot of abuse. The veto was overridden and the bill passed.

In the election of 1956, the Democratic majority in the House, though cut to 20, remained solid and substantial. It was now clear that 1954 was no freak and that we were a force to be reckoned with. Personally, I knew I'd learned a great deal in that freshman session—I bore plenty of scars from my lessons in human relations—and though the fire to reform still burned inside me, I knew how to go at the legislative process more patiently, and certainly more practically. And so armed, I indicated to my colleagues that I was available for the speakership of the Territorial House.

Two capable men also sought this post—O. Vincent Esposito and Elmer Cravalho—and in our contest we participated in many caucuses and I made several trips through the island chain. Actually, I was pretty confident of winning. I had polled the members privately and from what they told me, I had more than enough votes to win. Which simply goes to prove that I hadn't learned *everything* about politics in that first session. For many of the members had asked me if I could assure them certain legislative posts if I were named speaker, and my answer invariably was that I could assure them nothing, all positions would be decided by a caucus of the majority.

Then came the showdown, a secret ballot. I have always hoped that no one was watching me when the result was announced, for I am sure my jaw must have dropped wide open in astonishment. Of the 20 ballots cast, I had exactly 3—and one of them was my own!

Esposito was chosen speaker on the third ballot, and I was the almost unanimous choice for a second term as majority leader. I tried hard not to feel any bitterness—politics is full of triumphs and losses, disappointments and surprises—but I must say that my efforts at inner tranquility were severely jarred when immediately after the session no fewer than eight of my colleagues came up and, in confidential whispers, each informed me that his had been one of the three votes I'd received.

The second session moved smoothly along the legislative track. Esposito made a fine speaker, and with the Democratic approach leavened by experience, we carved out a record that even the two Republican papers said was acceptable.

All this time, I was theoretically engaged in the private practice of law. But the fact was that my tax return for the first quarter of the year showed an income of precisely zero.

I was simply too busy with my work in the legislature to seek out or properly represent any private clients. But Maggie, a girl of absolutely the rarest variety, never complained. She knew I was happy and for her that was enough.

Not that we really suffered financially. Maggie had returned to the University to teach, and between her salary and my pension we managed to keep going. Of course once the legislative sessions ended, I did make a little money in private practice, and anyway, we liked stew, corned beef and cabbage and spaghetti.

In 1958, I made what I then thought would be the most important political decision ever offered to me. I decided to leave the House and run for the Territorial Senate. Now it must be understood that in our Islands there is a great prestige attached to the Senate. True or not, that body is popularly considered to be occupied by Hawaii's statesmen, and I sincerely felt that to be elected a Territorial Senator would cap my career and give me gratifying political work for the rest of my days.

Well, when the votes were counted it turned out that I led the ticket. I was a Senator. Of course I ran into a little difficulty at the very outset; backing the wrong man for President of the Senate, I found myself appointed chairman of the relatively obscure veterans affairs committee. But I didn't brood about it. I was certainly interested in veterans, and maybe I could make the work of my committee more important. In any event, I was a happy man that year, certain I had achieved the limit of my political ambitions.

And then—statehood!

The matter of statehood for the Territory of Hawaii had been mentioned, rumored, discussed and shelved for many years. It would come some day, everyone said, and when Alaska began talking about statehood we in the Islands were even more encouraged. Surely, with our larger population and more viable economy, we would be taken into the union of states first. But though joint bills to admit both territories were introduced in Congress, still nothing happened.

Of course the opposition, both internal and on the mainland, was extremely potent. The people, by a 17-to-1 majority, had demonstrated in a referendum that they wanted to be a full and equal partner in the United States, but the tiny minority opposing it held very high cards. And their opposition was based on good and practical reasons—of their own.

As a territory, Hawaii's governor was chosen by the President and confirmed by the U.S. Senate. As long as this was the case, what voice did the little people have? What voice did Dan Inouye have? The suggestions and recommendations that were listened to were those made by men who had contributed handsomely to the campaign coffers of Mainland politicians—Democrats, as well as Republicans—for they were taking no chances, and surely a few thousand dollars a year was no stumbling block to them. These were the men of family, influence, social standing. They had run the Islands' economy for generations and, though they had recently lost control of the local legislature, their money and station retained for them a vast influence on the federal officialdom superimposed on Hawaii's home rule.

There were the judges and the federal bureaucracy. There was the military, particularly the Navy, which had long exercised a behind-the-scenes control of the Islands' affairs. And who entertained the admirals and the generals? Not the little people. Not anyone named Inouye. Try the Dillinghams. And so, for obvious reasons, you would not find *them* in the forefront of those fighting for statehood. As long as Hawaii remained a Territory, the Dillinghams didn't really have to worry about or work through Dan Inouye or Patsy Mink or Sparky Matsunaga. They could go directly to some admiral, who could put in a call to the White House on the spot.

But the power of the people, if they care and they persist, is, in the end, irresistible. The first significant step was the election of John Burns as Hawaii's Delegate to Congress in 1956. Jack pursued the dream of statehood along all the usual avenues and with all the customary diligence and rhetoric. And he was brought to a crashing dead stop by the steely opposition of powerful Southern congressmen. He listened to all the tiresome old arguments about noncontiguity and size and economic development, and he made all the standard answers—that Hawaii was ahead of many states in economic growth and population and statistically prepared for statehood years before. To no avail; for the real reason—expressed in remarks that never got into the *Congressional Record,* such as, "Sir, how would you like to be sitting in this chamber next to a Senator named Yamamoto?"—was neither numbers nor dollars but the fact that much of Hawaii's population was non-Caucasian and, in fact, heavily Japanese.

And faced with this grim truth, Jack Burns demonstrated a wisdom and political courage that ought to earn him a permanent place in the hearts of our people. He prevailed on the leaders to back him in withdrawing Hawaii from the statehood drive completely so that Alaska could have a clear shot at it.

You can imagine the hue and cry that this decision provoked. "Traitor!" was among the more polite adjectives used to characterize Jack Burns in those troubled days. But he took it all without whimper or apology. Of course he knew full well that by any realistic measure, Hawaii was better prepared for statehood than Alaska. But he had also come to realize that the joint bills, for all their theoretical reasoning about political balance—Alaska was supposed to go Democratic, Hawaii Republican—were killing us both. Alone, he reasoned, Alaska had a chance. And if they succeeded, how could Hawaii be denied?

His strategy was perfect. Alaska became the forty-ninth state in 1958, and during that vindictive election campaign in Hawaii, Jack Burns asked only one thing: send me back as your Delegate to Congress once more, and if the statehood bill for Hawaii fails to carry, I will disappear from the political scene and never return again.

And his essential faith in the Congress of the United States was not misplaced. With Alaska in, all the phony arguments about noncontiguity, population and economy were undercut. And the momentum generated by Alaska's drive overrode the opposition, and in March 1959, the U.S. Congress voted to accept Hawaii as the fiftieth state.

I will never forget that day. Burns telephoned the territorial legislature from Washington. "The roll call is still in progress," he said, "but we have the votes. We're in!"

It grew very quiet in the legislature when the announcement was made. This dream, this everlasting hope of nearly all of us in both parties, entailed too awesome a responsibility for anyone to feel like shouting in triumph in those first moments. The chaplain was called and led us in a prayer of thanksgiving. And that afternoon, both houses adjourned to go from Iolani Palace to Kawaihao Church, oldest in Hawaii and often called our Westminster Abbey, where the last of the Kamehamehas is buried.

Next day, while the newspapers which were to become collectors' items told the story in great glaring headlines and the people celebrated in the streets, I drove alone to the cemetery at Punchbowl. I like to do that when I can, not on national holidays or when the place is crowded with dignitaries, but by myself, on a day such as this, and sort of report to the boys. I wanted to tell them that it was a very great victory, perhaps the greatest, and that their sacrifice had helped to make it possible.

Let me offer one more insight into the character of Jack Burns. We Democrats wanted to share our great jubilation at statehood with him, not only because he richly deserved every reward that came our way, but because it was plain good politics. With happiness and honest pride we could say to the people, "We delivered! We promised statehood and we've got it, and here's the man who deserves the credit, John A. Burns!" We pictured his triumphal return from the mainland, the crowds lining the streets as his motorcade made its way through the city of Honolulu, the accolades as he traveled from island to island. And we sent urgent word to Washington that it was important for him to fly to Hawaii as soon as possible.

He phoned back immediately. No, he said, he was unable to return then because important legislation concerning the sugar industry was due up in Congress and he felt that he had to be on hand to defend Hawaii's interests. This was a special irony. The people who would most directly benefit from Jack's diligence were the wealthy planters, the Big Five, all of whom had long committed themselves to Burns' defeat. And though Jack knew it full well, he knew, too, that a healthy sugar industry was essential to the Islands' economy and to the well-being of the people. So in Washington he stayed and the statehood celebration proceeded without him.

But then the sugar battle was successfully waged and this time I called him myself; it was not too late for him to reap at least some of the political benefit for the job he'd done—if he returned immediately.

And again the answer was no. "Dan," he said, "I'm telling this only to you, but the reason I still can't come back is that Seishiro is graduating from college next week and I've promised Bea that we'd be there. I owe it to her. I owe it to the boy."

I think I understood. Here was a boy who wasn't supposed to have survived his birth, now about to get his degree from college. And politics or no politics, Jack Burns meant to be there with his wife. And he was. But this was a crucial period in the forming political pattern of the time and to this day some men believe that Jack Burns lost his first bid for the governorship then and there. He would win it eventually, yes, but there are those who say that had his conscience permitted him to forget the sugar industry, forget his son's graduation, he could have reversed his narrow margin of defeat and become the first governor of the *state* of Hawaii.

When the emotional binge tapered off and leaders of both parties settled themselves to the hard work of transforming a territory into a state, they realized that there was a lot more to it than met the eye. A special election was to be held in July and the time was upon them to weigh candidates for the U.S. Senate and House, and for Governor and Lieutenant-Governor.

It was a testing time and I'd be less than honest if I said I didn't see myself somewhere in that brand new political picture. Since there were no incumbents, everyone was starting out on an equal basis. Certainly the votes I'd run up in past elections were encouraging enough to persuade me that I might have a chance at one of the top state offices.

The one I tentatively decided to try for was the U.S. House of Representatives. But in discussing it with associates and party officials, I found them all but unanimous in urging me to declare for the Senate. Jack Burns was among those, although I knew that it was his own personal wish to go back to Washington as Senator. But nearly everyone in the party felt that it was more important that he run for Governor, and putting his own desires second, as always, he agreed.

I gave it some hard thought and came to the firm decision that I would give it a try. I withdrew my savings from the bank, borrowed $5,000, and my family pitched in some money on top of that. I ordered posters and bumper stickers —"Inouye for Senator"—and began planning my campaign.

At this point, only one other Democrat had declared for the Senate, a onetime marine named Frank Fasi, so the path to the nomination seemed fairly clear. About this time, a popular and articulate lady attorney, Mrs. Patsy Takemoto Mink, told me that she wanted to run for the Democratic nomination for the House. "I wouldn't do it if you were running against me, Dan," she said. "But if you're going for the Senate . . ."

"I think you'll make a great Congresswoman, Patsy," I assured her. "Good luck."

The next week, and within days of each other, two of the party's most distinguished elder statesmen announced their

candidacy for the two Senate seats. William Heen had been
the first Democratic president of the territorial senate, city
attorney and judge, and was an outstanding political talent.
Oren E. Long, then serving with me in the territorial senate,
was a former governor and superintendent of public instruction. It was Oren Long, nearly 20 years before, who had
handed me my high school diploma.

And now what was I supposed to do? In the next three
weeks, I was forced to face up to three choices, each of
which had repugnant aspects, and to make what I now *knew*
to be the most fateful decision of my career.

I could stay in the Senate race against two men to whom
the Democratic party owed everything and, incidentally,
violate my own heritage which decreed a constant respect
for honored elders.

I could run for the House of Representatives, despite a
commitment that had already cost me a great sum of money
and, much more to the point, despite the fact that I had all
but given Patsy Mink a clear field by assuring her I was in
the race for Senator.

Or I could completely withdraw from the federal elections, stifle what I honestly felt to be a chance at a larger
contribution to Hawaii and the nation, and stay in the state
legislature.

Those were not a happy three weeks, I can assure you.
Practically nothing in politics long stays private and personal, and soon the newspapers and the politicians, sensing
my dilemma, began to make public property of the intensely
personal question: what is Dan Inouye going to do? For
three bitter weeks the answer was: damned if I know.

I discussed it with Maggie and my closest friends, but
they could see how deeply all this was enmeshed with my

future, with what I myself had to decide and do, and what could they say? I went to see Jack Burns, the closest thing to a political godfather that I'll ever have, and Jack looked me in the eye and said, "You're young, Dan. You'll have other chances. So will Patsy. This chance belongs to Long and Heen."

Not long after that I made my lonely decision. The first thing I did was to arrange a dinner party for the six people most intimately involved—Maggie and me, her parents and my parents. We met, I remember, at the Evergreen Restaurant for what I'm sure the others thought was to be a festive family party. Instead, just before the dessert was served, I cleared my throat and said, "I have something to tell you that may disappoint you very much. But I believe it is what I must do. At 5 P.M. tomorrow, I am going to publicly withdraw from the Senate race and announce my candidacy for the House of Representatives."

My mother dropped her spoon. My in-laws looked at me as though I'd turned blue. My father tried once, twice, three times to speak, and failed. I knew how they felt. They were very proud of me and believed wholeheartedly that I would win and become Hawaii's first U.S. Senator. And how hard they had worked in my behalf! And now, over an issue I could never adequately explain to them, I was quitting.

Finally my father found voice. "Let us leave here and go somewhere to discuss this."

We went to my in-laws, which was closest, and for hours they tried to persuade me to stay in the race. Only Maggie really understood my devotion to Judge Heen and Senator Long, and she helped me convince them that my decision was the right one.

But that was only the beginning. Next morning I began

dictating the withdrawal announcement to my secretary and hadn't gotten two sentences into it when she looked up, tears starting to her eyes, and said, "Oh, no, Dan!"

"Oh, yes," I told her gently. "I have to. Now be a good girl and take it down."

Next I personally telephoned Governor Long, Judge Heen and several of the party leaders and invited them to "a private and important" luncheon at a Japanese teahouse. And finally, with all the arrangements made, I called Patsy Mink. I cut through the pleasantries as quickly as I could— the thing was bad enough without any additional hypocrisy.

"Patsy, I called to tell you that I'm withdrawing from the Senate race in favor of Governor Long and Judge Heen."

"Yes, Dan?" she said and, I'm sure, already knew what I had to say next.

"I'm going to announce my candidacy for the House of Representatives at 5 P.M. today."

There was an awful silence. I could almost feel her struggling between her natural, inevitable anger—that sense that she'd been betrayed—and her innate decency.

"Patsy, I'm sorry as hell it turned out this way. I didn't know Long and Heen would get in this thing. I meant it when I gave you my blessings."

"I know you did. I'm disappointed, but I think I understand."

"Thanks."

"Only I can't withdraw, Dan. Too many people have worked too hard for me to just pull out. So I guess we're in for a primary fight, you and I."

"There are lots of people I'd rather fight against," I told her. "But I promise you that as far as I'm concerned it will be the kind of campaign we can walk away from as friends."

So that was done. Then came the luncheon at which I informed the leaders. At 5 P.M., I made the news public and the reaction was stunning, the front pages full of the story the next day. And then, almost at once, the campaign was under way.

The first thing we had to do was get rid of those "Inouye for Senator" posters. We organized an impromptu committee consisting mostly of family, friends, Maggie and I, and feeling somewhat foolish, we went through the city tearing down posters, banners and signs. It was a totally unhappy operation—the thwarted hopes, the work involved and the constant reminder that more than $5,000 of extremely hard-to-come-by money was going down the drain. Well, not entirely. Although most of the signs were destroyed, a few of my devoutly loyal friends smuggled a handful of them away, and the time would come when they could serve for something more than a memento or keepsake.

Soon the new posters were printed and distributed and the primary fight was in full swing. It was a sad one for me and I did everything I could to make certain that it was conducted fairly and without mudslinging or bitterness. Patsy did her part, too, though she fought valiantly and with everything she had. Both of us traveled throughout the state, our paths crossing often, and with the Democratic party divided into two camps, there were huge crowds and plenty of excitement whenever we came together at rallies.

It was at one of these that I received an object lesson in how the heat of politics can sometimes make perfectly decent people terribly cruel. In the smaller towns and villages of Hawaii, it is the custom for the people to come forward before the speeches begin and to drape flower leis around each candidate's neck, often as many as ten or fifteen. It is a festive interval—the orchestra plays Hawaiian music, the people applaud their favorites as pretty girl after pretty girl comes forward to drape her lei around your neck, kiss your cheek and wish you well in the campaign. But behind the color and state fair camaraderie, there has grown up a coldly practical aspect of the lei ceremony: hard-eyed reporters have taken to counting the number of leis received by the respective candidates and, in the stories they write, tend to gauge each man's popularity with the voters by the weight of flowers around his neck.

At one village, which I shall leave nameless, where Patsy and I were scheduled to speak, a crowd of 700 or more had crowded into the ballpark, overflowing the seats and sprawling across the grass and car tops in every direction. I was introduced first and the presentation of leis began—and lasted fully ten minutes. One of the people on my campaign committee said I got 137 leis, each one accompanied by a fresh burst of applause. After I spoke it was Patsy's turn. And to my everlasting horror, she got only five leis and the briefest scattering of applause. By the time she had finished speaking, my horror had turned to cold fury. Maybe I was politically more popular than Patsy in this village—but not 132 leis more popular! And politics aside, the great spirit of aloha in all these villages ought to have insured her a more cordial reception than what she got. Somebody had been up to some skullduggery—somebody in my camp.

I sent for my campaign manager. I remember that in the course of a very brisk five-minute conversation, he got to say, "But, Dan," once or twice, and that's all. What I told him was that someone on our side had done a cruel and senseless thing for what I was damned sure was the last time. I wasn't interested in who or how, only that nothing remotely like it must ever happen again. And it didn't. As a matter of fact, I suspect that now and then, when it looked as though Patsy might not get her fair share of leis, my people arranged to have some of *mine* delivered to her. I never asked.

I think it was pretty clear, even to Patsy, that I was ahead so it couldn't have been a very serious shock to her when I won the primary by a decisive margin. She showed her caliber immediately afterward by announcing that she would support and work for me right up to election day. And nothing could have made me happier than when, five years later, I was able to back Patsy wholeheartedly for a seat in Congress, which she won and now fills with great skill and integrity.

My Republican opponent in that special election of 1959 was Dr. Charles Silva, a dentist from the Big Island, Hawaii, who had served capably in the state senate and won considerable popularity. The campaign was brief but extremely intense, and the outcome seemed clear from the moment the first returns began coming into our small headquarters on election eve. As early as 8:30 P.M., when it was obvious that I was going to roll up a huge majority, Dr. Silva gracefully conceded defeat and—it suddenly struck me with an enormous emotional impact—I was on my way to a place in the Congress of the United States.

Pandemonium had broken loose in the jam-packed headquarters. Movie and television cameramen tried to jostle their equipment around the reporters and well-wishers. Maggie clung to my hand, both of us deeply moved and sharply aware of the very special significance of this election: for the first time in the long history of the United

States, an American of Japanese ancestry had been elected to the House of Representatives. And there were the questions shouted at me:

"How does it feel, Mr. Congressman?"

"What's the first thing you're going to do in Washington, Dan?"

"Any future political plans?"

When they had finally simmered down and I could make myself heard, I said that I regarded my victory as a very special gift from the people, a sacred privilege. "I would hope that my service in the Congress would be a bridge between the Western world and the Orient. I would like to convey to the Mainland some small sense of our spirit of aloha."

It might have been a magnificent evening, perhaps the happiest I'd ever known, except that returns from the other contests brought sad news. Although Governor Long had been elected to the Senate handily, Judge Heen had been defeated by Hiram Fong and Jack Burns had lost his bid for the governorship.

A day or so later, I went up to the cemetery at Punchbowl and walked alone among the graves of the good men with whom I had served. I wanted to assure them that I would not let them down, never dishonor the cause and the country for which they had given so much. I wanted to promise them that I was not going to Washington to represent the 442nd, or the *nisei*, or any other separate group. I was going to represent all the people of Hawaii, and I asked God's help in this, the greatest undertaking of my life.

President Eisenhower had decreed August 21 as the official date for the signing of the proclamation that would

make Hawaii the fiftieth state in our Union. I was to be sworn
in as a Congressman two days later. Maggie and I came to
Washington early and were met at the airport by Delegate
Jack Burns, the chairman of the Democratic party and a
Congressional delegation. This was naturally very flattering
but I'm happy to say that it did not go to our heads. After
two luxurious nights at the Statler, we checked our bank
balance and moved over to the more reasonably-priced Congressional Hotel.

Promptly at noon on the twenty-first, there gathered in
the Oval Room of the White House an impressive group to
witness the signing of the statehood proclamation. Present
were the Vice-President, the Speaker of the House, members
of the Cabinet, Hawaii's new Congressional delegation, administrative assistants of every stripe, and honored guests—
but not Delegate Burns, the man most responsible for leading Hawaii to the point where in a few moments she would
be a state. I was astonished and angry—until that proclamation was signed, Burns was still Hawaii's official representative in Congress—and it was clear to me that someone on
the White House staff was exercising some cruel and petty
political revenge.

President Eisenhower took his seat, Richard Nixon on his
right and Speaker Sam Rayburn on the left. Everyone moved
a little closer as the President picked up the first pen from a
whole jar full, wrote a few letters, then handed it to Mr.
Nixon as a keepsake. He wrote a few more letters, then
offered the pen to Speaker Rayburn. And tough old bird that
he was, perfectly aware of the cruel slight to Jack Burns,
Rayburn said, "No, thank you, sir."

Considering my extremely junior rank in that gathering, I
know I should have held my peace. But if you've come this
far with me, you know that Inouye with something on his

mind is Inouye on the verge of speaking up. And that's how it was in that tense and historic moment. I leaned over Sam Rayburn's pink bald head and whispered, "Mr. Speaker, I know Jack Burns would deeply appreciate having one of those pens."

He craned around to look at me, then leaned back toward the President. "On second thought," he said very carefully, "noticing that Delegate Burns is not here, I'll just take one of those pens for him. I . . . uh . . . think he deserves it, sir."

There was an electric silent pause in the proceedings. Not a single man among all the dignitaries in that room was unaware of exactly what was happening and, as a matter of fact, most of them knew full well that Jack Burns, at this very instant which represented the great climax of his years of effort, was sitting alone in his office amid the packed trunks and the memories. And now courageous old Sam Rayburn had laid the truth right up there on the table for everyone to look at and I'm sure that except for the most hardhearted, it must have been an unpleasant sight. And at last Eisenhower managed a weak smile and handed the pen over. Later Rayburn personally delivered it to Burns, and it still sits in a place of honor on his desk.

Three years later, when I was leaving the House to campaign for a seat in the U.S. Senate, Congressman Leo O'Brien reminisced about the day I took my oath of office. O'Brien had been one of the most determined advocates of Hawaiian statehood in all the Congress. We had become good friends. But on that day when he stood up on the floor of the House to tell how I'd arrived on the national political scene, he had considerably more in mind than the usual intra-party back-patting. Let me quote from the *Congressional Record:*

"Tuesday last was the third anniversary of the admission

of Hawaii. Today is the third anniversary of one of the most dramatic and moving scenes ever to occur in this House.

"On that day, a young man, just elected to Congress from the brand new state, walked into the well of the House and faced the late Speaker Sam Rayburn.

"The House was very still. It was about to witness the swearing in, not only of the first Congressman from Hawaii, but the first American of Japanese descent to serve in either House of Congress.

" 'Raise your right hand and repeat after me,' intoned Speaker Rayburn.

"The hush deepened as the young Congressman raised not his right hand but his left, and he repeated the oath of office.

"There was no right hand, Mr. Speaker. It had been lost in combat by that young American soldier in World War II. Who can deny that, at that moment, a ton of prejudice slipped quietly to the floor of the House of Representatives."

Sam Rayburn was one of the great Americans of the twentieth century. Apart from his towering skills of statesmanship, he had an infinite regard for people, and the young Congressman on whom he turned a fatherly eye was very lucky indeed. I had been planning to call on him and pay my respects at the appropriate time, but only a few days after my arrival in Washington, the phone rang and that inimitable voice asked to speak to Congressman "Inn-oo-way, or Inn-way or however you say it."

"This is he," I said.

"This is Speaker Rayburn. I thought if you weren't too busy you might come around to see me."

"Yes, sir!" I said, and practically ran to his office.

He said he wanted to welcome me personally to Washington, and to take me on a little tour of the Capitol, something I never heard of him doing for any other freshman Congressman before or since. And it was an inspiring afternoon. He walked me around like a beneficent grandfather, through the galleries and the library and the chamber itself, the first time I had ever been on the floor, walking within these venerable and historic walls. He showed me where he sat and where I would sit. He pointed out the seals of the states—Hawaii's wasn't yet hung—and the fact that there were only two pictures on the walls: Washington's and Lafayette's. And through it all I listened and saw and walked with a sense of awe, a deep feeling for the continuing story of a great nation. Here I was, very newest legislator in Congress, in the presence of the great Sam Rayburn who, after the Vice-President, was next in line for the presidency of the United States.

Nor did he ignore the small but very practical aspects of life in Congress. Traditionally, he told me, shoeshine boys are not required by the rules to be paid by Congressmen, but, he harrumphed, a 25-cent tip would not be inappropriate. Here was the restaurant table where the Texas delegation usually sat, there was where the liberals gathered, and there the freshmen. "You are free to sit anywhere, of course," he said, "but I know I speak for all hands when I say the Texas delegation would be glad to have you."

We went back to sit in the cool calm of his office and he said, "How does it feel to be a U.S. Congressman?"

I looked around the room, searching for the right words. "I'm very proud and very happy and a little scared, Mr. Speaker."

He nodded. "That's the way I felt. That's the way we all feel the first time, I guess. But there's no reason to be scared.

If you're the right man you'll do well, and if you're the wrong man . . . well, being scared won't keep you from being found out."

He leaned back in that big chair and said, "I'll tell you a few things. The unwritten rules here are more important than the written ones. We don't sign contracts because a man's word is his bond. We are all different, representing a whole nation full of different people with different problems. In the beginning you'll find yourself hating some man for his position, cussing him out in your mind. But we get along here by respecting the needs and integrity of every man in the place—each one, remember, is an elected representative of the people—and we ask the same of you. And if you're convinced in your heart that something is right, do it, go after it, fight for it, even if you find yourself a minority of one."

He paused again, looked out the window on the summer streets of America's capital. "I'm going to start right out calling you Dan, all right? Because I'm damned if I can pronounce that last name of yours. Now, Dan, I'm sure you know that I am the best-known member of the House of Representatives."

"Yes, sir."

"Well, after me, do you know who the best-known member is?"

"No."

"You."

"Me?" I looked at him with astonishment. Was he pulling my leg?

"Of course, you," he said in that flat, no-nonsense way he had. "Oh, maybe not this very minute, not today. But very damned soon."

"But—why?"

"Why? Well, just think about it, son. How many one-arm Japanese do you think we have in the Congress of the United States?"

Chapter IX

For the U.S. Senate: Benjamin F. Dillingham III vs. Dan Inouye

❀ Early in the morning of the first Tuesday in November 1962, Maggie and I walked hand-in-hand to our precinct polling place in Honolulu. Somebody put leis on us and the photographers took our picture and the reporters yelled, "How does it look, Dan?"

I smiled at them. "I don't know. I'm not finished campaigning yet."

But I did know. I whispered to Maggie as we moved toward the voting booth: "How do you think you'll like being a Senator's lady?"

She looked up at me: "Being Dan Inouye's lady is what's important. The rest is just extra."

I squeezed her hand hard. After we'd voted, we drove around the precinct, stopping to talk to people, shake some hands, maybe even pick up a stray vote. I like to do that on election day, to be among the people. It strengthens me, somehow. We were back home by 5 P.M., cleaned up and had a simple dinner. Then Maggie said, "Well, shall we?"

And I said yes and we drove down to campaign headquarters to listen to the first returns in the contest between
Dan Inouye and Benjamin F. Dillingham III for the Senate
of the United States.

It had been a long step, perhaps the longest, in this
uniquely American journey. I had studied hard and worked
hard during my three and a half years in the House. There
was the strictly procedural but nonetheless urgent business
of learning how to get things done. What department
handles this problem? Which secretary has that information? Experience gradually taught me the answers, and
persistence helped me to answer the average of 120 letters
that flooded my office each day. I worked until midnight
three or four days each week, driving slowly across from the
House office building to our apartment still mulling over
questions, problems, lines of action. I had never been so
happy in my life.

I had real need for Sam Rayburn's excellent advice on my
very first vote. It was on the Landrum-Griffith labor management bill and after studying it until 5 o'clock one morning, I came to the conclusion that though we needed a law
to control corrupt labor practices, this bill was not it because
it was simply not fair. Why should labor leaders be required
to be bonded and take a loyalty oath and not management
leaders? Anyway, when my name was reached on the roll-
call, I stood up with a very distinct "No!" and felt a little
lonely when the bill passed with only 52 of us opposed. But I
had voted my conscience and no Congressman can do more.

I lived through a spate of publicity that seemed to lend
truth to Rayburn's astonishing prediction. *Life* and *Look*
had articles about me. The Junior Chamber of Commerce

named me one of the ten outstanding young men of the year. In every case I tried to convey my feelings—that I was happy to accept these honors, but that I did so on behalf of the people of Hawaii. In 1960, I won re-election with the greatest number of votes ever polled by any candidate in the Islands.

I made steady progress through those very intricate legislative chains of command. In 1960, the Speaker had offered me a seat on the House Foreign Affairs Committee, an assignment with considerable prestige and the opportunity to attract national attention. I thanked him for his confidence but requested instead a seat on the House Agriculture Committee. I was letting myself in for constant controversy and an unending political headache, but the simple fact is that Hawaii is basically an agricultural state, heavily dependent on its sugar and pineapple and cattle industries, and from a vantage point on the Agriculture Committee I could contribute the most to my state.

During the 1960 presidential campaign, I made no secret of my support for Lyndon B. Johnson. This was not the most popular position for me to uphold back home, for many of Hawaii's Democrats were strong backers of Adlai Stevenson or John F. Kennedy. The fact is that I had a soft spot in my heart for Stevenson myself and had been proud to cast my vote for him in the 1956 convention at Chicago. Certainly no one spoke more eloquently of the aspirations of men.

But as spring turned to summer in that year of decision and convention time came closer, it seemed clear to me that Stevenson was out of the race. And even more important, I felt myself honestly drawn to the leadership offered by Lyndon Johnson. I believed that the nation would greatly benefit from his practical approach to the art of government.

In Congress I had learned to appreciate his uncanny political finesse and knew of no one on the national scene with his raw courage: it is one thing to uphold a progressive and liberal position on civil rights from a secure political base in the north; it is quite another to do so as the United States Senator from Texas. Yet it was under Johnson's consummately skillful direction as majority leader that the first meaningful civil rights bill in generations was passed into law.

And so the Hawaiian delegation to the Democratic convention came to Los Angeles that summer of 1960 divided in their loyalties. A majority of my fellow delegates were prepared to cast their votes for Johnson, but the others held fast to their commitments to Stevenson and Kennedy. I might say that this was not an easy time to be a Johnson man; it seemed overwhelmingly likely that Kennedy was going to be nominated on the first or second ballot, which greatly intensified the feeling against those of us who persisted in holding out for "that Texan."

I had two key assignments in furtherance of the Johnson candidacy. The first was to make one of the seconding speeches to his nomination. Not long before, Speaker Rayburn had called me in and said that LBJ himself had suggested I do this. In his uncompromisingly honest way, Mr. Sam then told me that he had been against the idea because I was a newcomer to the political scene and Hawaii, after all, had only four electoral votes. But Johnson had insisted, and now Rayburn waited for my answer. I told him—in the understatement of the century—that I was surprised that Mr. Johnson had thought of me, but that I would be very proud to do it.

The second assignment had a somewhat less happy ending. A few days before the delegates convened, Johnson was invited by the National Association for the Advancement of Colored People to appear at a massive rally at the Los Angeles Shrine Auditorium. All the major civil rights groups were meeting there and had asked the Democratic contenders for the nomination to address them. This was certainly a worthy audience for any candidate, but as it happened, Johnson was already heavily committed for the day in question: he was to appear on *Meet the Press* and two other television programs, and had promised to meet with three separate state caucuses in the evening. Had the invitation been flexible enough so that he could squeeze out the time somewhere along the line, he would have been there. But he was allotted the time span between 2 and 2:30 P.M. and that was it.

Could he, then, send a spokesman? Johnson asked. Yes, that would be all right, they replied. Have him be at the Shrine Auditorium no later than 1:30.

The first I knew of all this was when Johnson headquarters called me and asked if I could pinch-hit on this very meaningful occasion. You can bet that I was there, ready and willing, by 1:30, led to a seat on the stage by some official, in company with a hundred or more civil rights leaders. Then I waited.

Jack Kennedy spoke, as did others in his behalf. Adlai Stevenson, also unable to appear personally, had sent as his emissaries, Eleanor Roosevelt and Governor Lehman of New York. Still I waited.

Perhaps I should have gleaned the tone and outcome of the meeting from the reception accorded Oscar Chapman, former Secretary of the Interior. Although Chapman was chairman of the Citizens for Johnson committee, he had been invited for valiant service in the cause of civil rights. As Interior Secretary, and with the permission and encouragement of President Truman, he had integrated his department's cafeteria, the first government official to do so, and had then gone on to do the same at our national parks.

Chapman spoke quietly but with obvious sincerity about his hopes for the civil and human rights of all people. Then he said that he was grateful for the invitation to appear, but that the honor for his efforts in behalf of the colored people ought to go to the man who had helped and supported him every step of the way, Harry S Truman.

At those words, almost as if on secret signal, there burst over the hall the loud and ugly sound of booing. It was obviously in response to an unfortunate but typically candid remark that Truman had made about certain aspects of the civil rights movement not long before, but the vehemence of the animosity suddenly turned loose in that place stunned me, and I could see that Oscar Chapman was badly shaken, especially since not one of the officials on that stage made any attempt to quiet the gathering.

When the audience had finally spent its venom, Chapman, courageous man that he is, raised his voice to say that he felt obliged to remind them that he was in Los Angeles as chairman of the Citizens for Johnson committee. And this time it sounded as though the roof would be blown off by the boos and cries and catcalls. Not for a long time after he left did the last of the mutterings die down.

And still I waited. At 4 P.M., I was due at a testimonial dinner in my honor, the proceeds for which were earmarked for the relief of victims of the recent tidal wave in Hawaii. But though 4 P.M. came and went, I wasn't about to leave there until I'd said what I had come to say in behalf of

Lyndon Johnson. Instead, I turned to the official seated next to me and asked him when I would have a chance to speak.

"Soon," he whispered, and kept repeating "Soon" each time I asked the same question over the next two hours.

At 6 o'clock Roy Wilkins strode to the podium. In dramatic tones he reminded the sea of faces in front of him that those who believed in civil rights believed also in freedom of speech. But not all Americans adhered to that time-honored precept, he said, for in the South a Negro was not allowed to speak his mind. But today, he went on, they had invited a spokesman of the South to address them. They wanted to give him a fair hearing. Where was he? he said then. Where was Lyndon B. Johnson?

I was furious. I twisted in my seat and said to the NAACP man next to me, "He knows I'm here! I've been here all day. Do I get to speak or not?"

He looked trapped and desperately uncomfortable. As Wilkins droned on, he suddenly sprang up and I watched as he crossed to the back of the stage and went into whispered conference with some of the others. I never took my eyes off him until he finally returned to say, "We decided we don't want a spokesman. We want Johnson or nobody."

"But you told me to come. I've been sitting in this place since 1:30 while you let other people speak for Kennedy and Stevenson. Do you just make up your mind as you go along who you believe in free speech *for?*"

"We want Johnson or nobody," he said again, and turned away.

Wilkins was telling them that their long wait had not been in vain for the next speaker was the man who was leading their great crusade, Martin Luther King. In the storm of applause that greeted the sound of that name, I got up and started to work my way to the exit. Then I turned back and said to my "friend" in the next seat: "Thanks for your hospitality. I hope you'll visit my office some day so I can reciprocate."

It was a bitter experience and I tasted the bitterness in my mouth all the way out of that place. Why had they kept me sitting there for four and a half hours? Why hadn't they at least given me a chance to tell them how someone from Hawaii, a member of a minority ethnic group, could be a supporter of Lyndon Johnson? Why were they afraid to hear the truth about his deep concern for all Americans, about his effectiveness in the fight for civil rights legislation? I wouldn't have pretended to them that it was a perfect law, the ultimate law. But I certainly would have reminded them that it was the first real step in the direction of civil rights in our lifetime. Then let them decide if Lyndon Johnson was an ogre!

It was 7 o'clock before I got to the testimonial dinner, and later than that before the worst of my anger slipped away. I think it is understandable that I haven't forgotten that little episode, but neither have I let it influence my attitude toward the aspirations of our Negro people. Although no leader of the NAACP has since visited my office—perhaps because of my sharp invitation that day—I am certain that no civil rights organization in the nation can say that I have ever voted or spoken against their great cause. But even now, with Lyndon Johnson as our President, skillfully fighting through bill after bill on their behalf, I sometimes wonder if the people who sat on the stage of the Shrine Auditorium ever remember that day.

I was honored to make a Johnson seconding speech a few days later, and was one of the first to know that he had agreed to accept the nomination for Vice-President under Jack Kennedy. And though we lost out in Los Angeles in 1960 and I campaigned hard for Kennedy, I have never once regretted backing LBJ and am proud today to call him my friend and political ally.

In September 1960, I was invited to serve on the American delegation to the Interparliamentary Union, the oldest such organization in the world, meeting in Tokyo that year. It was a busy and rewarding experience, to meet with representatives of all the nations, to address the plenary session gathered in the Japanese Diet, and to visit the universities for informal talks with students, many of who had been swayed toward an angry hostility to the United States. I hope I was able to cast some light where I found only heat.

Then the Ambassador suggested that as a further gesture of goodwill, I fly to the birthplace of my forefathers, Yokoyama village, and I leaped at the opportunity. He arranged for an American marine jet to fly me to Fukuoka City, some 600 miles south of Tokyo, for I could never have gotten there and back in the allotted time by any other means. And so early one morning, I clambered aboard and soon after had landed at Fukuoka, where a car was waiting to drive me to Yokoyama.

It was clear that the people had been given advance notice of my coming. An expectant crowd waited in front of the council hall and it was with deep feelings indeed that I responded to their warm greeting with words of thanks for their hospitality. As I spoke, I could almost feel the past surging through me. Here where I now stood, and everywhere along this long valley, uncounted generations of Inouyes had lived and worked in quiet simplicity and died and been laid to rest. Right here had my own odyssey begun.

A man stepped forward and was introduced to me as a member of the village's samurai family. He bowed and offered to me the traditional samurai sword that must have been handed down among his people for hundreds of years. Again I expressed my gratitude, then asked to be taken to the home of the relatives I had never seen.

We walked solemnly along the narrow, scrupulously clean streets, the people coming out of their houses to smile and nod. They were impressed, I later learned, not so much that I was an American Congressman, but because I was a member of a family where all four children had gone to college, and because I had risen to an officer's rank in the Army. And, perhaps most important of all, I was an Inouye, a name that would always represent the highest honor in this valley because of the heroic lengths two generations had gone to to pay a debt.

At last we came to the ancestral home, a thatched-roof building with a picture postcard courtyard. I wanted everything to be precisely correct and I ran through a last mental rehearsal as my uncle, now the head of the family, waited to greet me. I bowed to him, strained for my best Japanese, and said, "Dear sir, I have returned. I now desire to pay my respects to my ancestors and would be grateful if you would lead me to the burial ground."

He was enormously pleased, as were the other members of the family, who now edged closer to me, to think that I would have taken the trouble to learn the traditional procedure for a long-absent son. Obviously they had been hoping I would, for when we went to the little graveyard, the ground was absolutely clear of weeds and the tombstones freshly washed. I stood there for a long moment, paying my respects to men and women I'd never known but whose blood flowed in my veins, lost in thoughts of what might have happened to me if it hadn't been for a fire on a still night so long ago.

When we returned to the house, I was escorted to the place of honor, the other family members then seated according to their rank. We had a delightful meal and a warm reunion, and when the women and children had left, my uncle cleared his throat and said what had plainly been on his mind from the moment I arrived:

"My son, you understand that your dear father, had he stayed here, or even chosen to return, would now be the head of the Inouye household. Should you now desire to stay among us, we would be honored to have you choose any house in the family to be your own."

"I offer my thanks to you, Uncle, for your kindness and generosity. But my home is now in America and I must return to my people and my duties. Perhaps some time soon again I shall be able to visit you here."

A few hours later they were suiting me up in that jet outfit and helmet again and I was whistling back to Tokyo at more than 400 miles an hour. The marine colonel who met me at the airbase took one look at me crawling up from the cockpit with that samurai sword and said, "My God, Mr. Congressman, they made a *kamikaze* out of you!"

Sam Rayburn died of cancer on November 16, 1961. I flew from Honolulu to Texas for his funeral, feeling every mile of the way as though I had lost a father. And when my colleagues from all fifty states went to view the remains, I begged off and stayed behind. I could not bear to look at that vital, vibrant man cancer-shrunken to ninety pounds of clay.

Early in 1962, Senator Long told me that he was going to retire from active politics and that he wanted me to succeed him in the U.S. Senate. In April, he publicly announced that he would not seek re-election and further said that he hoped I would become a candidate for his seat. The following week I announced my candidacy.

It was a difficult campaign in many ways. Congress was in session and I couldn't get home except for short visits of a week or so, sometimes for only two days. My opponent was to be Ben Dillingham, son of the wealthiest man in Hawaii, a onetime territorial senator and member of the board of supervisors, articulate, friendly, and so well known in the Islands that he invariably led his ticket. Both *Time* and *Newsweek* listed my chances as doubtful.

But Ben Dillingham had a couple of handicaps to go with his attributes. He was an arch-conservative who had gone down the line opposing statehood for Hawaii. Tabbed by one of the magazines as "a fat old young man" because of his enormous bulk—he stood 6'5" and weighed nearly 250 pounds—and his turn-of-the-century view of politics, Ben worked tirelessly to live down the popular image of the rich *haole* who had exploited the people.

We made quite a contrast, the five-foot-six son of an immigrant, and the huge, rich, patrician Dillingham, and we got plenty of coverage. For a long time, with me stuck in Washington, Maggie carried the ball. She returned to Hawaii in June and spent seven days a week visiting every island and making hundreds of speeches in my behalf. When I finally did get back in October, my campaign manager met me at the airport and said, "We're glad to have you, but Maggie's been doing great."

As soon as I returned, Dillingham challenged me to a

television debate. I promptly accepted. The arrangements
proved difficult and time and again my people returned to
say that the other side was making impossible demands
about timing, subject matter and so on. Finally I instructed
them to go back one last time and agree to any format and
detail the Dillingham people wanted. All I asked was to get
in front of a TV camera with him.

The subject he chose, foreign affairs, seemed appropriate
enough on the night we met. President Kennedy had just
confronted Chairman Khrushchev with the evidence of
Russian missiles in Cuba and we were in that tense and
touchy period when for all anyone—including the White
House—knew, nuclear devices might be flying between the
continents at any moment. Dillingham, who had elected to
speak first, chose this occasion to denounce Kennedy for this
"political gimmick," to accuse the President of using Cuba
and a manufactured crisis as a trick to get more Democrats
elected to Congress.

The truth is that I could hardly believe my ears. Every
politician makes mistakes, but this was a catastrophe. When
it was my turn to speak, I began by saying, "Mr. Dillingham,
I am astounded by what you have just said," and I went on
from there. And that was the beginning of the end for Ben
Dillingham's hopes of winning.

So it was that on election night, Maggie and I went to
campaign headquarters feeling reasonably optimistic. Although the earliest returns seemed close, they came from
areas where voting was by machine, almost all Republican-
dominated. By 8 P.M., I had gotten out to a two-to-one lead,
and thereafter it just kept getting bigger. There was, as you
can imagine, intense excitement, which reached a fever peak

shortly after ten when Ben Dillingham, his wife and children all came to my headquarters to offer their congratulations. I thanked him sincerely—his coming was a mark of the inherently decent and courageous man that he was—and then sought a moment's peace to contemplate what had happened.

I was going to the Senate, to the very highest reaches of my government, I, Dan Inouye, who had been raised in respectable poverty and whose father had been born in a tiny Japanese village. My face and eyes and shape would be different from those of my colleagues. I was not of the Western world. But the fact is that there was really not so great a difference between my story and the stories of millions of other Americans who had come to this land from Ireland and Italy and Poland and Greece. They had come because America would permit any man to aspire to the topmost limits of his own talent and energy. I am proud to be one with these people.

Maggie and I spent New Year's Eve in Hawaii, then returned to Washington. The weather was unusually cold but we brought our own warmth with us: I was about to take my seat as a United States Senator and my father and two brothers had come along to see me take the oath of office. This was a special gladness because my father had suffered a heart attack some years before and had been unable to be in Washington when I was sworn in as a member of the House of Representatives. I know he always felt that to be a great loss. In a certain sense, January 9, 1963, belonged to him.

Because of my very junior status, there was no seat for him in the crowded family gallery to the left of the presiding officer. Instead, he sat at the other end of the chamber and, waiting my turn to take the oath, I kept searching the galleries for him. Then my name was called and I was escorted forward to where Vice-President Lyndon Johnson waited to administer the oath of office, a warm smile on his face. And as I raised my arm and swore to defend and protect the Constitution of the United States, I suddenly saw beyond the Vice-President's shoulder and directly in front of me the spellbound face of my father. Our eyes met and held fast. I tried to imagine what he was thinking. I felt an everlasting gratefulness to be alive, to be part of the turn of events that had brought Hyotaro Inouye to this time and this place.

In the hubbub following the conclusion of the ceremonies, I suddenly realized that Democratic Majority Leader Mike Mansfield was at my side. "Do you have any plans for lunch, Dan?" he was saying. "You and your family?"

"Well, I thought I'd take them down to the Senate restaurant."

"I imagine it'll be pretty jammed today," he said. "Why don't you all be my guests for lunch?"

The majority leader has a private dining room and I was greatly flattered that he would think to invite a most junior Senator and his family to join him there. After I got to know Mike Mansfield better, I realized that this was typical of this wise and gentle Montanan.

But the great glow of these days was not yet ended. As Maggie and my father and brothers and I were enjoying a sumptuous luncheon with Senator Mansfield, the telephone rang and I was informed that the White House wanted to talk with me. If I swallowed hard and tensed up, I hope no one noticed. In a moment, that unmistakably crisp voice came crackling over the line:

"I called to offer my congratulations, Senator," said President John F. Kennedy.

"Thank you very much, sir."

"I understand your father is in town. I'd like to meet him."

"He'd be delighted, Mr. President, and honored. When would it be convenient?"

"Any time."

"How about tomorrow morning?" I asked.

"Fine. I'll see you here at 9."

Their eyes widened when I repeated the conversation. Mike Mansfield smiled, but no one spoke for a long time.

Promptly at 9 o'clock next morning, Maggie, my father and brothers and I were escorted into the Oval Room of the White House. President Kennedy rose from his desk to greet us warmly. We made polite conversation for a moment or two—although my father, usually quite open and talkative, could hardly find words—then the President took us on a tour of the White House, from his office to the Rose Garden, commenting in that incisive way of his on the rich history all around us, graciously answering our questions, chatting about Caroline and John and his daily routine. Officially, we had been allotted five minutes for the appointment, but it was a solid half-hour before he let us say our goodbyes and leave.

Outside the Oval Room, a crowd of reporters and cameramen surged around us.

"Did the President give you any advice, Senator?"

"Senator, Senator! Did you discuss any legislation with the President?"

"Did you talk about a civil rights bill?"

I raised my hand but it was a long time before they

simmered down. When they finally did, I said, "Gentlemen, this is not my day. The President invited my father to the White House and I just happened to tag along. This is my father's day."

So they promptly besieged him:

"What did the President say, Mr. Inouye?"

"How did it feel to be in the White House?"

My father just kept shaking his head, a small smile on his lips, until at last they must have realized that he was totally unused to this rapid-fire press quiz and would not speak unless they were quiet. When they were, my father spoke quietly but with enormous dignity. "I want to thank the people of Hawaii for their goodness to my son," he said, "for sending him to the Senate. For me, for myself, I have seen my son become a Senator, I have been invited to eat with the Majority Leader of the Senate, and now I have met the President of the United States. Nothing that happens to me now can be greater. I will die a happy man."

I walked close to him out to the car. If he was proud of me, I was no less proud of him, this man whose American odyssey had begun in a little Japanese village and come to a supremely fulfilling culmination in the Oval Room of the White House. I know that his prized possession is a photograph taken that day, now framed and hung in the house on Coyne Street, a picture of Hyotaro Inouye and John Fitzgerald Kennedy.

On July 14, 1964, Maggie and I were blessed with our first child, a son. He is six times the eldest son of an eldest son, and Maggie named him Daniel Ken, Jr. And now no man can be more gratified than I, happier with his family and his work.

I will not deal in these pages with my service in the

Senate. Perhaps that will come later, the story of my part in the legislative process. I will only say the obvious, that I hope I have rewarded my country at least in small part for the great rewards America has offered me. I am now a member of the Senate Armed Services Committee and the Public Works Committee; I am a member of the Senate Democratic Policy Committee, the Senate Democratic Legislative Review Committee, Vice-Chairman of the Senate Democratic Campaign Committee, chairman of the speakers' bureau and assistant majority whip.

But I have been a Senator only a few short years and would hope that these are a prelude to a long and rewarding period of service. And in the long view of history, that is another story.